Mastering Linux Kernel Development

A kernel developer's reference manual

Raghu Bharadwaj

BIRMINGHAM - MUMBAI

D1379706

Mastering Linux Kernel Development

First published: October 2017

Production reference: 1091017

Published by Packt Publishing Ltd.
Livery Place
35 Livery Street
Birmingham
B3 2PB, UK.

ISBN 978-1-78588-305-7

www.packtpub.com

Credits

Author
Raghu Bharadwaj

Reviewer
Rami Rosen

Commissioning Editor
Kartikey Pandey

Acquisition Editor
Rahul Nair

Content Development Editor
Sharon Raj

Technical Editor
Mohit Hassija

Copy Editor
Madhusudan Uchil

Project Coordinator
Virginia Dias

Proofreader
Safis Editing

Indexer
Francy Puthiry

Graphics
Kirk D'Penha

Production Coordinator
Arvindkumar Gupta

About the Author

Raghu Bharadwaj is a leading consultant, contributor, and corporate trainer on the Linux kernel with experience spanning close to two decades. He is an ardent kernel enthusiast and expert, and has been closely following the Linux kernel since the late 90s. He is the founder of TECH VEDA, which specializes in engineering and skilling services on the Linux kernel, through technical support, kernel contributions, and advanced training. His precise understanding and articulation of the kernel has been a hallmark, and his penchant for software designs and OS architectures has garnered him special mention from his clients. Raghu is also an expert in delivering solution-oriented, customized training programs for engineering teams working on the Linux kernel, Linux drivers, and Embedded Linux. Some of his clients include major technology companies such as Xilinx, GE, Canon, Fujitsu, UTC, TCS, Broadcom, Sasken, Qualcomm, Cognizant, STMicroelectronics, Stryker, and Lattice Semiconductors.

I would first like to thank Packt for giving me this opportunity to come up with this book. I extend my sincere regards all the editors (Sharon and the team) at Packt for rallying behind me and ensuring that I stay on time and in line in delivering precise, crisp, and most up-to-date information through this book.
I would also like to thank my family, who supported me throughout my busy schedules. Lastly, but most importantly, I would like to thank my team at TECH VEDA who not only supported but also contributed in their own ways through valuable suggestions and feedback.

About the Reviewer

Rami Rosen is the author of *Linux Kernel Networking – Implementation and Theory* , a book published by Apress in 2013. Rami has worked for more than 20 years in high-tech companies—starting his way in three startups. Most of his work (past and present) is around kernel and userspace networking and virtualization projects, ranging from device drivers and kernel network stack and DPDK to NFV and OpenStack. Occasionally, he gives talks in international conferences and writes articles for LWN.net—the Linux Journal, and more.

I thank my wife, Yoonhwa, who allowed me to spend weekends reviewing this book.

www.PacktPub.com

For support files and downloads related to your book, please visit www.PacktPub.com.

Did you know that Packt offers eBook versions of every book published, with PDF and ePub files available? You can upgrade to the eBook version at www.PacktPub.com, and as a print book customer, you are entitled to a discount on the eBook copy. Get in touch with us at service@packtpub.com for more details.

At www.PacktPub.com, you can also read a collection of free technical articles, sign up for a range of free newsletters and receive exclusive discounts and offers on Packt books and eBooks.

https://www.packtpub.com/mapt

Get the most in-demand software skills with Mapt. Mapt gives you full access to all Packt books and video courses, as well as industry-leading tools to help you plan your personal development and advance your career.

Why subscribe?

- Fully searchable across every book published by Packt
- Copy and paste, print, and bookmark content
- On demand and accessible via a web browser

About the Reviewer

Rami Rosen is the author of *Linux Kernel Networking – Implementation and Theory* , a book published by Apress in 2013. Rami has worked for more than 20 years in high-tech companies—starting his way in three startups. Most of his work (past and present) is around kernel and userspace networking and virtualization projects, ranging from device drivers and kernel network stack and DPDK to NFV and OpenStack. Occasionally, he gives talks in international conferences and writes articles for LWN.net—the Linux Journal, and more.

I thank my wife, Yoonhwa, who allowed me to spend weekends reviewing this book.

www.PacktPub.com

For support files and downloads related to your book, please visit www.PacktPub.com.

Did you know that Packt offers eBook versions of every book published, with PDF and ePub files available? You can upgrade to the eBook version at www.PacktPub.com, and as a print book customer, you are entitled to a discount on the eBook copy. Get in touch with us at service@packtpub.com for more details.

At www.PacktPub.com, you can also read a collection of free technical articles, sign up for a range of free newsletters and receive exclusive discounts and offers on Packt books and eBooks.

https://www.packtpub.com/mapt

Get the most in-demand software skills with Mapt. Mapt gives you full access to all Packt books and video courses, as well as industry-leading tools to help you plan your personal development and advance your career.

Why subscribe?

- Fully searchable across every book published by Packt
- Copy and paste, print, and bookmark content
- On demand and accessible via a web browser

Customer Feedback

Thanks for purchasing this Packt book. At Packt, quality is at the heart of our editorial process. To help us improve, please leave us an honest review on this book's Amazon page at https://www.amazon.com/dp/1785883054.

If you'd like to join our team of regular reviewers, you can email us at customerreviews@packtpub.com. We award our regular reviewers with free eBooks and videos in exchange for their valuable feedback. Help us be relentless in improving our products!

Table of Contents

Preface

Mastering Linux Kernel Development looks at the Linux kernel, its internal arrangement and design, and various core subsystems, helping you to gain significant understanding of this open source marvel. You will look at how the Linux kernel, which possesses a kind of collective intelligence thanks to its scores of contributors, remains so elegant owing to its great design.

This book also looks at all the key kernel code, core data structures, functions, and macros, giving you a comprehensive foundation of the implementation details of the kernel's core services and mechanisms. You will also look at the Linux kernel as well-designed software, which gives us insights into software design in general that are easily scalable yet fundamentally strong and safe.

What this book covers

Chapter 1, Comprehending Processes, Address Space, and Threads, looks closely at one of the principal abstractions of Linux called the process and the whole ecosystem, which facilitate this abstraction. We will also spend time in understanding address space, process creation, and threads.

Chapter 2, *Deciphering the Process Scheduler*, explains process scheduling, which is a vital aspect of any operating system. Here we will build our understanding of the different scheduling policies engaged by Linux to deliver effective process execution.

Chapter 3, *Signal Management*, helps in understanding all core aspects of signal usage, their representation, data structures, and kernel routines for signal generation and delivery.

Chapter 4, *Memory Management and Allocators*, traverses us through one of the most crucial aspects of the Linux kernel, comprehending various nuances of memory representations and allocations. We will also gauge the efficiency of the kernel in maximizing resource usage at minimal costs.

Chapter 5, *Filesystems and File I/O*, imparts a generic understanding of a typical filesystem, its fabric, design, and what makes it an elemental part of an operating system. We will also look at abstraction, using the common, layered architecture design, which the kernel comprehensively imbibes through the VFS.

Chapter 6, *Interprocess Communication*, touches upon the various IPC mechanisms offered by the kernel. We will explore the layout and relationship between various data structures for each IPC mechanism, and look at both the SysV and POSIX IPC mechanisms.

Chapter 7, *Virtual Memory Management*, explains memory management with details of virtual memory management and page tables. We will look into the various aspects of the virtual memory subsystem such as process virtual address space and its segments, memory descriptor structure, memory mapping and VMA objects, page cache and address translation with page tables.

Chapter 8, *Kernel Synchronization and Locking*, enables us to understand the various protection and synchronization mechanisms provided by the kernel, and comprehend the merits and shortcomings of these mechanisms. We will try and appreciate the tenacity with which the kernel addresses these varying synchronization complexities.

Chapter 9, *Interrupts and Deferred work* , talks about interrupts, which are a key facet of any operating system to get necessary and priority tasks done. We will look at how interrupts are generated, handled, and managed in Linux. We will also look at various bottom halve mechanisms.

Chapter 10, *Clock and Time Management*, reveals how kernel measures and manages time. We will look at all key time-related structures, routines, and macros to help us gauge time management effectively.

Chapter 11, *Module Management*, quickly looks at modules, kernel's infrastructure in managing modules along with all the core data structures involved. This helps us understand how kernel inculcates dynamic extensibility.

What you need for this book

Apart from a deep desire to understand the nuances of the Linux kernel and its design, you need prior understanding of the Linux operating system in general, and the idea of an open-source software to start spending time with this book. However, this is not binding, and anyone with a keen eye to grab detailed information about the Linux system and its working can grab this book.

Who this book is for

- This book is for system programming enthusiasts and professionals who would like to deepen their understanding of the Linux kernel and its various integral components.
- This is a handy book for developers working on various kernel-related projects.
- Students of software engineering can use this as a reference guide for comprehending various aspects of Linux kernel and its design principles.

Conventions

In this book, you will find a number of text styles that distinguish between different kinds of information. Here are some examples of these styles and an explanation of their meaning. Code words in text, database table names, folder names, filenames, file extensions, pathnames, dummy URLs, user input, and Twitter handles are shown as follows: "In the `loop()` function, we read the value of the distance from the sensor and then display it on the serial port."

A block of code is set as follows:

```
/* linux-4.9.10/arch/x86/include/asm/thread_info.h */
struct thread_info {
 unsigned long flags; /* low level flags */
};
```

New terms and **important words** are shown in bold. Words that you see on the screen, for example, in menus or dialog boxes, appear in the text like this: "Go to **Sketch** | **Include Library** | **Manage Libraries** and you will get a dialog."

Warnings or important notes appear like this.

Tips and tricks appear like this.

Reader feedback

Feedback from our readers is always welcome. Let us know what you think about this book-what you liked or disliked. Reader feedback is important for us as it helps us develop titles that you will really get the most out of. To send us general feedback, simply email `feedback@packtpub.com`, and mention the book's title in the subject of your message. If there is a topic that you have expertise in and you are interested in either writing or contributing to a book, see our author guide at `www.packtpub.com/authors`.

Customer support

Now that you are the proud owner of a Packt book, we have a number of things to help you to get the most from your purchase.

Errata

Although we have taken every care to ensure the accuracy of our content, mistakes do happen. If you find a mistake in one of our books-maybe a mistake in the text or the code-we would be grateful if you could report this to us. By doing so, you can save other readers from frustration and help us improve subsequent versions of this book. If you find any errata, please report them by visiting`http://www.packtpub.com/submit-errata`, selecting your book, clicking on the **Errata Submission Form** link, and entering the details of your errata. Once your errata are verified, your submission will be accepted and the errata will be uploaded to our website or added to any list of existing errata under the Errata section of that title. To view the previously submitted errata, go to `https://www.packtpub.com/books/content/support` and enter the name of the book in the search field. The required information will appear under the **Errata** section.

Piracy

Piracy of copyrighted material on the internet is an ongoing problem across all media. At Packt, we take the protection of our copyright and licenses very seriously. If you come across any illegal copies of our works in any form on the internet, please provide us with the location address or website name immediately so that we can pursue a remedy. Please contact us at `copyright@packtpub.com` with a link to the suspected pirated material. We appreciate your help in protecting our authors and our ability to bring you valuable content.

Questions

If you have a problem with any aspect of this book, you can contact us at
questions@packtpub.com, and we will do our best to address the problem.

1
Comprehending Processes, Address Space, and Threads

When kernel services are invoked in the current process context, its layout throws open the right path for exploring kernels in more detail. Our effort in this chapter is centered around comprehending processes and the underlying ecosystem the kernel provides for them. We will explore the following concepts in this chapter:

- Program to process
- Process layout
- Virtual address spaces
- Kernel and user space
- Process APIs
- Process descriptors
- Kernel stack management
- Threads
- Linux thread API
- Data structures
- Namespace and cgroups

Processes

Quintessentially, computing systems are designed, developed, and often tweaked for running user applications efficiently. Every element that goes into a computing platform is intended to enable effective and efficient ways for running applications. In other words, computing systems exist to run diverse application programs. Applications can run either as firmware in dedicated devices or as a "process" in systems driven by system software (operating systems).

At its core, a process is a running instance of a program in memory. The transformation from a program to a process happens when the program (on disk) is fetched into memory for execution.

A program's binary image carries **code** (with all its binary instructions) and **data** (with all global data), which are mapped to distinct regions of memory with appropriate access permissions (read, write, and execute). Apart from code and data, a process is assigned additional memory regions called **stack** (for allocation of function call frames with auto variables and function arguments) and *heap* for dynamic allocations at runtime.

Multiple instances of the same program can exist with their respective memory allocations. For instance, for a web browser with multiple open tabs (running simultaneous browsing sessions), each tab is considered a process instance by the kernel, with unique memory allocations.

The following figure represents the layout of processes in memory:

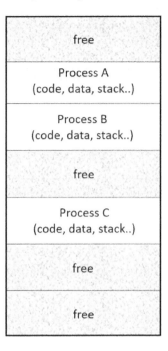

The illusion called address space

Modern-day computing platforms are expected to handle a plethora of processes efficiently. Operating systems thus must deal with allocating unique memory to all contending processes within the physical memory (often finite) and also ensure their reliable execution. With multiple processes contending and executing simultaneously (*multi-tasking*), the operating system must ensure that the memory allocation of every process is protected from accidental access by another process.

To address this issue, the kernel provides a level of abstraction between the process and the physical memory called *virtual address space*. Virtual address space is the process' view of memory; it is how the running program views the memory.

Virtual address space creates an illusion that every process exclusively owns the whole memory while executing. This abstracted view of memory is called *virtual memory* and is achieved by the kernel's memory manager in coordination with the CPU's MMU. Each process is given a contiguous 32 or 64-bit address space, bound by the architecture and unique to that process. With each process caged into its virtual address space by the MMU, any attempt by a process to access an address region outside its boundaries will trigger a hardware fault, making it possible for the memory manger to detect and terminate violating processes, thus ensuring protection.

The following figure depicts the illusion of address space created for every contending process:

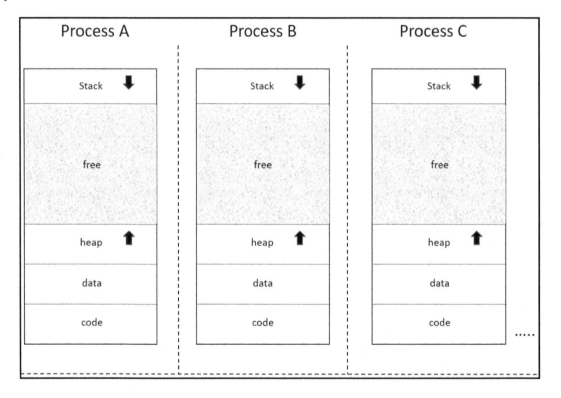

Kernel and user space

Modern operating systems not only prevent one process from accessing another but also prevent processes from accidentally accessing or manipulating kernel data and services (as the kernel is shared by all the processes).

Operating systems achieve this protection by segmenting the whole memory into two logical halves, the user and kernel space. This bifurcation ensures that all processes that are assigned address spaces are mapped to the user space section of memory and kernel data and services run in kernel space. The kernel achieves this protection in coordination with the hardware. While an application process is executing instructions from its code segment, the CPU is operating in user mode. When a process intends to invoke a kernel service, it needs to switch the CPU into privileged mode (kernel mode), which is achieved through special functions called APIs (application programming interfaces). These APIs enable user processes to switch into the kernel space using special CPU instructions and then execute the required services through *system calls*. On completion of the requested service, the kernel executes another mode switch, this time back from kernel mode to user mode, using another set of CPU instructions.

> System calls are the kernel's interfaces to expose its services to application processes; they are also called *kernel entry points*. As system calls are implemented in kernel space, the respective handlers are provided through APIs in the user space. API abstraction also makes it easier and convenient to invoke related system calls.

The following figure depicts a virtualized memory view:

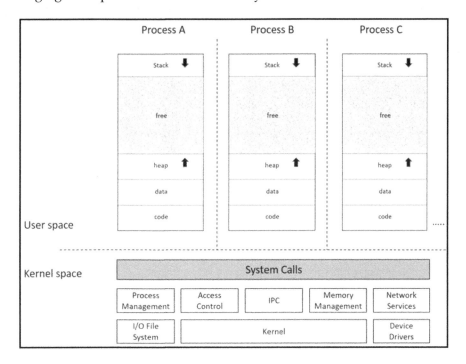

Process context

When a process requests a kernel service through a system call, the kernel will execute on behalf of the caller process. The kernel is now said to be executing in *process context*. Similarly, the kernel also responds to *interrupts* raised by other hardware entities; here, the kernel executes in *interrupt context*. When in interrupt context, the kernel is not running on behalf of any process.

Process descriptors

Right from the time a process is born until it exits, it's the kernel's process management subsystem that carries out various operations, ranging from process creation, allocating CPU time, and event notifications to destruction of the process upon termination.

Apart from the address space, a process in memory is also assigned a data structure called the *process descriptor*, which the kernel uses to identify, manage, and schedule the process. The following figure depicts process address spaces with their respective process descriptors in the kernel:

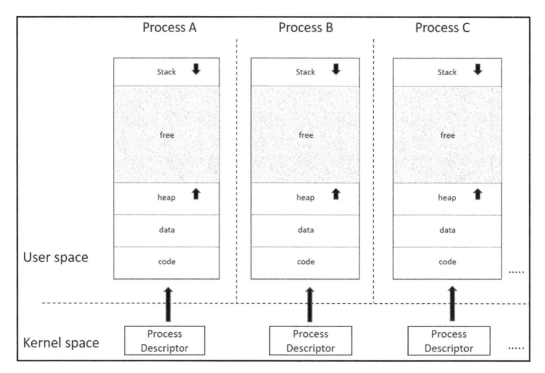

In Linux, a process descriptor is an instance of type `struct task_struct` defined in `<linux/sched.h>`, it is one of the central data structures, and contains all the attributes, identification details, and resource allocation entries that a process holds. Looking at `struct task_struct` is like a peek into the window of what the kernel sees or works with to manage and schedule a process.

Since the task structure contains a wide set of data elements, which are related to the functionality of various kernel subsystems, it would be out of context to discuss the purpose and scope of all the elements in this chapter. We shall consider a few important elements that are related to process management.

Process attributes - key elements

Process attributes define all the key and fundamental characteristics of a process. These elements contain the process's state and identifications along with other key values of importance.

state

A process right from the time it is spawned until it exits may exist in various states, referred to as *process states*--they define the process's current state:

- **TASK_RUNNING** (0): The task is either executing or contending for CPU in the scheduler run-queue.
- **TASK_INTERRUPTIBLE** (1): The task is in an interruptible wait state; it remains in wait until an awaited condition becomes true, such as the availability of mutual exclusion locks, device ready for I/O, lapse of sleep time, or an exclusive wake-up call. While in this wait state, any signals generated for the process are delivered, causing it to wake up before the wait condition is met.
- **TASK_KILLABLE**: This is similar to **TASK_INTERRUPTIBLE**, with the exception that interruptions can only occur on fatal signals, which makes it a better alternative to **TASK_INTERRUPTIBLE**.
- **TASK_UNINTERRUTPIBLE** (2): The task is in uninterruptible wait state similar to **TASK_INTERRUPTIBLE**, except that generated signals to the sleeping process do not cause wake-up. When the event occurs for which it is waiting, the process transitions to **TASK_RUNNING**. This process state is rarely used.
- **TASK_ STOPPED** (4): The task has received a STOP signal. It will be back to running on receiving the continue signal (SIGCONT).

- **TASK_TRACED** (8): A process is said to be in traced state when it is being combed, probably by a debugger.
- **EXIT_ZOMBIE** (32): The process is terminated, but its resources are not yet reclaimed.
- **EXIT_DEAD** (16): The child is terminated and all the resources held by it freed, after the parent collects the exit status of the child using *wait*.

The following figure depicts process states:

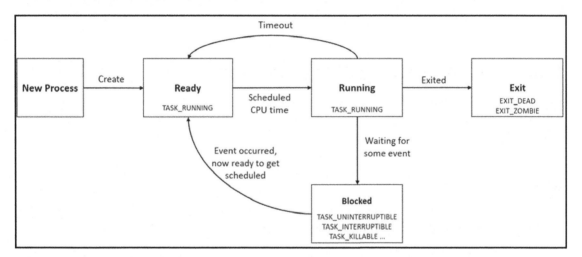

pid

This field contains a unique process identifier referred to as **PID**. PIDs in Linux are of the type `pid_t` (integer). Though a PID is an integer, the default maximum number PIDs is 32,768 specified through the `/proc/sys/kernel/pid_max` interface. The value in this file can be set to any value up to 2^{22} (`PID_MAX_LIMIT`, approximately 4 million).

To manage PIDs, the kernel uses a bitmap. This bitmap allows the kernel to keep track of PIDs in use and assign a unique PID for new processes. Each PID is identified by a bit in the PID bitmap; the value of a PID is determined from the position of its corresponding bit. Bits with value 1 in the bitmap indicate that the corresponding PIDs are in *use*, and those with value 0 indicate free PIDs. Whenever the kernel needs to assign a unique PID, it looks for the first unset bit and sets it to 1, and conversely to free a PID, it toggles the corresponding bit from 1 to 0.

tgid

This field contains the thread group id. For easy understanding, let's say when a new process is created, its PID and TGID are the same, as the process happens to be the only thread. When the process spawns a new thread, the new child gets a unique PID but inherits the TGID from the parent, as it belongs to the same thread group. The TGID is primarily used to support multi-threaded process. We will delve into further details in the threads section of this chapter.

thread info

This field holds processor-specific state information, and is a critical element of the task structure. Later sections of this chapter contain details about the importance of thread_info.

flags

The flags field records various attributes corresponding to a process. Each bit in the field corresponds to various stages in the lifetime of a process. Per-process flags are defined in <linux/sched.h>:

```
#define PF_EXITING              /* getting shut down */
#define PF_EXITPIDONE           /* pi exit done on shut down */
#define PF_VCPU                 /* I'm a virtual CPU */
#define PF_WQ_WORKER            /* I'm a workqueue worker */
#define PF_FORKNOEXEC           /* forked but didn't exec */
#define PF_MCE_PROCESS          /* process policy on mce errors */
#define PF_SUPERPRIV            /* used super-user privileges */
#define PF_DUMPCORE             /* dumped core */
#define PF_SIGNALED             /* killed by a signal */
#define PF_MEMALLOC             /* Allocating memory */
#define PF_NPROC_EXCEEDED       /* set_user noticed that RLIMIT_NPROC was
exceeded */
#define PF_USED_MATH            /* if unset the fpu must be initialized before
use */
#define PF_USED_ASYNC           /* used async_schedule*(), used by module init
*/
#define PF_NOFREEZE             /* this thread should not be frozen */
#define PF_FROZEN               /* frozen for system suspend */
#define PF_FSTRANS              /* inside a filesystem transaction */
#define PF_KSWAPD               /* I am kswapd */
#define PF_MEMALLOC_NOIO0       /* Allocating memory without IO involved */
#define PF_LESS_THROTTLE        /* Throttle me less: I clean memory */
#define PF_KTHREAD              /* I am a kernel thread */
```

```
#define PF_RANDOMIZE         /* randomize virtual address space */
#define PF_SWAPWRITE         /* Allowed to write to swap */
#define PF_NO_SETAFFINITY    /* Userland is not allowed to meddle with
cpus_allowed */
#define PF_MCE_EARLY         /* Early kill for mce process policy */
#define PF_MUTEX_TESTER      /* Thread belongs to the rt mutex tester */
#define PF_FREEZER_SKIP      /* Freezer should not count it as freezable */
#define PF_SUSPEND_TASK      /* this thread called freeze_processes and
should not be frozen */
```

exit_code and exit_signal

These fields contain the exit value of the task and details of the signal that caused the termination. These fields are to be accessed by the parent process through `wait()` on termination of the child.

comm

This field holds the name of the binary executable used to start the process.

ptrace

This field is enabled and set when the process is put into trace mode using the `ptrace()` system call.

Process relations - key elements

Every process can be related to a parent process, establishing a parent-child relationship. Similarly, multiple processes spawned by the same process are called *siblings*. These fields establish how the current process relates to another process.

real_parent and parent

These are pointers to the parent's task structure. For a normal process, both these pointers refer to the same `task_struct`; they only differ for multi-thread processes, implemented using `posix` threads. For such cases, `real_parent` refers to the parent thread task structure and parent refers the process task structure to which SIGCHLD is delivered.

children

This is a pointer to a list of child task structures.

sibling

This is a pointer to a list of sibling task structures.

group_leader

This is a pointer to the task structure of the process group leader.

Scheduling attributes - key elements

All contending processes must be given fair CPU time, and this calls for scheduling based on time slices and process priorities. These attributes contain necessary information that the scheduler uses when deciding on which process gets priority when contending.

prio and static_prio

`prio` helps determine the priority of the process for scheduling. This field holds static priority of the process within the range 1 to 99 (as specified by `sched_setscheduler()`) if the process is assigned a real-time scheduling policy. For normal processes, this field holds a dynamic priority derived from the nice value.

se, rt, and dl

Every task belongs to a scheduling entity (group of tasks), as scheduling is done at a per-entity level. `se` is for all normal processes, `rt` is for real-time processes, and `dl` is for deadline processes. We will discuss more on these attributes in the next chapter on scheduling.

policy

This field contains information about the scheduling policy of the process, which helps in determining its priority.

cpus_allowed

This field specifies the CPU mask for the process, that is, on which CPU(s) the process is eligible to be scheduled in a multi-processor system.

rt_priority

This field specifies the priority to be applied by real-time scheduling policies. For non-real-time processes, this field is unused.

Process limits - key elements

The kernel imposes resource limits to ensure fair allocation of system resources among contending processes. These limits guarantee that a random process does not monopolize ownership of resources. There are 16 different types of resource limits, and the `task` `structure` points to an array of type `struct rlimit`, in which each offset holds the current and maximum values for a specific resource.

```
/*include/uapi/linux/resource.h*/
struct rlimit {
  __kernel_ulong_t        rlim_cur;
  __kernel_ulong_t        rlim_max;
};
These limits are specified in include/uapi/asm-generic/resource.h

#define RLIMIT_CPU        0       /* CPU time in sec */
#define RLIMIT_FSIZE      1       /* Maximum filesize */
#define RLIMIT_DATA       2       /* max data size */
#define RLIMIT_STACK      3       /* max stack size */
#define RLIMIT_CORE       4       /* max core file size */
#ifndef RLIMIT_RSS
# define RLIMIT_RSS       5       /* max resident set size */
#endif
#ifndef RLIMIT_NPROC
# define RLIMIT_NPROC     6       /* max number of processes */
#endif
#ifndef RLIMIT_NOFILE
# define RLIMIT_NOFILE    7       /* max number of open files */
#endif
#ifndef RLIMIT_MEMLOCK
# define RLIMIT_MEMLOCK   8       /* max locked-in-memory
address space */
#endif
#ifndef RLIMIT_AS
```

```
# define RLIMIT_AS        9        /* address space limit */
#endif
#define RLIMIT_LOCKS     10        /* maximum file locks held */
#define RLIMIT_SIGPENDING 11       /* max number of pending signals */
#define RLIMIT_MSGQUEUE   12       /* maximum bytes in POSIX mqueues */
#define RLIMIT_NICE       13       /* max nice prio allowed to
raise to 0-39 for nice level 19 .. -20 */
#define RLIMIT_RTPRIO     14       /* maximum realtime priority */
#define RLIMIT_RTTIME     15       /* timeout for RT tasks in us */
#define RLIM_NLIMITS      16
```

File descriptor table - key elements

During the lifetime of a process, it may access various resource files to get its task done. This results in the process opening, closing, reading, and writing to these files. The system must keep track of these activities; file descriptor elements help the system know which files the process holds.

fs

Filesystem information is stored in this field.

files

The file descriptor table contains pointers to all the files that a process opens to perform various operations. The files field contains a pointer, which points to this file descriptor table.

Signal descriptor - key elements

For processes to handle signals, the *task structure* has various elements that determine how the signals must be handled.

signal

This is of type `struct signal_struct`, which contains information on all the signals associated with the process.

sighand

This is of type `struct sighand_struct`, which contains all signal handlers associated with the process.

sigset_t blocked, real_blocked

These elements identify signals that are currently masked or blocked by the process.

pending

This is of type `struct sigpending`, which identifies signals which are generated but not yet delivered.

sas_ss_sp

This field contains a pointer to an alternate stack, which facilitates signal handling.

sas_ss_size

This filed shows the size of the alternate stack, used for signal handling.

Kernel stack

With current-generation computing platforms powered by multi-core hardware capable of running simultaneous applications, the possibility of multiple processes concurrently initiating kernel mode switch when requesting for the same process is built in. To be able to handle such situations, kernel services are designed to be re-entrant, allowing multiple processes to step in and engage the required services. This mandated the requesting process to maintain its own private kernel stack to keep track of the kernel function call sequence, store local data of the kernel functions, and so on.

The kernel stack is directly mapped to the physical memory, mandating the arrangement to be physically in a contiguous region. The kernel stack by default is 8kb for x86-32 and most other 32-bit systems (with an option of 4k kernel stack to be configured during kernel build), and 16kb on an x86-64 system.

When kernel services are invoked in the current process context, they need to validate the process's prerogative before it commits to any relevant operations. To perform such validations, the kernel services must gain access to the task structure of the current process and look through the relevant fields. Similarly, kernel routines might need to have access to the current `task structure` for modifying various resource structures such as signal handler tables, looking for pending signals, file descriptor table, and memory descriptor among others. To enable accessing the `task structure` at runtime, the address of the current `task structure` is loaded into a processor register (register chosen is architecture specific) and made available through a kernel global macro called `current` (defined in architecture-specific kernel header `asm/current.h`):

```
/* arch/ia64/include/asm/current.h */
#ifndef _ASM_IA64_CURRENT_H
#define _ASM_IA64_CURRENT_H
/*
 * Modified 1998-2000
 *      David Mosberger-Tang <davidm@hpl.hp.com>, Hewlett-Packard Co
 */
#include <asm/intrinsics.h>
/*
 * In kernel mode, thread pointer (r13) is used to point to the
   current task
 * structure.
 */
#define current ((struct task_struct *) ia64_getreg(_IA64_REG_TP))
#endif /* _ASM_IA64_CURRENT_H */
/* arch/powerpc/include/asm/current.h */
#ifndef _ASM_POWERPC_CURRENT_H
#define _ASM_POWERPC_CURRENT_H
#ifdef __KERNEL__
/*
 * This program is free software; you can redistribute it and/or
 * modify it under the terms of the GNU General Public License
 * as published by the Free Software Foundation; either version
 * 2 of the License, or (at your option) any later version.
 */
struct task_struct;
#ifdef __powerpc64__
#include <linux/stddef.h>
#include <asm/paca.h>
static inline struct task_struct *get_current(void)
{
        struct task_struct *task;

        __asm__ __volatile__("ld %0,%1(13)"
        : "=r" (task)
```

```
                : "i" (offsetof(struct paca_struct, __current)));
                return task;
    }
    #define current get_current()
    #else
    /*
    * We keep `current' in r2 for speed.
    */
    register struct task_struct *current asm ("r2");
    #endif
    #endif /* __KERNEL__ */
    #endif /* _ASM_POWERPC_CURRENT_H */
```

However, in register-constricted architectures, where there are few registers to spare, reserving a register to hold the address of the current task structure is not viable. On such platforms, the task structure of the current process is directly made available at the top of the kernel stack that it owns. This approach renders a significant advantage with respect to locating the task structure, by just masking the least significant bits of the stack pointer.

With the evolution of the kernel, the task structure grew and became too large to be contained in the kernel stack, which is already restricted in physical memory (8Kb). As a result, the task structure was moved out of the kernel stack, barring a few key fields that define the process's CPU state and other low-level processor-specific information. These fields were then wrapped in a newly created structure called struct thread_info. This structure is contained on top of the kernel stack and provides a pointer that refers to the current task structure, which can be used by kernel services.

The following code snippet shows struct thread_info for x86 architecture (kernel 3.10):

```
/* linux-3.10/arch/x86/include/asm/thread_info.h */

struct thread_info {
struct task_struct *task; /* main task structure */
struct exec_domain *exec_domain; /* execution domain */
__u32 flags; /* low level flags */
__u32 status; /* thread synchronous flags */
__u32 cpu; /* current CPU */
int preempt_count; /* 0 => preemptable, <0 => BUG */
mm_segment_t addr_limit;
struct restart_block restart_block;
void __user *sysenter_return;
#ifdef CONFIG_X86_32
unsigned long previous_esp; /* ESP of the previous stack in case of
nested (IRQ) stacks */
__u8 supervisor_stack[0];
```

```
#endif
unsigned int sig_on_uaccess_error:1;
unsigned int uaccess_err:1; /* uaccess failed */
};
```

With `thread_info` containing process-related information, apart from `task structure`, the kernel has multiple viewpoints to the current process structure: `struct task_struct`, an architecture-independent information block, and `thread_info`, an architecture-specific one. The following figure depicts **thread_info** and **task_struct**:

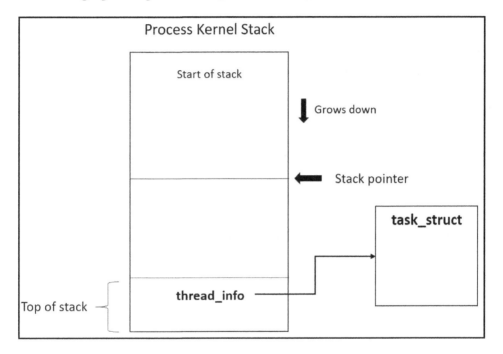

For architectures that engage `thread_info`, the current macro's implementation is modified to look into the top of kernel stack to obtain a reference to the current `thread_info` and through it the `current task structure`. The following code snippet shows the implementation of current for an x86-64 platform:

```
#ifndef __ASM_GENERIC_CURRENT_H
#define __ASM_GENERIC_CURRENT_H
#include <linux/thread_info.h>
#define get_current() (current_thread_info()->task)
#define current get_current()
#endif /* __ASM_GENERIC_CURRENT_H */
/*
 * how to get the current stack pointer in C
```

```
*/
register unsigned long current_stack_pointer asm ("sp");
/*
 * how to get the thread information struct from C
 */
static inline struct thread_info *current_thread_info(void)
__attribute_const__;
static inline struct thread_info *current_thread_info(void)
{
        return (struct thread_info *)
                (current_stack_pointer & ~(THREAD_SIZE - 1));
}
```

As use of PER_CPU variables has increased in recent times, the process scheduler is tuned to cache crucial current process-related information in the PER_CPU area. This change enables quick access to current process data over looking up the kernel stack. The following code snippet shows the implementation of the current macro to fetch the current task data through the PER_CPU variable:

```
#ifndef _ASM_X86_CURRENT_H
#define _ASM_X86_CURRENT_H
#include <linux/compiler.h>
#include <asm/percpu.h>
#ifndef __ASSEMBLY__
struct task_struct;
DECLARE_PER_CPU(struct task_struct *, current_task);
static __always_inline struct task_struct *get_current(void)
{
        return this_cpu_read_stable(current_task);
}

#define current get_current()
#endif /* __ASSEMBLY__ */

#endif /* _ASM_X86_CURRENT_H */
```

The use of PER_CPU data led to a gradual reduction of information in thread_info. With thread_info shrinking in size, kernel developers are considering getting rid of thread_info altogether by moving it into the task structure. As this involves changes to low-level architecture code, it has only been implemented for the x86-64 architecture, with other architectures planned to follow. The following code snippet shows the current state of the thread_info structure with just one element:

```
/* linux-4.9.10/arch/x86/include/asm/thread_info.h */
struct thread_info {
 unsigned long flags; /* low level flags */
};
```

The issue of stack overflow

Unlike user mode, the kernel mode stack lives in directly mapped memory. When a process invokes a kernel service, which may internally be deeply nested, chances are that it may overrun into immediate memory range. The worst part of it is the kernel will be oblivious to such occurrences. Kernel programmers usually engage various debug options to track stack usage and detect overruns, but these methods are not handy to prevent stack breaches on production systems. Conventional protection through the use of *guard pages* is also ruled out here (as it wastes an actual memory page).

Kernel programmers tend to follow coding standards--minimizing the use of local data, avoiding recursion, and avoiding deep nesting among others--to cut down the probability of a stack breach. However, implementation of feature-rich and deeply layered kernel subsystems may pose various design challenges and complications, especially with the storage subsystem where filesystems, storage drivers, and networking code can be stacked up in several layers, resulting in deeply nested function calls.

The Linux kernel community has been pondering over preventing such breaches for quite long, and toward that end, the decision was made to expand the kernel stack to 16kb (x86-64, since kernel 3.15). Expansion of the kernel stack might prevent some breaches, but at the cost of engaging much of the directly mapped kernel memory for the per-process kernel stack. However, for reliable functioning of the system, it is expected of the kernel to elegantly handle stack breaches when they show up on production systems.

With the 4.9 release, the kernel has come with a new system to set up virtually mapped kernel stacks. Since virtual addresses are currently in use to map even a directly mapped page, principally the kernel stack does not actually require physically contiguous pages. The kernel reserves a separate range of addresses for virtually mapped memory, and addresses from this range are allocated when a call to vmalloc() is made. This range of memory is referred as the **vmalloc range**. Primarily this range is used when programs require huge chunks of memory which are virtually contiguous but physically scattered. Using this, the kernel stack can now be allotted as individual pages, mapped to the vmalloc range. Virtual mapping also enables protection from overruns as a no-access guard page can be allocated with a page table entry (without wasting an actual page). Guard pages would prompt the kernel to pop an oops message on memory overrun and initiate a kill against overrunning process.

Virtually mapped kernel stacks with guard pages are currently available only for the x86-64 architecture (support for other architectures seemingly to follow). This can be enabled by choosing the HAVE_ARCH_VMAP_STACK or CONFIG_VMAP_STACK build-time options.

Process creation

During kernel boot, a kernel thread called init is spawned, which in turn is configured to initialize the first user-mode process (with the same name). The init (pid 1) process is then configured to carry out various initialization operations specified through configuration files, creating multiple processes. Every child process further created (which may in turn create its own child process(es)) are all descendants of the *init* process. Processes thus created end up in a tree-like structure or a single hierarchy model. The shell, which is one such process, becomes the interface for users to create user processes, when programs are called for execution.

Fork, vfork, exec, clone, wait and exit are the core kernel interfaces for the creation and control of new process. These operations are invoked through corresponding user-mode APIs.

fork()

Fork() is one of the core "Unix thread APIs" available across *nix systems since the inception of legacy Unix releases. Aptly named, it forks a new process from a running process. When fork() succeeds, the new process is created (referred to as child) by duplicating the caller's address space and task structure. On return from fork(), both caller (parent) and new process (child) resume executing instructions from the same code segment which was duplicated under copy-on-write. Fork() is perhaps the only API that enters kernel mode in the context of caller process, and on success returns to user mode in the context of both caller and child (new process).

Most resource entries of the parent's task structure such as memory descriptor, file descriptor table, signal descriptors, and scheduling attributes are inherited by the child, except for a few attributes such as memory locks, pending signals, active timers, and file record locks (for the full list of exceptions, refer to the fork(2) man page). A child process is assigned a unique pid and will refer to its parent's pid through the ppid field of its task structure; the child's resource utilization and processor usage entries are reset to zero.

The parent process updates itself about the child's state using the wait() system call and normally waits for the termination of the child process. Failing to call wait(), the child may terminate and be pushed into a zombie state.

Copy-on-write (COW)

Duplication of parent process to create a child needs cloning of the user mode address space (stack, data, code, and heap segments) and task structure of the parent for the child; this would result in execution overhead that leads to un-deterministic process-creation time. To make matters worse, this process of cloning would be rendered useless if neither parent nor child did not initiate any state-change operations on cloned resources.

As per COW, when a child is created, it is allocated a unique task structure with all resource entries (including page tables) referring to the parent's task structure, with read-only access for both parent and child. Resources are truly duplicated when either of the processes initiates a state change operation, hence the name *copy-on-write* (write in COW implies a state change). COW does bring effectiveness and optimization to the fore, by deferring the need for duplicating process data until write, and in cases where only read happens, it avoids it altogether. This on-demand copying also reduces the number of swap pages needed, cuts down the time spent on swapping, and might help reduce demand paging.

exec

At times creating a child process might not be useful, unless it runs a new program altogether: the `exec` family of calls serves precisely this purpose. `exec` replaces the existing program in a process with a new executable binary:

```
#include <unistd.h>
int execve(const char *filename, char *const argv[],
char *const envp[]);
```

The `execve` is the system call that executes the program binary file, passed as the first argument to it. The second and third arguments are null-terminated arrays of arguments and environment strings, to be passed to a new program as command-line arguments. This system call can also be invoked through various `glibc` (library) wrappers, which are found to be more convenient and flexible:

```
#include <unistd.h>
extern char **environ;
int execl(const char *path, const char *arg, ...);
int execlp(const char *file, const char *arg, ...);
int execle(const char *path, const char *arg,
..., char * const envp[]);
int execv(const char *path, char *constargv[]);
int execvp(const char *file, char *constargv[]);
int execvpe(const char *file, char *const argv[],
char *const envp[]);
```

Command-line user-interface programs such as `shell` use the `exec` interface to launch user-requested program binaries.

vfork()

Unlike `fork()`, `vfork()` creates a child process and blocks the parent, which means that the child runs as a single thread and does not allow concurrency; in other words, the parent process is temporarily suspended until the child exits or call `exec()`. The child shares the data of the parent.

Linux support for threads

The flow of execution in a process is referred to as a **thread**, which implies that every process will at least have one thread of execution. Multi-threaded means the existence of multiple flows of execution contexts in a process. With modern many-core architectures, multiple flows of execution in a process can be truly concurrent, achieving fair multitasking.

Threads are normally enumerated as pure user-level entities within a process that are scheduled for execution; they share parent's virtual address space and system resources. Each thread maintains its code, stack, and thread local storage. Threads are scheduled and managed by the thread library, which uses a structure referred to as a thread object to hold a unique thread identifier, for scheduling attributes and to save the thread context. User-level thread applications are generally lighter on memory, and are the preferred model of concurrency for event-driven applications. On the flip side, such user-level thread model is not suitable for parallel computing, since they are tied onto the same processor core to which their parent process is bound.

Linux doesn't support user-level threads directly; it instead proposes an alternate API to enumerate a special process, called **light weight process** (**LWP**), that can share a set of configured resources such as dynamic memory allocations, global data, open files, signal handlers, and other extensive resources with the parent process. Each LWP is identified by a unique PID and task structure, and is treated by the kernel as an independent execution context. In Linux, the term thread invariably refers to LWP, since each thread initialized by the thread library (Pthreads) is enumerated as an LWP by the kernel.

clone()

clone() is a Linux-specific system call to create a new process; it is considered a generic version of the fork() system call, offering finer controls to customize its functionality through the flags argument:

```
int clone(int (*child_func)(void *), void *child_stack, int flags, void
*arg);
```

It provides more than twenty different CLONE_* flags that control various aspects of the clone operation, including whether the parent and child process share resources such as virtual memory, open file descriptors, and signal dispositions. The child is created with the appropriate memory address (passed as the second argument) to be used as the stack (for storing the child's local data). The child process starts its execution with its start function (passed as the first argument to the clone call).

When a process attempts to create a thread through the `pthread` library, `clone()` is invoked with the following flags:

```
/*clone flags for creating threads*/
flags=CLONE_VM|CLONE_FS|CLONE_FILES|CLONE_SIGHAND|CLONE_THREAD|CLONE_SYSVSE
M|CLONE_SETTLS|CLONE_PARENT_SETTID|CLONE_CHILD_CLEARTID;
```

Flag	Meaning
CLONE_VM	Enables sharing(read/write) of parents virtual address space including active memory maps
CLONE_FS	Enables sharing parent's file system information.(current working directory, umask)
CLONE_FILES	Enables sharing the same file descriptor table. Any file descriptor created by the calling process or by the child process is also valid in the other process
CLONE_SIGHAND	Enables parent and child to share signal handler tables, Note that this option does not affect signal mask, and pending signals list
CLONE_THREAD	Recall that each LWP has its own pid. However thread library standard mandates all threads of a multithreaded application to bind with same PID. To achieve this Linux uses concept of thread groups, with distinct group-ids. When this flag is set the child is placed in the same thread group as the parent process
CLONE_SYSVSEM	Enables child and the calling process to share a single list of System V semaphore adjustment values
CLONE_SETTLS	Creates a new thread local storage descriptor for the child
CLONE_PARENT_SETTID	Child process spawned through fork() system may at times exit even before its PID is returned in the parent's context; when this occurs (happens when parent loses race) parent would no longer be able to track child status. This flag can be enabled by pthread library to store the child TID at the location ptid in the parent's memory even before child thread begins execution
CLONE_CHILD_CLEARTID	When thread exits its stack must be deallocated, this flag enables clearing child tid at a memory location on which parent waits through futex, upon wakeup parent frees the thread stack.

The `clone()` can also be used to create a regular child process that is normally spawned using `fork()` and `vfork()`:

```
/* clone flags for forking child */
flags = SIGCHLD;
/* clone flags for vfork child */
flags = CLONE_VFORK | CLONE_VM | SIGCHLD;
```

Kernel threads

To augment the need for running background operations, the kernel spawns threads
(similar to processes). These kernel threads are similar to regular processes, in that they are
represented by a task structure and assigned a PID. Unlike user processes, they do not have
any address space mapped, and run exclusively in kernel mode, which makes them non-
interactive. Various kernel subsystems use kthreads to run periodic and asynchronous
operations.

All kernel threads are descendants of kthreadd (pid 2), which is spawned by the
kernel (pid 0) during boot. The kthreadd enumerates other kernel threads; it provides
interface routines through which other kernel threads can be dynamically spawned at
runtime by kernel services. Kernel threads can be viewed from the command line with the
ps -ef command--they are shown in [square brackets]:

```
UID PID PPID C STIME TTY TIME CMD
root 1 0 0 22:43 ? 00:00:01 /sbin/init splash
root 2 0 0 22:43 ? 00:00:00 [kthreadd]
root 3 2 0 22:43 ? 00:00:00 [ksoftirqd/0]
root 4 2 0 22:43 ? 00:00:00 [kworker/0:0]
root 5 2 0 22:43 ? 00:00:00 [kworker/0:0H]
root 7 2 0 22:43 ? 00:00:01 [rcu_sched]
root 8 2 0 22:43 ? 00:00:00 [rcu_bh]
root 9 2 0 22:43 ? 00:00:00 [migration/0]
root 10 2 0 22:43 ? 00:00:00 [watchdog/0]
root 11 2 0 22:43 ? 00:00:00 [watchdog/1]
root 12 2 0 22:43 ? 00:00:00 [migration/1]
root 13 2 0 22:43 ? 00:00:00 [ksoftirqd/1]
root 15 2 0 22:43 ? 00:00:00 [kworker/1:0H]
root 16 2 0 22:43 ? 00:00:00 [watchdog/2]
root 17 2 0 22:43 ? 00:00:00 [migration/2]
root 18 2 0 22:43 ? 00:00:00 [ksoftirqd/2]
root 20 2 0 22:43 ? 00:00:00 [kworker/2:0H]
root 21 2 0 22:43 ? 00:00:00 [watchdog/3]
root 22 2 0 22:43 ? 00:00:00 [migration/3]
root 23 2 0 22:43 ? 00:00:00 [ksoftirqd/3]
root 25 2 0 22:43 ? 00:00:00 [kworker/3:0H]
root 26 2 0 22:43 ? 00:00:00 [kdevtmpfs]
/*kthreadd creation code (init/main.c) */
static noinline void __ref rest_init(void)
{
 int pid;

 rcu_scheduler_starting();
 /*
 * We need to spawn init first so that it obtains pid 1, however
```

```
 * the init task will end up wanting to create kthreads, which, if
 * we schedule it before we create kthreadd, will OOPS.
 */
kernel_thread(kernel_init, NULL, CLONE_FS);
numa_default_policy();
pid = kernel_thread(kthreadd, NULL, CLONE_FS | CLONE_FILES);
rcu_read_lock();
kthreadd_task = find_task_by_pid_ns(pid, &init_pid_ns);
rcu_read_unlock();
complete(&kthreadd_done);

/*
 * The boot idle thread must execute schedule()
 * at least once to get things moving:
 */
init_idle_bootup_task(current);
schedule_preempt_disabled();
/* Call into cpu_idle with preempt disabled */
cpu_startup_entry(CPUHP_ONLINE);
}
```

The previous code shows the kernel boot routine `rest_init()` invoking the `kernel_thread()` routine with appropriate arguments to spawn both the `kernel_init` thread (which then goes on to start the user-mode `init` process) and `kthreadd`.

The `kthread` is a perpetually running thread that looks into a list called `kthread_create_list` for data on new `kthreads` to be created:

```
/*kthreadd routine(kthread.c) */
int kthreadd(void *unused)
{
 struct task_struct *tsk = current;

 /* Setup a clean context for our children to inherit. */
 set_task_comm(tsk, "kthreadd");
 ignore_signals(tsk);
 set_cpus_allowed_ptr(tsk, cpu_all_mask);
 set_mems_allowed(node_states[N_MEMORY]);

 current->flags |= PF_NOFREEZE;

 for (;;) {
 set_current_state(TASK_INTERRUPTIBLE);
 if (list_empty(&kthread_create_list))
 schedule();
 __set_current_state(TASK_RUNNING);
```

```
spin_lock(&kthread_create_lock);
while (!list_empty(&kthread_create_list)) {
struct kthread_create_info *create;

create = list_entry(kthread_create_list.next,
struct kthread_create_info, list);
list_del_init(&create->list);
spin_unlock(&kthread_create_lock);

create_kthread(create); /* creates kernel threads with attributes enqueued
*/

spin_lock(&kthread_create_lock);
}
spin_unlock(&kthread_create_lock);
}

return 0;
}
```

Kernel threads are created by invoking either `kthread_create` or through its wrapper `kthread_run` by passing appropriate arguments that define the `kthreadd` (start routine, ARG data to start routine, and name). The following code snippet shows `kthread_create` invoking `kthread_create_on_node()`, which by default creates threads on the current Numa node:

```
struct task_struct *kthread_create_on_node(int (*threadfn)(void *data),
void *data,
int node,
const char namefmt[], ...);

/**
 * kthread_create - create a kthread on the current node
 * @threadfn: the function to run in the thread
 * @data: data pointer for @threadfn()
 * @namefmt: printf-style format string for the thread name
 * @...: arguments for @namefmt.
 *
 * This macro will create a kthread on the current node, leaving it in
 * the stopped state. This is just a helper for
 * kthread_create_on_node();
 * see the documentation there for more details.
 */
#define kthread_create(threadfn, data, namefmt, arg...)
kthread_create_on_node(threadfn, data, NUMA_NO_NODE, namefmt, ##arg)
```

```
struct task_struct *kthread_create_on_cpu(int (*threadfn)(void *data),
 void *data,
 unsigned int cpu,
 const char *namefmt);

/**
 * kthread_run - create and wake a thread.
 * @threadfn: the function to run until signal_pending(current).
 * @data: data ptr for @threadfn.
 * @namefmt: printf-style name for the thread.
 *
 * Description: Convenient wrapper for kthread_create() followed by
 * wake_up_process(). Returns the kthread or ERR_PTR(-ENOMEM).
 */
#define kthread_run(threadfn, data, namefmt, ...)
({
 struct task_struct *__k
 = kthread_create(threadfn, data, namefmt, ## __VA_ARGS__);
 if (!IS_ERR(__k))
 wake_up_process(__k);
 __k;
})
```

`kthread_create_on_node()` instantiates details (received as arguments) of `kthread` to be created into a structure of type `kthread_create_info` and queues it at the tail of `kthread_create_list`. It then wakes up `kthreadd` and waits for thread creation to complete:

```
/* kernel/kthread.c */
static struct task_struct *__kthread_create_on_node(int (*threadfn)(void
*data),
 void *data, int node,
 const char namefmt[],
 va_list args)
{
 DECLARE_COMPLETION_ONSTACK(done);
 struct task_struct *task;
 struct kthread_create_info *create = kmalloc(sizeof(*create),
 GFP_KERNEL);

 if (!create)
 return ERR_PTR(-ENOMEM);
 create->threadfn = threadfn;
 create->data = data;
 create->node = node;
 create->done = &done;

 spin_lock(&kthread_create_lock);
```

```
        list_add_tail(&create->list, &kthread_create_list);
        spin_unlock(&kthread_create_lock);

        wake_up_process(kthreadd_task);
        /*
         * Wait for completion in killable state, for I might be chosen by
         * the OOM killer while kthreadd is trying to allocate memory for
         * new kernel thread.
         */
        if (unlikely(wait_for_completion_killable(&done))) {
        /*
         * If I was SIGKILLed before kthreadd (or new kernel thread)
         * calls complete(), leave the cleanup of this structure to
         * that thread.
         */
        if (xchg(&create->done, NULL))
        return ERR_PTR(-EINTR);
        /*
         * kthreadd (or new kernel thread) will call complete()
         * shortly.
         */
        wait_for_completion(&done); // wakeup on completion of thread creation.
         }
        ...
        ...
        ...
        }

struct task_struct *kthread_create_on_node(int (*threadfn)(void *data),
 void *data, int node,
 const char namefmt[],
 ...)
{
 struct task_struct *task;
 va_list args;

 va_start(args, namefmt);
 task = __kthread_create_on_node(threadfn, data, node, namefmt, args);
 va_end(args);

 return task;
}
```

Recall that `kthreadd` invokes the `create_thread()` routine to start kernel threads as per data queued into the list. This routine creates the thread and signals completion:

```c
/* kernel/kthread.c */
static void create_kthread(struct kthread_create_info *create)
{
 int pid;

#ifdef CONFIG_NUMA
 current->pref_node_fork = create->node;
#endif

 /* We want our own signal handler (we take no signals by default). */
 pid = kernel_thread(kthread, create, CLONE_FS | CLONE_FILES |
 SIGCHLD);
 if (pid < 0) {
 /* If user was SIGKILLed, I release the structure. */
 struct completion *done = xchg(&create->done, NULL);

 if (!done) {
 kfree(create);
 return;
 }
 create->result = ERR_PTR(pid);
 complete(done); /* signal completion of thread creation */
 }
}
```

do_fork() and copy_process()

All of the process/thread creation calls discussed so far invoke different system calls (except `create_thread`) to step into kernel mode. All of those system calls in turn converge into the common kernel `function _do_fork()`, which is invoked with distinct `CLONE_*` flags. `do_fork()` internally falls back on `copy_process()` to complete the task. The following figure sums up the call sequence for process creation:

```c
/* kernel/fork.c */
/*
 * Create a kernel thread.
 */
```

```
pid_t kernel_thread(int (*fn)(void *), void *arg, unsigned long flags)
{
 return _do_fork(flags|CLONE_VM|CLONE_UNTRACED, (unsigned long)fn,
 (unsigned long)arg, NULL, NULL, 0);
}

/* sys_fork: create a child process by duplicating caller */
SYSCALL_DEFINE0(fork)
{
#ifdef CONFIG_MMU
 return _do_fork(SIGCHLD, 0, 0, NULL, NULL, 0);
#else
 /* cannot support in nommu mode */
 return -EINVAL;
#endif
}

/* sys_vfork: create vfork child process */
SYSCALL_DEFINE0(vfork)
{
 return _do_fork(CLONE_VFORK | CLONE_VM | SIGCHLD, 0,
 0, NULL, NULL, 0);
}

/* sys_clone: create child process as per clone flags */

#ifdef __ARCH_WANT_SYS_CLONE
#ifdef CONFIG_CLONE_BACKWARDS
SYSCALL_DEFINE5(clone, unsigned long, clone_flags, unsigned long, newsp,
 int __user *, parent_tidptr,
 unsigned long, tls,
 int __user *, child_tidptr)
#elif defined(CONFIG_CLONE_BACKWARDS2)
SYSCALL_DEFINE5(clone, unsigned long, newsp, unsigned long, clone_flags,
 int __user *, parent_tidptr,
 int __user *, child_tidptr,
 unsigned long, tls)
#elif defined(CONFIG_CLONE_BACKWARDS3)
SYSCALL_DEFINE6(clone, unsigned long, clone_flags, unsigned long, newsp,
 int, stack_size,
 int __user *, parent_tidptr,
 int __user *, child_tidptr,
 unsigned long, tls)
#else
SYSCALL_DEFINE5(clone, unsigned long, clone_flags, unsigned long, newsp,
 int __user *, parent_tidptr,
 int __user *, child_tidptr,
 unsigned long, tls)
```

```
#endif
{
 return _do_fork(clone_flags, newsp, 0, parent_tidptr, child_tidptr, tls);
}
#endif
```

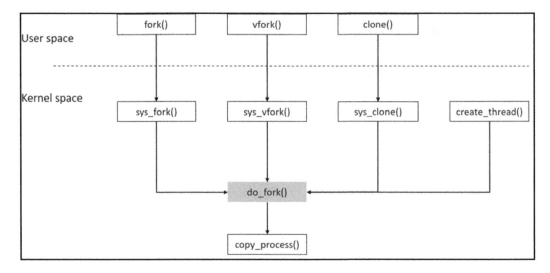

Process status and termination

During the lifetime of a process, it traverses through many states before it ultimately terminates. Users must have proper mechanisms to be updated with all that happens to a process during its lifetime. Linux provides a set of functions for this purpose.

wait

For processes and threads created by a parent, it might be functionally useful for the parent to know the execution status of the child process/thread. This can be achieved using the wait family of system calls:

```
#include <sys/types.h>
#include <sys/wait.h>
pid_t wait(int *status);
pid_t waitpid(pid_t pid, int *status, intoptions);
int waitid(idtype_t idtype, id_t id, siginfo_t *infop, int options)
```

These system calls update the calling process with the state change events of a child. The following state change events are notified:

- Termination of child
- Stopped by a signal
- Resumed by a signal

In addition to reporting the status, these APIs allow the parent process to reap a terminated child. A process on termination is put into zombie state until the immediate parent engages the `wait` call to reap it.

exit

Every process must end. Process termination is done either by the process calling `exit()` or when the main function returns. A process may also be terminated abruptly on receiving a signal or exception that forces it to terminate, such as the `KILL` command, which sends a signal to kill the process, or when an exception is raised. Upon termination, the process is put into exit state until the immediate parent reaps it.

The `exit` calls the `sys_exit` system call, which internally calls the `do_exit` routine. The `do_exit` primarily performs the following tasks (`do_exit` sets many values and makes multiple calls to related kernel routines to complete its task):

- Takes the exit code returned by the child to the parent.
- Sets the `PF_EXITING` flag, indicating process exiting.
- Cleans up and reclaims the resources held by the process. This includes releasing `mm_struct`, removal from the queue if it is waiting for an IPC semaphore, release of filesystem data and files, if any, and calling `schedule()` as the process is no longer executable.

After `do_exit`, the process remains in zombie state and the process descriptor is still intact for the parent to collect the status, after which the resources are reclaimed by the system.

Namespaces and cgroups

Users logged into a Linux system have a transparent view of various system entities such as global resources, processes, kernel, and users. For instance, a valid user can access PIDs of all running processes on the system (irrespective of the user to which they belong). Users can observe the presence of other users on the system, and they can run commands to view the state of global system global resources such as memory, filesystem mounts, and devices. Such operations are not deemed as intrusions or considered security breaches, as it is always guaranteed that one user/process can never intrude into other user/process.

However, such transparency is unwarranted on a few server platforms. For instance, consider cloud service providers offering **PaaS (platform as a service)**. They offer an environment to host and deploy custom client applications. They manage runtime, storage, operating system, middleware, and networking services, leaving customers to manage their applications and data. PaaS services are used by various e-commerce, financial, online gaming, and other related enterprises.

For efficient and effective isolation and resource management for clients, PaaS service providers use various tools. They virtualize the system environment for each client to achieve security, reliability, and robustness. The Linux kernel provides low-level mechanisms in the form of cgroups and namespaces for building various lightweight tools that can virtualize the system environment. Docker is one such framework that builds on cgroups and namespaces.

Namespaces fundamentally are mechanisms to abstract, isolate, and limit the visibility that a group of processes has over various system entities such as process trees, network interfaces, user IDs, and filesystem mounts. Namespaces are categorized into several groups, which we will now see.

Mount namespaces

Traditionally, mount and unmount operations will change the filesystem view as seen by all processes in the system; in other words, there is one global mount namespace seen by all processes. The mount namespaces confine the set of filesystem mount points visible within a process namespace, enabling one process group in a mount namespace to have an exclusive view of the filesystem list compared to another process.

UTS namespaces

These enable isolating the system's host and domain name within a uts namespace. This makes initialization and configuration scripts able to be guided based on the respective namespaces.

IPC namespaces

These demarcate processes from using System V and POSIX message queues. This prevents one process from an ipc namespace accessing the resources of another.

PID namespaces

Traditionally, *nix kernels (including Linux) spawn the `init` process with PID 1 during system boot, which in turn starts other user-mode processes and is considered the root of the process tree (all the other processes start below this process in the tree). The PID namespace allows a process to spin off a new tree of processes under it with its own root process (PID 1 process). PID namespaces isolate process ID numbers, and allow duplication of PID numbers across different PID namespaces, which means that processes in different PID namespaces can have the same process ID. The process IDs within a PID namespace are unique, and are assigned sequentially starting with PID 1.

PID namespaces are used in containers (lightweight virtualization solution) to migrate a container with a process tree, onto a different host system without any changes to PIDs.

Network namespaces

This type of namespace provides abstraction and virtualization of network protocol services and interfaces. Each network namespace will have its own network device instances that can be configured with individual network addresses. Isolation is enabled for other network services: routing table, port number, and so on.

User namespaces

User namespaces allow a process to use unique user and group IDs within and outside a namespace. This means that a process can use privileged user and group IDs (zero) within a user namespace and continue with non-zero user and group IDs outside the namespace.

Cgroup namespaces

A cgroup namespace virtualizes the contents of the `/proc/self/cgroup` file. Processes inside a cgroup namespace are only able to view paths relative to their namespace root.

Control groups (cgroups)

Cgroups are kernel mechanisms to restrict and measure resource allocations to each process group. Using cgroups, you can allocate resources such as CPU time, network, and memory.

Similar to the process model in Linux, where each process is a child to a parent and relatively descends from the `init` process thus forming a single-tree like structure, cgroups are hierarchical, where child cgroups inherit the attributes of the parent, but what makes is different is that multiple cgroup hierarchies can exist within a single system, with each having distinct resource prerogatives.

Applying cgroups on namespaces results in isolation of processes into `containers` within a system, where resources are managed distinctly. Each *container* is a lightweight virtual machine, all of which run as individual entities and are oblivious of other entities within the same system.

The following are namespace APIs described in the Linux man page for `namespaces`:

```
clone(2)
The clone(2) system call creates a new process. If the flags argument of
the call specifies one or more of the CLONE_NEW* flags listed below, then
new namespaces are created for each flag, and the child process is made a
member of those namespaces.(This system call also implements a number of
features unrelated to namespaces.)

setns(2)
The setns(2) system call allows the calling process to join an existing
namespace. The namespace to join is specified via a file descriptor that
refers to one of the /proc/[pid]/ns files described below.

unshare(2)
The unshare(2) system call moves the calling process to a new namespace. If
the flags argument of the call specifies one or more of the CLONE_NEW*
flags listed below, then new namespaces are created for each flag, and the
calling process is made a member of those namespaces. (This system call
also implements a number of features unrelated to namespaces.)
Namespace     Constant             Isolates
Cgroup        CLONE_NEWCGROUP      Cgroup root directory
IPC           CLONE_NEWIPC         System V IPC, POSIX message queues
```

```
Network     CLONE_NEWNET     Network devices, stacks, ports, etc.
Mount       CLONE_NEWNS      Mount points
PID         CLONE_NEWPID     Process IDs
User        CLONE_NEWUSER    User and group IDs
UTS         CLONE_NEWUTS     Hostname and NIS domain name
```

Summary

We understood one of the principal abstractions of Linux called the process, and the whole ecosystem that facilitates this abstraction. The challenge now remains in running the scores of processes by providing fair CPU time. With many-core systems imposing a multitude of processes with diverse policies and priorities, the need for deterministic scheduling is paramount.

In our next chapter, we will delve into process scheduling, another critical aspect of process management, and comprehend how the Linux scheduler is designed to handle this diversity.

2
Deciphering the Process Scheduler

Process scheduling is one of the most crucial executive jobs of any operating system, Linux being no different. The heuristics and efficiency in scheduling processes is what make any operating system tick and also give it an identity, such as a general-purpose operating system, server, or a real-time system. In this chapter, we will get under the skin of the Linux scheduler, deciphering concepts such as:

- Linux scheduler design
- Scheduling classes
- Scheduling policies and priorities
- Completely Fair Scheduler
- Real-Time Scheduler
- Deadline Scheduler
- Group scheduling
- Preemption

Process schedulers

The effectiveness of any operating system is proportional to its ability to fairly schedule all contending processes. The process scheduler is the core component of the kernel, which computes and decides when and for how long a process gets CPU time. Ideally, processes require a *timeslice* of the CPU to run, so schedulers essentially need to allocate slices of processor time fairly among processes.

A scheduler typically has to:

- Avoid process starvation
- Manage priority scheduling
- Maximize throughput of all processes
- Ensure low turnaround time
- Ensure even resource usage
- Avoid CPU hogging
- Consider process' behavioral patterns for prioritization
- Elegantly subsidize under heavy load
- Handle scheduling on multiple cores efficiently

Linux process scheduler design

Linux, which was primarily developed for desktop systems, has unassumingly evolved into a multi-dimensional operating system with its usage spread across embedded devices, mainframes, and supercomputers to room-sized servers. It has also seamlessly accommodated the ever-evolving diverse computing platforms such as SMP, virtualization, and real-time systems. The diversity of these platforms is brought forth by the kind of processes that run on these systems. For instance, a highly interactive desktop system may run processes that are I/O bound, and a real-time system thrives on deterministic processes. Every kind of process thus calls for a different kind of heuristic when it needs to be fairly scheduled, as a CPU-intensive process may require more CPU time than a normal process, and a real-time process would require deterministic execution. Linux, which caters to a wide spectrum of systems, is thus confronted with addressing the varying scheduling challenges that come along when managing these diverse processes.

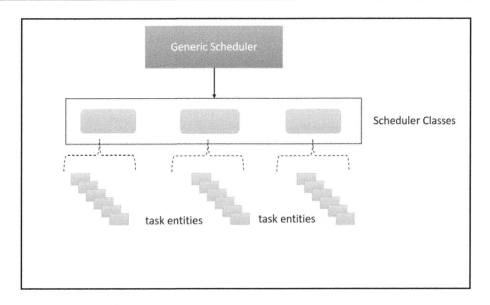

The intrinsic design of Linux's process scheduler elegantly and deftly handles this challenge by adopting a simple two-layered model, with its first layer, the **Generic Scheduler**, defining abstract operations that serve as entry functions for the scheduler, and the second layer, the scheduling class, implementing the actual scheduling operations, where each class is dedicated to handling the scheduling heuristics of a particular kind of process. This model enables the generic scheduler to remain abstracted from the implementation details of every scheduler class. For instance, normal processes (I/O bound) can be handled by one class, and processes that require deterministic execution, such as real-time processes, can be handled by another class. This architecture also enables adding a new scheduling class seamlessly. The previous figure depicts the layered design of the process scheduler.

The generic scheduler defines abstract interfaces through a structure called `sched_class`:

```
struct sched_class {
    const struct sched_class *next;

    void (*enqueue_task) (struct rq *rq, struct task_struct *p, int
flags);
    void (*dequeue_task) (struct rq *rq, struct task_struct *p, int flags);
    void (*yield_task) (struct rq *rq);
        bool (*yield_to_task) (struct rq *rq, struct task_struct *p, bool
preempt);

    void (*check_preempt_curr) (struct rq *rq, struct task_struct *p, int
flags);
```

```
        /*
         * It is the responsibility of the pick_next_task() method that
will
         * return the next task to call put_prev_task() on the @prev task or
    * something equivalent.
     *
         * May return RETRY_TASK when it finds a higher prio class has
runnable
     * tasks.
 */
        struct task_struct * (*pick_next_task) (struct rq *rq,
                                        struct task_struct *prev,
                                    struct rq_flags *rf);
     void (*put_prev_task) (struct rq *rq, struct task_struct *p);

#ifdef CONFIG_SMP
        int   (*select_task_rq)(struct task_struct *p, int task_cpu, int
sd_flag, int flags);
      void (*migrate_task_rq)(struct task_struct *p);

      void (*task_woken) (struct rq *this_rq, struct task_struct *task);

   void (*set_cpus_allowed)(struct task_struct *p,
                            const struct cpumask *newmask);

     void (*rq_online)(struct rq *rq);
  void (*rq_offline)(struct rq *rq);
#endif

      void (*set_curr_task) (struct rq *rq);
    void (*task_tick) (struct rq *rq, struct task_struct *p, int queued);
     void (*task_fork) (struct task_struct *p);
        void (*task_dead) (struct task_struct *p);

   /*
         * The switched_from() call is allowed to drop rq->lock, therefore
we
     * cannot assume the switched_from/switched_to pair is serialized by
         * rq->lock. They are however serialized by p->pi_lock.
      */
       void (*switched_from) (struct rq *this_rq, struct task_struct
*task);
      void (*switched_to) (struct rq *this_rq, struct task_struct *task);
        void (*prio_changed) (struct rq *this_rq, struct task_struct *task,
                        int oldprio);

   unsigned int (*get_rr_interval) (struct rq *rq,
                                    struct task_struct *task);
```

```
        void (*update_curr) (struct rq *rq);

#define TASK_SET_GROUP   0
#define TASK_MOVE_GROUP   1

#ifdef CONFIG_FAIR_GROUP_SCHED
        void (*task_change_group) (struct task_struct *p, int type);
#endif
};
```

Every scheduler class implements operations as defined in the sched_class structure. As of the 4.12.x kernel, there are three scheduling classes: the **Completely Fair Scheduling (CFS)** class , Real-Time Scheduling class, and Deadline Scheduling class, with each class handling processes with specific scheduling requirements. The following code snippets show how each class populates its operations as per the sched_class structure.

CFS class:

```
const struct sched_class fair_sched_class = {
        .next                   = &idle_sched_class,
        .enqueue_task           = enqueue_task_fair,
        .dequeue_task           = dequeue_task_fair,
        .yield_task             = yield_task_fair,
        .yield_to_task          = yield_to_task_fair,

        .check_preempt_curr     = check_preempt_wakeup,

        .pick_next_task         = pick_next_task_fair,
        .put_prev_task          = put_prev_task_fair,
....
}
```

Real-Time Scheduling class:

```
const struct sched_class rt_sched_class = {
        .next                   = &fair_sched_class,
        .enqueue_task           = enqueue_task_rt,
        .dequeue_task           = dequeue_task_rt,
        .yield_task             = yield_task_rt,

        .check_preempt_curr     = check_preempt_curr_rt,

        .pick_next_task         = pick_next_task_rt,
        .put_prev_task          = put_prev_task_rt,
....
}
```

Deadline Scheduling class:

```
const struct sched_class dl_sched_class = {
        .next                   = &rt_sched_class,
        .enqueue_task           = enqueue_task_dl,
        .dequeue_task           = dequeue_task_dl,
        .yield_task             = yield_task_dl,

        .check_preempt_curr     = check_preempt_curr_dl,

        .pick_next_task         = pick_next_task_dl,
        .put_prev_task          = put_prev_task_dl,
   ....
   }
```

Runqueue

Conventionally, the runqueue contains all the processes that are contending for CPU time on a given CPU core (a runqueue is per-CPU). The generic scheduler is designed to look into the runqueue whenever it is invoked to schedule the next best runnable task. Maintaining a common runqueue for all the runnable processes would not be a possible since each scheduling class deals with specific scheduling policies and priorities.

The kernel addresses this by bringing its design principles to the fore. Each scheduling class defined the layout of its runqueue data structure as best suitable for its policies. The generic scheduler layer implements an abstract runqueue structure with common elements that serves as the runqueue interface. This structure is extended with pointers that refer to class-specific runqueues. In other words, all scheduling classes embed their runqueues into the main runqueue structure. This is a classic design hack, which lets every scheduler class choose an appropriate layout for its runqueue data structure.

The following code snippet of struct rq (runqueue) will help us comprehend the concept (elements related to SMP have been omitted from the structure to keep our focus on what's relevant):

```
struct rq {
      /* runqueue lock: */
      raw_spinlock_t lock;
  /*
   * nr_running and cpu_load should be in the same cacheline because
   * remote CPUs use both these fields when doing load calculation.
   */
      unsigned int nr_running;
  #ifdef CONFIG_NUMA_BALANCING
```

```
                unsigned int nr_numa_running;
                unsigned int nr_preferred_running;
        #endif
                #define CPU_LOAD_IDX_MAX 5
                unsigned long cpu_load[CPU_LOAD_IDX_MAX];
#ifdef CONFIG_NO_HZ_COMMON
#ifdef CONFIG_SMP
                unsigned long last_load_update_tick;
#endif /* CONFIG_SMP */
                unsigned long nohz_flags;
#endif /* CONFIG_NO_HZ_COMMON */
#ifdef CONFIG_NO_HZ_FULL
                unsigned long last_sched_tick;
#endif
                /* capture load from *all* tasks on this cpu: */
                struct load_weight load;
                unsigned long nr_load_updates;
                u64 nr_switches;

                struct cfs_rq cfs;
                struct rt_rq rt;
                struct dl_rq dl;

#ifdef CONFIG_FAIR_GROUP_SCHED
                /* list of leaf cfs_rq on this cpu: */
                struct list_head leaf_cfs_rq_list;
                struct list_head *tmp_alone_branch;
#endif /* CONFIG_FAIR_GROUP_SCHED */

                 unsigned long nr_uninterruptible;

                struct task_struct *curr, *idle, *stop;
                unsigned long next_balance;
                struct mm_struct *prev_mm;

                unsigned int clock_skip_update;
                u64 clock;
                u64 clock_task;

                atomic_t nr_iowait;

#ifdef CONFIG_IRQ_TIME_ACCOUNTING
                u64 prev_irq_time;
#endif
#ifdef CONFIG_PARAVIRT
                u64 prev_steal_time;
#endif
#ifdef CONFIG_PARAVIRT_TIME_ACCOUNTING
```

```
        u64 prev_steal_time_rq;
#endif

        /* calc_load related fields */
        unsigned long calc_load_update;
        long calc_load_active;

#ifdef CONFIG_SCHED_HRTICK
#ifdef CONFIG_SMP
        int hrtick_csd_pending;
        struct call_single_data hrtick_csd;
#endif
        struct hrtimer hrtick_timer;
#endif
...
#ifdef CONFIG_CPU_IDLE
        /* Must be inspected within a rcu lock section */
        struct cpuidle_state *idle_state;
#endif
};
```

You can see how the scheduling classes (`cfs`, `rt`, and `dl`) embed themselves into the runqueue. Other elements of interest in the runqueue are:

- `nr_running`: This denotes the number of processes in the runqueue
- `load`: This denotes the current load on the queue (all runnable processes)
- `curr` and `idle`: These point to the *task_struct* of the current running task and the idle task, respectively. The idle task is scheduled when there are no other tasks to run.

The scheduler's entry point

The process of scheduling starts with a call to the generic scheduler, that is, the `schedule()` function, defined in `<kernel/sched/core.c>`. This is perhaps one of the most invoked routines in the kernel. The functionality of `schedule()` is to pick the next best runnable task. The `pick_next_task()` of the `schedule()` function iterates through all the corresponding functions contained in the scheduler classes and ends up picking the next best task to run. Each scheduler class is linked using a single linked list, which enables the `pick_next_task()` to iterate through these classes.

Considering that Linux was primarily designed to cater to highly interactive systems, the function first looks for the next best runnable task in the CFS class if there are no higher-priority runnable tasks in any of the other classes (this is done by checking whether the total number of runnable tasks (`nr_running`) in the runqueue is equal to the total number of runnable tasks in the CFS class's sub-runqueue); else, it iterates through all the other classes and picks the next best runnable task. Finally, if no tasks are found, it invokes the idle, background tasks (which always returns a non-null value).

The following code block shows the implementation of `pick_next_task()`:

```
/*
 * Pick up the highest-prio task:
 */
static inline struct task_struct *
pick_next_task(struct rq *rq, struct task_struct *prev, struct rq_flags
*rf)
{
    const struct sched_class *class;
  struct task_struct *p;

      /*
        * Optimization: we know that if all tasks are in the fair class we
can
    * call that function directly, but only if the @prev task wasn't of a
        * higher scheduling class, because otherwise those loose the
      * opportunity to pull in more work from other CPUs.
        */
      if (likely((prev->sched_class == &idle_sched_class ||
                prev->sched_class == &fair_sched_class) &&
            rq->nr_running == rq->cfs.h_nr_running)) {

        p = fair_sched_class.pick_next_task(rq, prev, rf);
            if (unlikely(p == RETRY_TASK))
                goto again;
```

```
            /* Assumes fair_sched_class->next == idle_sched_class */
                if (unlikely(!p))
                    p = idle_sched_class.pick_next_task(rq, prev, rf);

            return p;
    }

again:
        for_each_class(class) {
            p = class->pick_next_task(rq, prev, rf);
                if (p) {
                    if (unlikely(p == RETRY_TASK))
                            goto again;
                        return p;
            }
    }

    /* The idle class should always have a runnable task: */
    BUG();
}
```

Process priorities

The decision of which process to run depends on the priority of the process. Every process is labelled with a priority value, giving it an immediate position in terms of when it will be given CPU time. Priorities are fundamentally classified into *dynamic* and *static* priorities on *nix systems. **Dynamic priorities** are basically applied to normal processes dynamically by the kernel, considering various factors such as the nice value of the process, its historic behavior (I/O bound or processor bound), lapsed execution, and waiting time. **Static priorities** are applied to real-time processes by the user and the kernel does not change their priorities dynamically. Processes with static priorities are thus given higher priority when scheduling.

I/O bound process: When the execution of a process is heavily punctuated with I/O operations (waiting for a resource or an event), for instance a text editor, which almost alternates between running and waiting for a key press, such processes are called I/O bound. Due to this nature, the scheduler normally allocates short processor time slices to I/O-bound processes and multiplexes them with other processes, adding the overhead of context switching and the subsequent heuristics of computing the next best process to run.

Processor bound process: These are processes that love to stick on to CPU time slices, as they require maximum utilization of the processor's computing capacity. Processes requiring heavy computations such as complex scientific calculations, and video rendering codecs are processor bound. Though the need for a longer CPU slice looks desirable, the expectation to run them under fixed time periods is not often a requirement. Schedulers on interactive operating systems tend to favor more I/O-bound processes than processor-bound ones. Linux, which aims for good interactive performance, is more optimized for faster response time, inclining towards I/O bound processes, even though processor-bound processes are run less frequently they are ideally given longer timeslices to run.

Processes can also be **multi-faceted**, with an I/O-bound process needing to perform serious scientific computations, burning the CPU.

The *nice* value of any normal process ranges between 19 (lowest priority) and -20 (highest priority), with 0 being the default value. A higher nice value indicates a lower priority (the process is being nicer to other processes). Real-time processes are prioritized between 0 and 99 (static priority). All these priority ranges are from the perspective of the user.

Kernel's perspective of priorities

Linux however looks at process priorities from its own perspective. It adds a lot more computation for arriving at the priority of a process. Basically, it scales all priorities between 0 to 139, where 0 to 99 is assigned for real-time processes and 100 to 139 represents the nice value range (-20 to 19).

Scheduler classes

Let's now go deeper into each scheduling class and understand the operations, policies, and heuristics it engages in managing scheduling operations adeptly and elegantly for its processes. As mentioned earlier, an instance of `struct sched_class` must be provided by each scheduling class; let's look at some of the key elements from that structure:

- `enqueue_task`: Basically adds a new process to the run queue
- `dequeue_task`: When the process is taken off the runqueue
- `yield_task`: When the process wants to relinquish CPU voluntarily
- `pick_next_task`: The corresponding function of the *pick_next_task* called by *schedule()*. It picks up the next best runnable task from its class.

Completely Fair Scheduling class (CFS)

All processes with dynamic priorities are handled by the CFS class, and as most processes in general-purpose *nix systems are normal (non-realtime), CFS remains the busiest scheduler class in the kernel.

CFS relies on maintaining *balance* in allocating processor time to tasks, based on policies and dynamic priorities assigned per task. Process scheduling under CFS is implemented under the premise that it has an "ideal, precise multi-tasking CPU," that equally powers all processes at its peak capacity. For instance, if there are two processes, the perfectly multi-tasking CPU ensures that both processes run simultaneously, each utilizing 50% of its power. As this is practically impossible (achieving parallelism), CFS allocates processor time to a process by maintaining proper balance across all contending processes. If a process fails to receive a fair amount of time, it is considered out of balance, and thus goes in next as the best runnable process.

CFS does not rely on the traditional time slices for allocating processor time, but rather uses a concept of virtual runtime (*vruntime*): it denotes the amount of time a process got CPU time, which means a low `vruntime` value indicates that the process is processor deprived and a high `vruntime` value denotes that the process acquired considerable processor time. Processes with low `vruntime` values get maximum priority when scheduling. CFS also engages *sleeper fairness* for processes that are ideally waiting for an I/O request. Sleeper fairness demands that waiting processes be given considerable CPU time when they eventually wake up, post event. Based on the `vruntime` value, CFS decides what amount of time the process is to run. It also uses the nice value to weigh a process in relation to all contending processes: a higher-value, low-priority process gets less weight, and a lower-value, high-priority task gets more weight. Even handling processes with varying priorities is elegant in Linux, as a lower-priority task gets considerable factors of delay compared to a higher-priority task; this makes the time allocated to a low-priority task dissipate quickly.

Computing priorities and time slices under CFS

Priorities are assigned based on how long the process is waiting, how long the process ran, the process's historical behavior, and its nice value. Normally, schedulers engage complex algorithms to end up with the next best process to run.

In computing the timeslice every process gets, CFS not just relies on the nice value of the process but also looks at the load weight of the process. For every jump in the nice value of a process by 1, there will be a 10% reduction in the CPU timeslice, and for every decrease in the nice value by 1, there will be a 10% addition in the CPU timeslice, indicating that nice values are multiplicative by a 10% change for every jump. To compute the load weight for corresponding nice values, the kernel maintains an array called `prio_to_weight`, where each nice value corresponds to a weight:

```
static const int prio_to_weight[40] = {
 /* -20 */       88761,      71755,      56483,      46273,      36291,
 /* -15 */       29154,      23254,      18705,      14949,      11916,
 /* -10 */        9548,       7620,       6100,       4904,       3906,
 /*  -5 */        3121,       2501,       1991,       1586,       1277,
 /*   0 */        1024,        820,        655,        526,        423,
 /*   5 */         335,        272,        215,        172,        137,
 /*  10 */         110,         87,         70,         56,         45,
 /*  15 */          36,         29,         23,         18,         15,
};
```

The load value of a process is stored in the `weight` field of `struct load_weight`.

Like a process's weight, the runqueue of CFS is also assigned a weight, which is the gross weight of all the tasks in the runqueue. Now the timeslice is computed by factoring the entity's load weight, the runqueue's load weight, and the `sched_period` (scheduling period).

CFS's runqueue

CFS sheds the need for a normal runqueue and uses a self-balancing, red-black tree instead to get to the next best process to run in the shortest possible time. The *RB tree* holds all the contending processes and facilitates easy and quick insertion, deletion, and searching of processes. The highest-priority process is placed to its leftmost node. The `pick_next_task()` function now just picks the leftmost node from the `rb tree` to schedule.

Group scheduling

To ensure fairness when scheduling, CFS is designed to guarantee that every runnable process gets at least one run on the processor under a defined time duration, called the **scheduling period**. Within a scheduling period, CFS rudimentarily ensures fairness or, in other words, ensures that unfairness is kept at a minimum, as each process at least runs once. CFS divides the scheduling period into timeslices among all threads of execution to avoid process starvation; however, imagine a scenario where process A spawns 10 threads of execution and process B spawns 5 threads of execution: here CFS divides timeslices to all the threads equally, leading to process A and its spawned threads getting the maximum time and process B to be dealt with unfairly. If process A keeps on spawning more threads, the situation may become grave for process B and its spawned threads, as process B will have to contend with the minimum scheduling granularity or timeslice (which is 1 millisecond). Fairness in this scenario demands process A and B getting equal timeslices with spawned threads to share these timeslices internally. For instance, if process A and B get 50% of the time each, then process A shall divide its 50% time among its spawned 10 threads, with each thread getting 5% time internally.

To address this issue and to keep up the fairness, CFS introduced **group scheduling**, where timeslices are allotted to groups of threads instead of individual threads. Continuing the same example, under group scheduling, process A and its spawned threads belong to one group and process B and its spawned threads belong to another. As scheduling granularity is imposed at a group level and not at a thread level, it gives process A and B equal share of processor time, with process A and B dividing the timeslice among its group members internally. Here, a thread spawned under process A suffers as it is penalized for spawning more threads of execution. To ensure group scheduling, CONFIG_FAIR_GROUP_SCHED is to be set when configuring the kernel. CFS task groups are represented by the structure sched_entity, and every group is referred as a **scheduling entity**. The following code snippet shows key elements of the scheduling entity structure:

```
struct sched_entity {
        struct load_weight       load;   /* for load-balancing */
        struct rb_node           run_node;
        struct list_head         group_node;
        unsigned int             on_rq;

        u64                      exec_start;
        u64                      sum_exec_runtime;
        u64                      vruntime;
        u64                      prev_sum_exec_runtime;

        u64                      nr_migrations;

#ifdef CONFIG_SCHEDSTATS
        struct sched_statistics statistics;
#endif

#ifdef CONFIG_FAIR_GROUP_SCHED
        int depth;
        struct sched_entity *parent;
         /* rq on which this entity is (to be) queued: */
        struct cfs_rq            *cfs_rq;
        /* rq "owned" by this entity/group: */
        struct cfs_rq            *my_q;
#endif

....
};
```

- load: Denotes the amount of load each entity bears on the total load of the queue
- vruntime: Denotes the amount of time the process ran

Scheduling entities under many-core systems

Task groups can in a many-core system run on any CPU core, but to facilitate this, creating only one scheduling entity will not suffice. Groups thus must create a scheduling entity for every CPU core on the system. Scheduling entities across CPUs are represented by `struct task_group`:

```
/* task group related information */
struct task_group {
        struct cgroup_subsys_state css;

#ifdef CONFIG_FAIR_GROUP_SCHED
 /* schedulable entities of this group on each cpu */
        struct sched_entity **se;
 /* runqueue "owned" by this group on each cpu */
  struct cfs_rq **cfs_rq;
    unsigned long shares;

#ifdef CONFIG_SMP
        /*
          * load_avg can be heavily contended at clock tick time, so put
    * it in its own cacheline separated from the fields above which
    * will also be accessed at each tick.
      */
        atomic_long_t load_avg ____cacheline_aligned;
#endif
#endif

#ifdef CONFIG_RT_GROUP_SCHED
    struct sched_rt_entity **rt_se;
   struct rt_rq **rt_rq;

        struct rt_bandwidth rt_bandwidth;
#endif

        struct rcu_head rcu;
       struct list_head list;

       struct task_group *parent;
         struct list_head siblings;
         struct list_head children;

#ifdef CONFIG_SCHED_AUTOGROUP
        struct autogroup *autogroup;
#endif

    struct cfs_bandwidth cfs_bandwidth;
```

```
};
```

Now every task group has a scheduling entity for every CPU core along with a CFS runqueue associated with it. When a task from one task group migrates from one CPU core (x) to another CPU core (y), the task is dequeued from the CFS runqueue of CPU x and enqueued to the CFS runqueue of CPU y.

Scheduling policies

Scheduling policies are applied to processes, and help in determining scheduling decisions. If you recall, in `Chapter 1`, *Comprehending Processes, Address Space, and Threads*, we described the `int policy` field under the scheduling attributes of struct `task_struct`. The `policy field` contains the value indicating which policy is to be applied to the process when scheduling. The CFS class handles all normal processes using the following two policies:

- `SCHED_NORMAL (0)`: This is used for all normal processes. All non-realtime processes can be summarized as normal processes. As Linux aims to be a highly responsive and interactive system, most of the scheduling activity and heuristics are centered to fairly schedule normal processes. Normal processes are referred to as `SCHED_OTHER` as per POSIX.
- `SCHED_BATCH (3)`: Normally in servers, where processes are non-interactive, CPU-bound batch processing is employed. These processes that are CPU intensive are given less priority than a `SCHED_NORMAL` process, and they do not preempt normal processes, which are scheduled.
- The CFS class also handles scheduling the idle process, which is specified by the following policy:
- `SCHED_IDLE (5)`: When there are no processes to run, the *idle* process (low-priority background processes) is scheduled. The *idle* process is assigned the least priority among all processes.

Real-time scheduling class

Linux supports soft real-time tasks and they are scheduled by the real-time scheduling class. rt processes are assigned static priorities and are unchanged dynamically by the kernel. As real-time tasks aim at deterministic runs and desire control over when and how long they are to be scheduled, they are always given preference over normal tasks (SCHED_NORMAL). Unlike CFS, which uses rb tree as its sub-runqueue, the rt scheduler, which is less complicated, uses a simple linked list per priority value (1 to 99). Linux applies two real-time policies, rr and fifo, when scheduling static priority processes; these are indicated by the policy element of struct task_struct.

- SCHED_FIFO (1): This uses the first in, first out method to schedule soft real-time processes
- SCHED_RR (2): This is the round-robin policy used to schedule soft real-time processes

FIFO

FIFO is a scheduling mechanism applied to processes with priorities higher than 0 (0 is assigned to normal processes). FIFO processes run sans any timeslice allocation; in other words, they invariably run until they block for some event or explicitly yield to another process. A FIFO process also gets preempted when the scheduler encounters a higher-priority runnable FIFO, RR, or deadline task. When scheduler encounters more than one fifo task with the same priority, it runs the processes in round robin, starting with the first process at the head of the list. On preemption, the process is added back to the tail of the list. If a higher-priority process preempts the FIFO process, it waits at the head of the list, and when all other high-priority tasks are preempted, it is again picked up to run. When a new fifo process becomes runnable, it is added to the tail of the list.

RR

The round-robin policy is similar to FIFO, with the only exception being that it is allocated a timeslice to run. This is kind of an enhancement to FIFO (as a FIFO process may run until it yields or waits). Similar to FIFO, the RR process at the head of the list is picked for execution (if no other higher-priority task is available) and on completion of the timeslice gets preempted and is added back to the tail end of the list. RR processes with the same priority run round robin until preempted by a high-priority task. When a high-priority task preempts an RR task, it waits at the head of the list, and on resumption runs for the remainder of its timeslice only.

Real-time group scheduling

Similar to group scheduling under CFS, real-time processes can also be grouped for scheduling with CONFIG_RT_GROUP_SCHED set. For group scheduling to succeed, each group must be assigned a portion of CPU time, with a guarantee that the timeslice is enough to run the tasks under each entity, or it fails. So "run time" (a portion of how much time a CPU can spend running in a period) is allocated per group. The run time allocated to one group will not be used by another group. CPU time that is not allocated for real-time groups will be used by normal-priority tasks and any time unused by the real-time entities will also be picked by the normal tasks. FIFO and RR groups are represented by struct sched_rt_entity:

```
struct sched_rt_entity {
  struct list_head              run_list;
  unsigned long                 timeout;
   unsigned long                 watchdog_stamp;
    unsigned int                  time_slice;
       unsigned short                on_rq;
     unsigned short                on_list;

     struct sched_rt_entity        *back;
#ifdef CONFIG_RT_GROUP_SCHED
   struct sched_rt_entity        *parent;
   /* rq on which this entity is (to be) queued: */
   struct rt_rq                  *rt_rq;
    /* rq "owned" by this entity/group: */
    struct rt_rq                  *my_q;
#endif
};
```

Deadline scheduling class (sporadic task model deadline scheduling)

Deadline represents the new breed of RT processes on Linux (added since the 3.14 kernel). Unlike FIFO and RR, where processes may hog CPU or be bound by timeslices, a deadline process, which is based on GEDF (Global Earliest Deadline First) and CBS (Constant Bandwidth Server) algorithms, predetermines its runtime requirements. A sporadic process internally runs multiple tasks, with each task having a relative deadline within which it must complete executing and a computation time, defining the time that the CPU needs to complete process execution. To ensure that the kernel succeeds in executing deadline processes, the kernel runs an admittance test based on the deadline parameters, and on failure returns an error, EBUSY. Processes with the deadline policy gets precedence over all other processes. Deadline processes use SCHED_DEADLINE (6) as their policy element.

Scheduler related system calls

Linux provides an entire family of system calls that manage various scheduler parameters, policies, and priorities and retrieve a multitude of scheduling-related information for the calling threads. It also enables threads to yield CPU explicitly:

```
nice(int inc)
```

nice() takes an *int* parameter and adds it to the nice value of the calling thread. On success, it returns the new nice value of the thread. Nice values are within the range 19 (lowest priority) to -20 (highest priority). *Nice* values can be incremented only within this range:

```
getpriority(int which, id_t who)
```

This returns the nice value of the thread, group, user, or set of threads of a specified user as indicated by its parameters. It returns the highest priority held by any of the processes:

```
setpriority(int which, id_t who, int prio)
```

The scheduling priority of the thread, group, user, or set of threads of a specified user as indicated by its parameters is set by setpriority. It returns zero on success:

```
sched_setscheduler(pid_t pid, int policy, const struct sched_param *param)
```

This sets both the scheduling policy and parameters of a specified thread, indicated by its `pid`. If the `pid` is zero, the policy of the calling thread will be set. The `param` argument, which specifies the scheduling parameters, points to a structure `sched_param`, which holds `int sched_priority`. `sched_priority` must be zero for normal processes and a priority value in the range 1 to 99 for FIFO and RR policies (mentioned in policy argument). It returns zero on success:

```
sched_getscheduler(pid_t pid)
```

It returns the scheduling policy of a thread (`pid`). If the `pid` is zero, the policy of the calling thread will be retrieved:

```
sched_setparam(pid_t pid, const struct sched_param *param)
```

It sets the scheduling parameters associated with the scheduling policy of the given thread (`pid`). If the `pid` is zero, the parameters of the calling process are set. On success, it returns zero:

```
sched_getparam(pid_t pid, struct sched_param *param)
```

This sets the scheduling parameters for the specified thread (`pid`). If the `pid` is zero, the scheduling parameters of the calling thread will be retrieved. On success, it returns zero:

```
sched_setattr(pid_t pid, struct sched_attr *attr, unsigned int flags)
```

It sets the scheduling policy and related attributes for the specified thread (`pid`). If the `pid` is zero, the policy and attributes of the calling process are set. This is a Linux-specific call and is the superset of the functionality provided by `sched_setscheduler()` and `sched_setparam()` calls. On success, it returns zero.

```
sched_getattr(pid_t pid, struct sched_attr *attr, unsigned int size,
unsigned int flags)
```

It fetches the scheduling policy and related attributes of the specified thread (`pid`). If the `pid` is zero the scheduling policy and related attributes of the calling thread will be retrieved. This is a Linux-specific call and is a superset of the functionality provided by `sched_getscheduler()` and `sched_getparam()` calls. On success, it returns zero.

```
sched_get_priority_max(int policy)
sched_get_priority_min(int policy)
```

This returns the max and min priority respectively for the specified `policy`. `fifo`, `rr`, `deadline`, `normal`, `batch`, and `idle` are supported values of policy.

> **sched_rr_get_interval(pid_t** pid, **struct timespec** *tp)

It fetches the time quantum of the specified thread (`pid`) and writes it into the `timespec` `struct`, specified by `tp`. If the `pid` is zero, the time quantum of the calling process is fetched into `tp`. This is only applicable to processes with the *rr* policy. On success, it returns zero.

> **sched_yield**(void)

This is called to relinquish the CPU explicitly. The thread is now added back to the queue. On success, it returns zero.

Processor affinity calls

Linux-specific processor affinity calls are provided, which help the threads define on which CPU(s) they want to run. By default, every thread inherits the processor affinity of its parent, but it can define its affinity mask to determine its processor affinity. On many-core systems, CPU affinity calls help in enhancing the performance, by helping the process stick to one core (Linux however attempts to keep a thread on one CPU). The affinity bitmask information is contained in the `cpu_allowed` field of `struct task_struct`. The affinity calls are as follows:

> **sched_setaffinity(pid_t** pid, **size_t** cpusetsize, **const cpu_set_t** *mask)

It sets the CPU affinity mask of the thread (`pid`) to the value mentioned by `mask`. If the thread (`pid`) is not running in one of the specified CPU's queues, it is migrated to the specified `cpu`. On success, it returns zero.

> **sched_getaffinity(pid_t** pid, **size_t** cpusetsize, **cpu_set_t** *mask)

This fetches the affinity mask of the thread (`pid`) into the `cpusetsize` structure, pointed to by *mask*. If the `pid` is zero, the mask of the calling thread is returned. On success, it returns zero.

Process preemption

Understanding preemption and context switching is key to fully comprehending scheduling and the impact it has on the kernel in maintaining low latency and consistency. Every process must be preempted either implicitly or explicitly to make way for another process. Preemption might lead to context switching, which requires a low-level architecture-specific operation, carried out by the function `context_switch()`. There are two primary tasks that need to be done for a processor to switch its context: switch the virtual memory mapping of the old process with the new one, and switch the processor state from that of the old process to the new one. These two tasks are carried out by `switch_mm()` and `switch_to()`.

Preemption can happen for any of the following reasons:

When a high-priority process becomes runnable. For this, the scheduler will have to periodically check for a high-priority runnable thread. On return from interrupts and system calls, `TIF_NEED_RESCHEDULE` (kernel-provided flag that indicates the need for a reschedule) is set, invoking the scheduler. Since there is a periodic timer interrupt that is guaranteed to occur at regular intervals, invocation of the scheduler is guaranteed. Preemption also happens when a process enters a blocking call or on occurrence of an interrupt event.

The Linux kernel historically has been non-preemptive, which means a task in kernel mode is non-preemptible unless an interrupt event occurs or it chooses to explicitly relinquish CPU. Since the 2.6 kernel, preemption has been added (needs to be enabled during kernel build). With kernel preemption enabled, a task in kernel mode is preemptible for all the reasons listed, but a kernel-mode task is allowed to disable kernel preemption while carrying out critical operations. This has been made possible by adding a preemption counter (`preempt_count`) to each process's `thread_info` structure. Tasks can disable/enable preemption through the kernel macros `preempt_disable()` and `preempt_enable()`, which in turn increment and decrement the `preempt_counter`. This ensures that the kernel is preemptible only when the `preempt_counter` is zero (indicating no acquired locks).

Critical sections in the kernel code are executed by disabling preemption, which is enforced by invoking `preempt_disable` and `preempt_enable` calls within kernel lock operations (spinlock, mutex).

Linux kernels build with "preempt rt", supporting *fully preemptible kernel* option, which when enabled makes all the kernel code including critical sections be fully preemptible.

Summary

Process scheduling is an ever-evolving aspect of the kernel, and as Linux evolves and diversifies further into many computing domains, finer tweaks and changes to the process scheduler will be mandated. However, with our understanding established over this chapter, gaining deeper insights or comprehending any new changes will be quite easy. We are now equipped to go further and explore another important aspect of job control and signal management. We will brush through basics of signals and move on into signal management data structures and routines of the kernel.

3
Signal Management

Signals provide a fundamental infrastructure in which any process can be notified of a system event asynchronously. They can also be engaged as communication mechanisms between processes. Understanding how the kernel provides and manages smooth throughput of the entire signal-handling mechanism lets us gain more grounding on the kernel. In this chapter, we shall pile on our understanding of signals, right from how processes can usher them to how the kernel deftly manages the routines to ensure signal events tick. We shall look at the following topics in great detail:

- Overview of signals and their types
- Process-level signal-management calls
- Signal data structures in process descriptors
- Kernel's signal generation and delivery mechanisms

Signals

Signals are short messages delivered to a process or a process group. The kernel uses signals to notify processes about the occurrence of a system event; signals are also used for communication between processes. Linux categorizes signals into two groups, namely general-purpose POSIX (classic Unix signals) and real-time signals. Each group consists of 32 distinct signals, identified by a unique ID:

```
#define _NSIG 64
#define _NSIG_BPW __BITS_PER_LONG
#define _NSIG_WORDS (_NSIG / _NSIG_BPW)

#define SIGHUP 1
#define SIGINT 2
#define SIGQUIT 3
```

```
#define SIGILL 4
#define SIGTRAP 5
#define SIGABRT 6
#define SIGIOT 6
#define SIGBUS 7
#define SIGFPE 8
#define SIGKILL 9
#define SIGUSR1 10
#define SIGSEGV 11
#define SIGUSR2 12
#define SIGPIPE 13
#define SIGALRM 14
#define SIGTERM 15
#define SIGSTKFLT 16
#define SIGCHLD 17
#define SIGCONT 18
#define SIGSTOP 19
#define SIGTSTP 20
#define SIGTTIN 21
#define SIGTTOU 22
#define SIGURG 23
#define SIGXCPU 24
#define SIGXFSZ 25
#define SIGVTALRM 26
#define SIGPROF 27
#define SIGWINCH 28
#define SIGIO 29
#define SIGPOLL SIGIO
/*
#define SIGLOST 29
*/
#define SIGPWR 30
#define SIGSYS 31
#define SIGUNUSED 31

/* These should not be considered constants from userland. */
#define SIGRTMIN 32
#ifndef SIGRTMAX
#define SIGRTMAX _NSIG
#endif
```

Signals in the general-purpose category are bound to a specific system event and are named appropriately through macros. Those in the real-time category aren't bound to a specific event, and are free for applications to engage for process communication; the kernel refers to them with generic names: SIGRTMIN and SIGRTMAX.

Upon generation of a signal, the kernel delivers the signal event to the destination process, which in turn can respond to the signal as per the configured action, called **signal disposition**.

The following is the list of actions that a process can set up as its signal disposition. A process can set up any one of the actions as its signal disposition at a point in time, but it can switch between these actions any number of times without any restrictions.

- **Kernel handler**: The kernel implements a default handler for each signal. These handlers are available to a process through the signal handler table of its task structure. Upon reception of a signal, a process can request execution of the appropriate signal handler. This is the default disposition.

- **Process defined handler:** A process is allowed to implement its own signal handlers, and set them up to be executed in response to a signal event. This is made possible through the appropriate system call interface, which allows the process to bind its handler routine with a signal. On occurrence of a signal, the process handler would be invoked asynchronously.

- **Ignore:** A process is also allowed to ignore the occurrence of a signal, but it needs to announce its intent to ignore by invoking the appropriate system call.

Kernel-defined default handler routines can execute any of the following actions:

- **Ignore**: Nothing happens.
- **Terminate**: Kill the process, that is, all threads in the group (similar to `exit_group`). The group leader (only) reports the `WIFSIGNALED` status to its parent.
- **Coredump**: Write a core dump file describing all threads using the same mm and then kill all those threads
- **Stop**: Stop all the threads in the group, that is, the `TASK_STOPPED` state.

Following is the summarized table that lists out actions executed by default handlers:

```
* +-------------------+-----------------+
* | POSIX signal      | default action  |
* +-------------------+-----------------+
* | SIGHUP            | terminate
* | SIGINT            | terminate
* | SIGQUIT           | coredump
* | SIGILL            | coredump
* | SIGTRAP           | coredump
* | SIGABRT/SIGIOT    | coredump
```

```
*  | SIGBUS             | coredump
*  | SIGFPE             | coredump
*  | SIGKILL            | terminate
*  | SIGUSR1            | terminate
*  | SIGSEGV            | coredump
*  | SIGUSR2            | terminate
*  | SIGPIPE            | terminate
*  | SIGALRM            | terminate
*  | SIGTERM            | terminate
*  | SIGCHLD            | ignore
*  | SIGCONT            | ignore
*  | SIGSTOP            | stop
*  | SIGTSTP            | stop
*  | SIGTTIN            | stop
*  | SIGTTOU            | stop
*  | SIGURG             | ignore
*  | SIGXCPU            | coredump
*  | SIGXFSZ            | coredump
*  | SIGVTALRM          | terminate
*  | SIGPROF            | terminate
*  | SIGPOLL/SIGIO      | terminate
*  | SIGSYS/SIGUNUSED   | coredump
*  | SIGSTKFLT          | terminate
*  | SIGWINCH           | ignore
*  | SIGPWR             | terminate
*  | SIGRTMIN-SIGRTMAX  | terminate
*  +------------------+-----------------+
*  | non-POSIX signal | default action  |
*  +------------------+-----------------+
*  | SIGEMT             | coredump |
*  +--------------------+-----------------+
```

Signal-management APIs

Applications are provided with various APIs for managing signals; we shall take a look at few of the important ones:

1. Sigaction(): User-mode processes use the POSIX API sigaction() to examine or change the disposition of a signal. This API provides a variety of attribute flags that can further define the behavior of a signal:

```
#include <signal.h>
int sigaction(int signum, const struct sigaction *act, struct sigaction
*oldact);
```

The sigaction structure is defined as something like:

```
struct sigaction {
void (*sa_handler)(int);
void (*sa_sigaction)(int, siginfo_t *, void *);
sigset_t sa_mask;
int sa_flags;
void (*sa_restorer)(void);
};
```

- `int signum` is the identifier number of a recognized `signal`. `sigaction()` examines and sets the action to be associated with this signal.
- `const struct sigaction *act` can be assigned with the address of a `struct sigaction` instance. The action specified in this structure becomes the new action bound to the signal. When the *act* pointer is left uninitialized (NULL), the current disposition is left unchanged.
- `struct sigaction *oldact` is an outparam and needs to be initialized with the address of an uninitialized `sigaction` instance; `sigaction()` returns the action currently associated with the signal through this argument.
- Following are the various `flag` options:
- `SA_NOCLDSTOP`: This flag is relevant only while binding the handler for `SIGCHLD`. It's used to disable `SIGCHLD` notifications for stop (`SIGSTP`) and resume (`SIGCONT`) events on the child process.
- `SA_NOCLDWAIT`: This flag is relevant only while binding the handler for the `SIGCHLD` or setting its disposition to `SIG_DFL`. Setting this flag causes the child process to be instantly destroyed on termination rather than having it in a *zombie* state.
- `SA_NODEFER`: Setting this flag causes the generated signal to be delivered even if the corresponding handler is in execution.
- `SA_ONSTACK`: This flag is relevant only while binding a signal handler. Setting this flag causes the signal handler to use an alternate stack; the alternate stack must be set up by the caller process through the `sigaltstack()` API. In the absence of an alternate stack, the handler will be invoked on the current stack.
- `SA_RESETHAND`: When this flag is applied with `sigaction()`, it makes the signal handler one-shot, that is, the action for the specified signal is reset to `SIG_DFL` for subsequent occurrences of this signal.
- `SA_RESTART`: This flag enables the re-entry of system call operations, interrupted by the current signal handler.

- `SA_SIGINFO`: This flag is used to indicate to the system that the signal handler is assigned--the `sa_sigaction` pointer of the `sigaction` structure instead of `sa_handler`. Handlers assigned to `sa_sigaction` receive two additional arguments:

  ```
  void handler_fn(int signo, siginfo_t *info, void *context);
  ```

  The first argument is `signum`, to which the handler is bound. The second argument is an outparam that is a pointer to an object of type `siginfo_t`, which provides additional information about the source of the signal. Following is the full definition of `siginfo_t`:

```
siginfo_t {
int si_signo; /* Signal number */
int si_errno; /* An errno value */
int si_code; /* Signal code */
int si_trapno; /* Trap number that caused hardware-generated signal
(unused on most          architectures) */
pid_t si_pid; /* Sending process ID */
uid_t si_uid; /* Real user ID of sending process */
int si_status; /* Exit value or signal */
clock_t si_utime; /* User time consumed */
clock_t si_stime; /* System time consumed */
sigval_t si_value; /* Signal value */
int si_int; /* POSIX.1b signal */
void *si_ptr; /* POSIX.1b signal */
int si_overrun; /* Timer overrun count; POSIX.1b timers */
int si_timerid; /* Timer ID; POSIX.1b timers */
void *si_addr; /* Memory location which caused fault */
long si_band; /* Band event (was int in glibc 2.3.2 and earlier) */
int si_fd; /* File descriptor */
short si_addr_lsb; /* Least significant bit of address (since Linux
2.6.32) */
void *si_call_addr; /* Address of system call instruction (since Linux
3.5) */
 int si_syscall; /* Number of attempted system call (since Linux 3.5) */
 unsigned int si_arch; /* Architecture of attempted system call (since
Linux 3.5) */
 }
```

2. `Sigprocmask()`: Apart from changing the signal disposition, which specifies the action to be executed on receipt of a signal, applications are also allowed to block or unblock signal delivery. Applications might need to carry out such operations while executing critical code blocks without preemption by an asynchronous signal handler. For instance, a network communication application might not want to handle signals while entering a code block that initiates a connection with its peers:

- `sigprocmask()` is a POSIX API, used to examine, block, and unblock signals.

```
int sigprocmask(int how, const sigset_t *set, sigset_t *oldset);
```

Any occurrence of blocked signals is queued in a per-process pending signals list. The pending queue is designed to hold one occurrence of a blocked general-purpose signal while it queues every occurrence of a real-time signal. User-mode processes can probe for pending signals using the `sigpending()` and `rt_sigpending()` APIs. These routines return a list of pending signals into an instance pointed to by the `sigset_t` pointer.

```
int sigpending(sigset_t *set);
```

The operations are applicable for all signals except `SIGKILL` and `SIGSTOP`; in other words, processes are not allowed to alter the default disposition or block `SIGSTOP` and `SIGKILL` signals.

Raising signals from a program

`kill()` and `sigqueue()` are POSIX APIs through which a process can raise a signal for another process or process group. These APIs facilitate utilization of signals as **process-communication** mechanisms:

```
int kill(pid_t pid, int sig);
int sigqueue(pid_t pid, int sig, const union sigval value);

union sigval {
int sival_int;
void *sival_ptr;
};
```

While both APIs provide arguments to specify the receiver PID and signum to be raised, sigqueue() provides an additional argument (union signal) through which *data* can be sent to the receiver process along with the signal. The destination process can access the data through struct siginfo_t (si_value) instances. Linux extends these functions with native APIs that can queue the signal to a thread group, or even to a lightweight process (LWP) in a thread group:

```
/* queue signal to specific thread in a thread group */
int tgkill(int tgid, int tid, int sig);

/* queue signal and data to a thread group */
int rt_sigqueueinfo(pid_t tgid, int sig, siginfo_t *uinfo);

/* queue signal and data to specific thread in a thread group */
int rt_tgsigqueueinfo(pid_t tgid, pid_t tid, int sig, siginfo_t *uinfo);
```

Waiting for queued signals

When applying signals for process communication, it might be more appropriate for a process to suspend itself until the occurrence of a specific signal, and resume execution on the arrival of a signal from another process. The POSIX calls sigsuspend(), sigwaitinfo(), and sigtimedwait() provide this functionality:

```
int sigsuspend(const sigset_t *mask);
int sigwaitinfo(const sigset_t *set, siginfo_t *info);
int sigtimedwait(const sigset_t *set, siginfo_t *info, const struct
timespec *timeout);
```

While all of these APIs allow a process to wait for a specified signal to occur, sigwaitinfo() provides additional data about the signal through the siginfo_t instance returned through the info pointer. sigtimedwait() extends the functionality by providing an additional argument that allows the operation to time out, making it a bounded wait call. The Linux kernel provides an alternate API that allows the process to be notified about the occurrence of a signal through a special file descriptor called signalfd():

```
#include <sys/signalfd.h>
int signalfd(int fd, const sigset_t *mask, int flags);
```

On success, signalfd() returns a file descriptor, on which the process needs to invoke read(), which blocks until any of the signals specified in the mask occur.

Signal data structures

The kernel maintains per-process signal data structures to keep track of, *signal disposition*, *blocked signals*, and *pending signal queues*. The process task structure contains appropriate references to these data structures:

```
struct task_struct {

....
....
....
/* signal handlers */
 struct signal_struct *signal;
 struct sighand_struct *sighand;

 sigset_t blocked, real_blocked;
 sigset_t saved_sigmask; /* restored if set_restore_sigmask() was used */
 struct sigpending pending;

 unsigned long sas_ss_sp;
 size_t sas_ss_size;
 unsigned sas_ss_flags;
  ....
  ....
  ....
  ....

};
```

Signal descriptors

Recall from our earlier discussions in the first chapter that Linux supports multi-threaded applications through lightweight processes. All LWPs of a threaded application are part of a *process group* and share signal handlers; each LWP (thread) maintains its own pending, and blocked signal queues.

The **signal** pointer of the task structure refers to the instance of type `signal_struct`, which is the signal descriptor. This structure is shared by all LWPs of a thread group and maintains elements such as a shared pending signal queue (for signals queued to a thread group), which is common to all threads in a process group.

The following figure represents the data structures involved in maintaining shared pending signals:

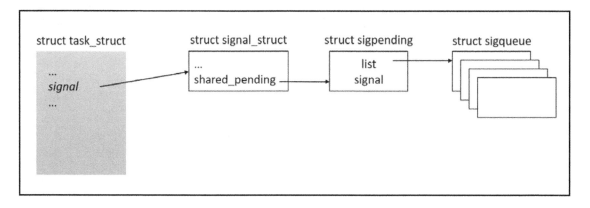

Following are a few important fields of `signal_struct`:

```
struct signal_struct {
 atomic_t sigcnt;
 atomic_t live;
 int nr_threads;
 struct list_head thread_head;

 wait_queue_head_t wait_chldexit; /* for wait4() */

 /* current thread group signal load-balancing target: */
 struct task_struct *curr_target;

 /* shared signal handling: */
 struct sigpending shared_pending;

 /* thread group exit support */
 int group_exit_code;
 /* overloaded:
 * - notify group_exit_task when ->count is equal to notify_count
 * - everyone except group_exit_task is stopped during signal delivery
 * of fatal signals, group_exit_task processes the signal.
 */
 int notify_count;
 struct task_struct *group_exit_task;

 /* thread group stop support, overloads group_exit_code too */
 int group_stop_count;
 unsigned int flags; /* see SIGNAL_* flags below */
```

Blocked and pending queues

`blocked` and `real_blocked` instances in the task structure are bit masks of blocked signals; these queues are per-process. Each LWP in a thread group thus has its own blocked signal mask. The `pending` instance of the task structure is used to queue private pending signals; all signals queued to a normal process and a specific LWP in a thread group are queued into this list:

```
struct sigpending {
  struct list_head list; // head to double linked list of struct sigqueue
  sigset_t signal; // bit mask of pending signals
};
```

The following figure represents the data structures involved in maintaining private pending signals:

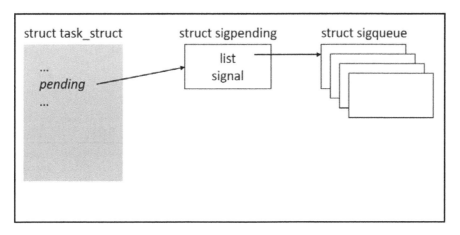

Signal handler descriptor

The sighand pointer of the task structure refers to an instance of the struct sighand_struct, which is the signal handler descriptor shared by all processes in a thread group. This structure is also shared by all processes created using clone() with the CLONE_SIGHAND flag. This structure holds an array of k_sigaction instances, each wrapping an instance of sigaction that describes the current disposition of each signal:

```
struct k_sigaction {
  struct sigaction sa;
#ifdef __ARCH_HAS_KA_RESTORER
  __sigrestore_t ka_restorer;
#endif
};

struct sighand_struct {
  atomic_t count;
  struct k_sigaction action[_NSIG];
  spinlock_t siglock;
  wait_queue_head_t signalfd_wqh;
};
```

The following figure represents the signal handler descriptor:

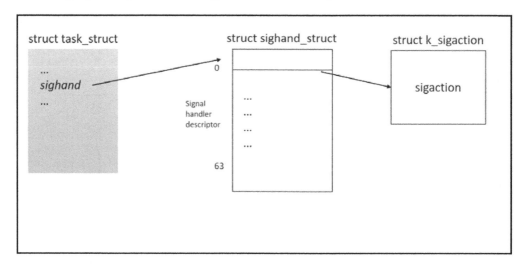

Signal generation and delivery

A signal is said to be **generated** when its occurrence is enqueued, to list of pending signals in the task structure of the receiver process or processes. The signal is generated (on a process or a group) upon request from a user-mode process, kernel, or any of the kernel services. A signal is considered to be **delivered** when the receiver process or processes are made aware of its occurrence and are forced to execute the appropriate response handler; in other words, signal delivery is equal to initialization of the corresponding handler. Ideally, every signal generated is assumed to be instantly delivered; however, there is a possibility of delay between signal generation, and it eventual delivery. To facilitate possible deferred delivery, the kernel provides separate functions for signal generation and delivery.

Signal-generation calls

The kernel provides two separate group of functions for signal generation: one set for generating signals on individual process and another for process thread groups.

- Following is the list of important functions to generate signals on a process: `send_sig()`: Generates a specified signal on a process; this function is used widely by kernel services
- `end_sig_info()`: Extends `send_sig()` with additional `siginfo_t` instances
- `force_sig()`: Used to generate priority non-maskable signals which cannot be ignored or blocked
- `force_sig_info()`: Extends `force_sig()` with additional `siginfo_t` instances.

All of these routines eventually invoke the core kernel function `send_signal()` which is programmed to generate a specified signal.

Following is the list of important functions to generate signals on a process group:

- `kill_pgrp()`: Generates the specified signal on all thread groups in a process group
- `kill_pid()`: Generates the specified signal to a thread group identified by a PID
- `kill_pid_info()`: Extends `kill_pid()` with additional `siginfo_t` instances

All of these routines invoke a function `group_send_sig_info()` which eventually invokes `send_signal()` with appropriate parameters.

The `send_signal()` function is the core signal-generation function; it invokes the `__send_signal()` routine with appropriate arguments:

```
    static int send_signal(int sig, struct siginfo *info, struct task_struct
    *t,
     int group)
    {
     int from_ancestor_ns = 0;

    #ifdef CONFIG_PID_NS
     from_ancestor_ns = si_fromuser(info) &&
     !task_pid_nr_ns(current, task_active_pid_ns(t));
    #endif

     return __send_signal(sig, info, t, group, from_ancestor_ns);
    }
```

Following are important steps executed by `__send_signal()`:

1. Check for the source of the signal from the `info` argument. If signal generation was initiated by the kernel for non-maskable `SIGKILL` or `SIGSTOP`, it immediately sets the appropriate bit of the sigpending bitmask, sets the `TIF_SIGPENDING` flag, and initiates the delivery process by waking up the target thread:

```
/*
 * fast-pathed signals for kernel-internal things like SIGSTOP
 * or SIGKILL.
 */
if (info == SEND_SIG_FORCED)
goto out_set;
....
....
....
out_set:
 signalfd_notify(t, sig);
 sigaddset(&pending->signal, sig);
 complete_signal(sig, t, group);
```

2. Invoke the __sigqeueue_alloc() function, which checks if the number of pending signals for the receiver process is less than the resource limit. If true, it increments the pending signal counter and returns the address of the struct sigqueue instance:

```
q = __sigqueue_alloc(sig, t, GFP_ATOMIC | __GFP_NOTRACK_FALSE_POSITIVE,
override_rlimit);
```

3. Enqueue the sigqueue instance into the pending list and fill out the signal information into siginfo_t:

```
if (q) {
list_add_tail(&q->list, &pending->list);
switch ((unsigned long) info) {
case (unsigned long) SEND_SIG_NOINFO:
     q->info.si_signo = sig;
     q->info.si_errno = 0;
     q->info.si_code = SI_USER;
     q->info.si_pid = task_tgid_nr_ns(current,
     task_active_pid_ns(t));
     q->info.si_uid = from_kuid_munged(current_user_ns(), current_uid());
     break;
case (unsigned long) SEND_SIG_PRIV:
     q->info.si_signo = sig;
     q->info.si_errno = 0;
     q->info.si_code = SI_KERNEL;
     q->info.si_pid = 0;
     q->info.si_uid = 0;
     break;
default:
     copy_siginfo(&q->info, info);
     if (from_ancestor_ns)
     q->info.si_pid = 0;
     break;
}
```

4. Set the appropriate signal bit in the pending signal's bitmask, and attempt signal delivery by invoking complete_signal(), which in turn sets the TIF_SIGPENDING flag:

```
sigaddset(&pending->signal, sig);
complete_signal(sig, t, group);
```

Signal delivery

After a signal is **generated** by updating appropriate entries in the receiver's task structure, through any of the previously mentioned signal-generation calls, the kernel moves into delivery mode. The signal is instantly delivered if the receiver process was on CPU and has not blocked the specified signal. Priority signals SIGSTOP and SIGKILL are delivered even if the receiver is not on CPU by waking up the process; however, for the rest of the signals, **delivery** is deferred until the process is ready to receive signals. To facilitate deferred delivery, the kernel checks for nonblocked pending signals of a process on return from **interrupt** and **system calls** before allowing a process to resume user-mode execution. When the process scheduler (invoked on return from interrupt and exceptions) finds the TIF_SIGPENDING flag set, it invokes the kernel function do_signal() to initiate delivery of the pending signal before resuming the user-mode context of the process.

Upon entry into kernel mode, the user-mode register state of the process is stored in the process kernel stack in a structure called pt_regs (architecture specific):

```
struct pt_regs {
/*
 * C ABI says these regs are callee-preserved. They aren't saved on kernel
entry
 * unless syscall needs a complete, fully filled "struct pt_regs".
 */
unsigned long r15;
unsigned long r14;
unsigned long r13;
unsigned long r12;
unsigned long rbp;
unsigned long rbx;
/* These regs are callee-clobbered. Always saved on kernel entry. */
unsigned long r11;
unsigned long r10;
unsigned long r9;
unsigned long r8;
unsigned long rax;
unsigned long rcx;
unsigned long rdx;
unsigned long rsi;
unsigned long rdi;
/*
 * On syscall entry, this is syscall#. On CPU exception, this is error
code.
 * On hw interrupt, it's IRQ number:
 */
unsigned long orig_rax;
/* Return frame for iretq */
unsigned long rip;
```

```
  unsigned long cs;
  unsigned long eflags;
  unsigned long rsp;
  unsigned long ss;
/* top of stack page */
};
```

The do_signal() routine is invoked with the address of pt_regs in the kernel stack. Though do_signal() is meant to deliver nonblocked pending signals, its implementation is architecture specific.

Following is the x86 version of do_signal():

```
void do_signal(struct pt_regs *regs)
{
struct ksignal ksig;
if (get_signal(&ksig)) {
/* Whee! Actually deliver the signal. */
handle_signal(&ksig, regs);
return;
}
/* Did we come from a system call? */
if (syscall_get_nr(current, regs) >= 0) {
/* Restart the system call - no handlers present */
switch (syscall_get_error(current, regs)) {
case -ERESTARTNOHAND:
case -ERESTARTSYS:
case -ERESTARTNOINTR:
regs->ax = regs->orig_ax;
regs->ip -= 2;
break;
case -ERESTART_RESTARTBLOCK:
regs->ax = get_nr_restart_syscall(regs);
regs->ip -= 2;
break;
}
}
/*
 * If there's no signal to deliver, we just put the saved sigmask
 * back.
 */
restore_saved_sigmask();
}
```

do_signal() invokes the get_signal() function with the address of an instance of type struct ksignal (we shall briefly consider important steps of this routine, skipping other details). This function contains a loop that invokes dequeue_signal() until all non-blocked pending signals from both private and shared pending lists are dequeued. It begins with lookup into the private pending signal queue, starting from the lowest-numbered signal, and follows into pending signals in the shared queue, and then updates the data structures to indicate that the signal is no longer pending and returns its number:

```
signr = dequeue_signal(current, &current->blocked, &ksig->info);
```

For each pending signal returned by dequeue_signal()), get_signal() retrieves the current signal disposition through a pointer of type struct ksigaction *ka:

```
ka = &sighand->action[signr-1];
```

If signal disposition is set to SIG_IGN, it silently ignores the current signal and continues iteration to retrieve another pending signal:

```
if (ka->sa.sa_handler == SIG_IGN) /* Do nothing. */
  continue;
```

If disposition is not equal to SIG_DFL, it retrieves the address of **sigaction** and initializes it into arguments ksig->ka for further execution of the user-mode handler. It further checks for the SA_ONESHOT (SA_RESETHAND) flag in the user's **sigaction** and, if set, resets the signal disposition to SIG_DFL, breaks out of the loop, and returns to the caller. do_signal() now invokes the handle_signal() routine to execute the user-mode handler (we shall discuss this in detail in the next section).

```
 if (ka->sa.sa_handler != SIG_DFL) {
/* Run the handler. */
ksig->ka = *ka;

if (ka->sa.sa_flags & SA_ONESHOT)
ka->sa.sa_handler = SIG_DFL;

break; /* will return non-zero "signr" value */
 }
```

If disposition is set to SIG_DFL, it invokes a set of macros to check for the **default action** of the kernel handler. Possible default actions are:

- **Term**: Default action is to terminate the process
- **Ign**: Default action is to ignore the signal

- **Core**: Default action is to terminate the process and dump core
- **Stop**: Default action is to stop the process
- **Cont**: Default action is to continue the process if it is currently stopped

Following is a code snippet from `get_signal()` that initiates the default action as per the set disposition:

```
/*
 * Now we are doing the default action for this signal.
 */
if (sig_kernel_ignore(signr)) /* Default is nothing. */
continue;

/*
 * Global init gets no signals it doesn't want.
 * Container-init gets no signals it doesn't want from same
 * container.
 *
 * Note that if global/container-init sees a sig_kernel_only()
 * signal here, the signal must have been generated internally
 * or must have come from an ancestor namespace. In either
 * case, the signal cannot be dropped.
 */
if (unlikely(signal->flags & SIGNAL_UNKILLABLE) &&
!sig_kernel_only(signr))
continue;

if (sig_kernel_stop(signr)) {
/*
 * The default action is to stop all threads in
 * the thread group. The job control signals
 * do nothing in an orphaned pgrp, but SIGSTOP
 * always works. Note that siglock needs to be
 * dropped during the call to is_orphaned_pgrp()
 * because of lock ordering with tasklist_lock.
 * This allows an intervening SIGCONT to be posted.
 * We need to check for that and bail out if necessary.
 */
if (signr != SIGSTOP) {
spin_unlock_irq(&sighand->siglock);

/* signals can be posted during this window */

if (is_current_pgrp_orphaned())
goto relock;

spin_lock_irq(&sighand->siglock);
```

```
}

if (likely(do_signal_stop(ksig->info.si_signo))) {
/* It released the siglock. */
goto relock;
}

/*
 * We didn't actually stop, due to a race
 * with SIGCONT or something like that.
 */
continue;
}

spin_unlock_irq(&sighand->siglock);

/*
 * Anything else is fatal, maybe with a core dump.
 */
current->flags |= PF_SIGNALED;

if (sig_kernel_coredump(signr)) {
if (print_fatal_signals)
print_fatal_signal(ksig->info.si_signo);
proc_coredump_connector(current);
/*
 * If it was able to dump core, this kills all
 * other threads in the group and synchronizes with
 * their demise. If we lost the race with another
 * thread getting here, it set group_exit_code
 * first and our do_group_exit call below will use
 * that value and ignore the one we pass it.
 */
do_coredump(&ksig->info);
}

/*
 * Death signals, no core dump.
 */
do_group_exit(ksig->info.si_signo);
/* NOTREACHED */
}
```

First, the macro `sig_kernel_ignore` checks for the default action ignore. If true, it continues loop iteration to look for the next pending signal. The second macro `sig_kernel_stop` checks for the default action stop; if true, it invokes the `do_signal_stop()` routine, which puts each thread in the process group into the `TASK_STOPPED`state. The third macro `sig_kernel_coredump` checks for the default action dump; if true, it invokes the `do_coredump()` routine, which generates the coredump binary file and terminates all the processes in the thread group. Next, for signals with default action terminate, all threads in the group are killed by invoking the `do_group_exit()` routine.

Executing user-mode handlers

Recall from our discussion in the previous section that `do_signal()` invokes the `handle_signal()` routine for delivery of pending signals whose disposition is set to user handler. The user-mode signal handler resides in the process code segment and requires access to the user-mode stack of the process; therefore, the kernel needs to switch to the user-mode stack for executing the signal handler. Successful return from the signal handler requires a switch back to the kernel stack to restore the user context for normal user-mode execution, but such an operation would fail since the kernel stack would no longer contain the user context (`struct pt_regs`) since it is emptied on each entry of the process from user to kernel mode.

To ensure smooth transition of the process for its normal execution in user mode (on return from the signal handler), `handle_signal()` moves the user-mode hardware context (`struct pt_regs`) in the kernel stack into the user-mode stack (`struct ucontext`) and sets up the handler frame to invoke the `_kernel_rt_sigreturn()` routine during return; this function copies the hardware context back into the kernel stack and restores the user-mode context for resuming normal execution of the current process.

The following figure depicts the execution of a user-mode signal handler:

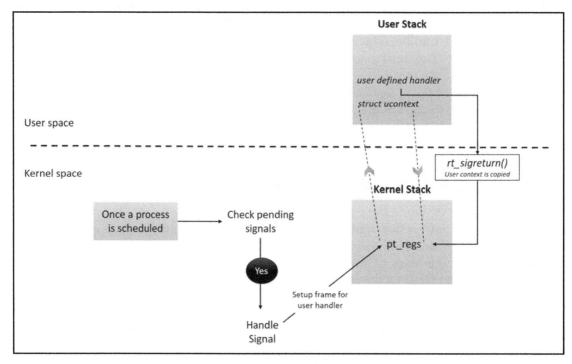

Setting up user-mode handler frames

To set up a stack frame for a user-mode handler, `handle_signal()` invokes `setup_rt_frame()` with the address of the instance of `ksignal`, which contains the `k_sigaction` associated with the signal and the pointer to `struct pt_regs` in the kernel stack of the current process.

Following is x86 implementation of `setup_rt_frame()`:

```
setup_rt_frame(struct ksignal *ksig, struct pt_regs *regs)
{
 int usig = ksig->sig;
 sigset_t *set = sigmask_to_save();
 compat_sigset_t *cset = (compat_sigset_t *) set;

 /* Set up the stack frame */
 if (is_ia32_frame(ksig)) {
 if (ksig->ka.sa.sa_flags & SA_SIGINFO)
 return ia32_setup_rt_frame(usig, ksig, cset, regs); // for 32bit systems
```

```
with SA_SIGINFO
 else
 return ia32_setup_frame(usig, ksig, cset, regs); // for 32bit systems
without SA_SIGINFO
 } else if (is_x32_frame(ksig)) {
 return x32_setup_rt_frame(ksig, cset, regs);// for systems with x32 ABI
 } else {
 return __setup_rt_frame(ksig->sig, ksig, set, regs);// Other variants of
x86
 }
}
```

It checks for the specific variant of x86 and invokes the appropriate frame setup routine. For further discussion, we shall focus on __setup_rt_frame(), which applies for x86-64. This function populates an instance of a structure called struct rt_sigframe with information needed to handle the signal, sets up a return path (through the _kernel_rt_sigreturn() function), and pushes it into the user-mode stack:

```
/*arch/x86/include/asm/sigframe.h */
#ifdef CONFIG_X86_64

struct rt_sigframe {
 char __user *pretcode;
 struct ucontext uc;
 struct siginfo info;
 /* fp state follows here */
};


-----------------------


/*arch/x86/kernel/signal.c */
static int __setup_rt_frame(int sig, struct ksignal *ksig,
 sigset_t *set, struct pt_regs *regs)
{
 struct rt_sigframe __user *frame;
 void __user *restorer;
 int err = 0;
 void __user *fpstate = NULL;

 /* setup frame with Floating Point state */
 frame = get_sigframe(&ksig->ka, regs, sizeof(*frame), &fpstate);

 if (!access_ok(VERIFY_WRITE, frame, sizeof(*frame)))
 return -EFAULT;

 put_user_try {
 put_user_ex(sig, &frame->sig);
```

```
put_user_ex(&frame->info, &frame->pinfo);
put_user_ex(&frame->uc, &frame->puc);

/* Create the ucontext. */
if (boot_cpu_has(X86_FEATURE_XSAVE))
put_user_ex(UC_FP_XSTATE, &frame->uc.uc_flags);
else
put_user_ex(0, &frame->uc.uc_flags);
put_user_ex(0, &frame->uc.uc_link);
save_altstack_ex(&frame->uc.uc_stack, regs->sp);

/* Set up to return from userspace. */
restorer = current->mm->context.vdso +
vdso_image_32.sym___kernel_rt_sigreturn;
if (ksig->ka.sa.sa_flags & SA_RESTORER)
restorer = ksig->ka.sa.sa_restorer;
put_user_ex(restorer, &frame->pretcode);

/*
 * This is movl $__NR_rt_sigreturn, %ax ; int $0x80
 *
 * WE DO NOT USE IT ANY MORE! It's only left here for historical
 * reasons and because gdb uses it as a signature to notice
 * signal handler stack frames.
 */
put_user_ex(*((u64 *)&rt_retcode), (u64 *)frame->retcode);
} put_user_catch(err);

err |= copy_siginfo_to_user(&frame->info, &ksig->info);
err |= setup_sigcontext(&frame->uc.uc_mcontext, fpstate,
regs, set->sig[0]);
err |= __copy_to_user(&frame->uc.uc_sigmask, set, sizeof(*set));

if (err)
return -EFAULT;

/* Set up registers for signal handler */
regs->sp = (unsigned long)frame;
regs->ip = (unsigned long)ksig->ka.sa.sa_handler;
regs->ax = (unsigned long)sig;
regs->dx = (unsigned long)&frame->info;
regs->cx = (unsigned long)&frame->uc;

regs->ds = __USER_DS;
regs->es = __USER_DS;
regs->ss = __USER_DS;
regs->cs = __USER_CS;
```

```
    return 0;
  }
```

The *pretcode field of the rt_sigframe structure is assigned the return address of the signal-handler function, which is the _kernel_rt_sigreturn() routine. struct ucontext uc is initialized with sigcontext, which contains the user-mode context copied from pt_regs of the kernel stack, bit array of regular blocked signals, and floating point state. After setting up and pushing the frame instance to the user-mode stack, __setup_rt_frame() alters pt_regs of the process in the kernel stack to hand over control to the signal handler when the current process resumes execution. The **instruction pointer (ip)** is set to the base address of the signal handler and the **stack pointer (sp)** is set to the top address of the frame pushed earlier; these changes cause the signal handler to execute.

Restarting interrupted system calls

We understood in Chapter 1, *Comprehending Processes, Address Space, and Threads* that user-mode processes invoke *system calls* to switch into kernel mode for executing kernel services. When a process enters a kernel service routine, there is a possibility of the routine being blocked for availability of resources (for example, wait on exclusion lock) or occurrence of an event (such as interrupts). Such blocking operations require the caller process to be put into the TASK_INTERRUPTIBLE, TASK_UNINTERRUPTIBLE, *or* TASK_KILLABLE state. The specific state effected depends on the choice of blocking call invoked in the system calls.

If the caller task is put into the TASK_UNINTERRUPTIBLE state, occurrences of signals on that task are generated, causing them to enter the pending list, and are delivered to the process only after completion of the service routine (on its return path to user mode). However, if the task was put into the TASK_INTERRUPTIBLE state, occurrences of signals on that task are generated and an immediate delivery is attempted by altering its state to TASK_RUNNING, which causes the task to wake up on a blocked system call even before the system call is completed (resulting in the system call operation to fail). Such interruptions are indicated by returning the appropriate failure code. The effect of signals on a task in the TASK_KILLABLE state is similar to TASK_INTERRUPTIBLE, except that wake-up is only effected on occurrence of the fatal SIGKILL signal.

EINTR, ERESTARTNOHAND, ERESTART_RESTARTBLOCK, ERESTARTSYS, or ERESTARTNOINTR are various kernel-defined failure codes; system calls are programmed to return appropriate error flags on failure. Choice of error code determines whether failed system call operations are restarted after the interrupting signal is handled:

```
(include/uapi/asm-generic/errno-base.h)
#define EPERM 1 /* Operation not permitted */
#define ENOENT 2 /* No such file or directory */
#define ESRCH 3 /* No such process */
#define EINTR 4 /* Interrupted system call */
#define EIO 5 /* I/O error */
#define ENXIO 6 /* No such device or address */
#define E2BIG 7 /* Argument list too long */
#define ENOEXEC 8 /* Exec format error */
#define EBADF 9 /* Bad file number */
#define ECHILD 10 /* No child processes */
#define EAGAIN 11 /* Try again */
#define ENOMEM 12 /* Out of memory */
#define EACCES 13 /* Permission denied */
#define EFAULT 14 /* Bad address */
#define ENOTBLK 15 /* Block device required */
#define EBUSY 16 /* Device or resource busy */
#define EEXIST 17 /* File exists */
#define EXDEV 18 /* Cross-device link */
#define ENODEV 19 /* No such device */
#define ENOTDIR 20 /* Not a directory */
#define EISDIR 21 /* Is a directory */
#define EINVAL 22 /* Invalid argument */
#define ENFILE 23 /* File table overflow */
#define EMFILE 24 /* Too many open files */
#define ENOTTY 25 /* Not a typewriter */
#define ETXTBSY 26 /* Text file busy */
#define EFBIG 27 /* File too large */
#define ENOSPC 28 /* No space left on device */
#define ESPIPE 29 /* Illegal seek */
#define EROFS 30 /* Read-only file system */
#define EMLINK 31 /* Too many links */
#define EPIPE 32 /* Broken pipe */
#define EDOM 33 /* Math argument out of domain of func */
#define ERANGE 34 /* Math result not representable */
linux/errno.h)
#define ERESTARTSYS 512
#define ERESTARTNOINTR 513
#define ERESTARTNOHAND 514 /* restart if no handler.. */
#define ENOIOCTLCMD 515 /* No ioctl command */
#define ERESTART_RESTARTBLOCK 516 /* restart by calling
sys_restart_syscall */
```

```
#define EPROBE_DEFER 517 /* Driver requests probe retry */
#define EOPENSTALE 518 /* open found a stale dentry */
```

On return from an interrupted system call, the user-mode API always returns the EINTR error code, irrespective of the specific error code returned by the underlying kernel service routine. The remaining error codes are used by the signal-delivery routines of the kernel to determine whether interrupted system calls can be restarted on return from the signal handler.

The following table shows the error codes for when system call execution gets interrupted and the effect it has for various signal dispositions:

Disposition	EINTR	ERESTARTSYS	ERESTARTNOHAND ERESTART_RESTARTBLOCK	ERESTARTNOINTR
Default Handler	No Restart	Auto Restart	Auto Restart	Auto Restart
Ignore	No Restart	Auto Restart	Auto Restart	Auto Restart
User Defined	No Restart	Explicit Restart	No Restart	Auto Restart

This is what they mean:

- **No Restart**: The system call will not be restarted. The process will resume execution in user mode from the instruction that follows the system call (int $0x80 or sysenter).
- **Auto Restart**: The kernel forces the user process to re-initiate the system call operation by loading the corresponding syscall identifier into *eax* and executing the syscall instruction (int $0x80 or sysenter).
- **Explicit Restart**: The system call is restarted only if the process has enabled the SA_RESTART flag while setting up the handler (through sigaction) for the interrupting signal.

Summary

Signals, though a rudimentary form of communication engaged by processes and kernel services, provide an easy and effective way to get asynchronous responses from a running process on occurrence of various events. By understanding all core aspects of signal usage, their representation, data structures and kernel routines for signal generation and delivery, we are now more kernel aware and also better prepared to look at more sophisticated means of communication between processes, in a later part of this book. After having spent the first three chapters on processes and their related aspects, we shall now delve into other subsystems of the kernel to notch up our visibility. In the next chapter, we will build our understanding of one of the core aspects of the kernel, the memory subsystem.

Throughout the next chapter, we will go through comprehending step by step many critical aspects of memory management such as memory initialization, paging and protection, and kernel memory allocation algorithms, among others.

4
Memory Management and Allocators

The efficiency of memory management broadly sets the efficiency of the whole kernel. Casually managed memory systems can seriously impact the performance of other subsystems, making memory a critical component of the kernel. This subsystem sets all processes and kernel services in motion by virtualizing physical memory and managing all dynamic allocation requests initiated by them. The memory subsystem also handles a wide spectrum of operations in sustaining operational efficiency and optimizing resources. The operations are both architecture specific and independent, which mandates the overall design and implementation to be just and tweakable. We will closely look at the following aspects in this chapter in our effort to comprehend this colossal subsystem:

- Physical memory representation
- Concepts of nodes and zones
- Page allocator
- Buddy system
- Kmalloc allocations
- Slab caches
- Vmalloc allocations
- Contiguous memory allocations

Initialization operations

In most architectures, on *reset*, processor is initialized in normal or physical address mode (also called **real mode** in x86) and begins executing the platform's firmware instructions found at the **reset vector**. These firmware instructions (which can be single binary or multi-stage binary) are programmed to carry out various operations, which include initialization of the memory controller, calibration of physical RAM, and loading the binary kernel image into a specific region of physical memory, among others.

When in real mode, processors do not support virtual addressing, and Linux, which is designed and implemented for systems with **protected mode**, requires **virtual addressing** to enable process protection and isolation, a crucial abstraction provided by the kernel (recall from Chapter 1, *Comprehending Processes, Address Space, and Threads*). This mandates the processor to be switched into protected mode and turn on virtual address support before the kernel kicks in and begins its boot operations and initialization of subsystems. Switching to protected mode requires the MMU chipset to be initialized, by setting up appropriate core data structures, in the process enabling *paging*. These operations are architecture specific and are implemented in *arch* branch of the kernel source tree. During kernel build these sources are compiled and linked as a header to protected mode kernel image; this header is referred as the **kernel bootstrap** or **real mode kernel**.

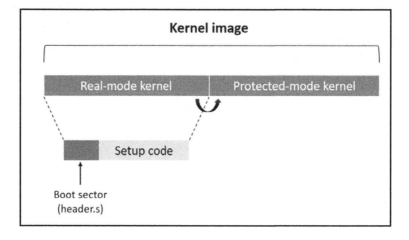

Following is the `main()` routine of x86 architecture's boot strap; this function is executed in real mode and is responsible for allocating appropriate resources before stepping into protected mode by invoking `go_to_protected_mode()`:

```c
/* arch/x86/boot/main.c */
void main(void)
{
 /* First, copy the boot header into the "zeropage" */
 copy_boot_params();

 /* Initialize the early-boot console */
 console_init();
 if (cmdline_find_option_bool("debug"))
 puts("early console in setup coden");

 /* End of heap check */
 init_heap();

 /* Make sure we have all the proper CPU support */
 if (validate_cpu()) {
 puts("Unable to boot - please use a kernel appropriate "
 "for your CPU.n");
 die();
 }

 /* Tell the BIOS what CPU mode we intend to run in. */
 set_bios_mode();

 /* Detect memory layout */
 detect_memory();

 /* Set keyboard repeat rate (why?) and query the lock flags */
 keyboard_init();

 /* Query Intel SpeedStep (IST) information */
 query_ist();

 /* Query APM information */
#if defined(CONFIG_APM) || defined(CONFIG_APM_MODULE)
 query_apm_bios();
#endif

 /* Query EDD information */
#if defined(CONFIG_EDD) || defined(CONFIG_EDD_MODULE)
 query_edd();
#endif

 /* Set the video mode */
```

```
set_video();

/* Do the last things and invoke protected mode */
go_to_protected_mode();
}
```

Real mode kernel routines that are invoked for setting up MMU and handle transition into protected mode are architecture specific (we will not be touching on those routines here). Irrespective of the architecture-specific code engaged, the primary objective is to enable support for **virtual addressing** by turning on **paging**. With paging enabled, system begins to perceive physical memory (RAM) as an array of blocks of fixed size, called page frames. Size of a page frame is configured by programming the paging unit of MMU appropriately; most MMUs support 4k, 8k, 16k, 64k up to 4MB options for frame size configuration. However, Linux kernel's default build configuration for most architectures chooses 4k as its standard page frame size.

Page descriptor

Page frames are the smallest possible allocation units of memory and kernel needs to utilize them for all its memory needs. Some page frames would be required for mapping physical memory to virtual address spaces of user mode processes, some for kernel code and its data structures, and some for processing dynamic allocation requests raised by process or a kernel service. For efficient management of such operations, kernel needs to distinguish between page frames currently in *use* from those which are free and available. This purpose is achieved through an architecture-independent data structure called `struct page`, which is defined to hold all meta data pertaining to a page frame, including its current state. An instance of `struct page` is allocated for each physical page frame found, and kernel has to maintain a list of page instances in main memory all the time.

Page structure is one of the heavily used data structures of the kernel, and is referred from various kernel code paths. This structure is populated with diverse elements, whose relevance is entirely based on the state of the physical frame. For instance, specific members of page structure specify if corresponding physical page is mapped to virtual address space of a process, or a group of process. Such fields are not considered valid when the physical page has been reserved for dynamic allocations. To ensure that page instance in memory is allocated only with relevant fields, unions are heavily used to populate member fields. This is a prudent choice, since it enables cramming more information into the page structure without increasing its size in memory:

```
/*include/linux/mm-types.h */
/* The objects in struct page are organized in double word blocks in
 * order to allows us to use atomic double word operations on portions
```

```
 * of struct page. That is currently only used by slub but the arrangement
 * allows the use of atomic double word operations on the flags/mapping
 * and lru list pointers also.
 */
struct page {
        /* First double word block */
        unsigned long flags; /* Atomic flags, some possibly updated
asynchronously */   union {
            struct address_space *mapping;
            void *s_mem; /* slab first object */
            atomic_t compound_mapcount; /* first tail page */
            /* page_deferred_list().next -- second tail page */
    };
    ....
    ....

}
```

Following is a brief description of important members of page structure. Note that a lot of the details here assume your familiarity with other aspects of memory subsystem which we discuss in further sections of this chapter, such as memory allocators, page tables, and so forth. I recommend new readers to skip and revisit this section after you get acquainted with the necessary prerequisites.

Flags

This is an `unsigned long` bit-field that holds flags which describe state of the physical page. Flag constants are defined through an `enum` in kernel header `include/linux/page-flags.h`. The following table lists out important flag constants:

Flag	Description
PG_locked	Used to indicate if page is locked; this bit is set while initiating I/O operations on page and cleared on completion.
PG_error	Used to indicate an error page. Set on occurrence of an I/O error on the page.
PG_referenced	Set to indicate page reclaim for page cache.
PG_uptodate	Set to indicate if page is valid after read operation from disk.
PG_dirty	Set when file backed page is modified and is out-of-sync with disk image of the same.

PG_lru	Used to indicate that the least recently used bit is set which helps handle page reclaim.
PG_active	Used to indicate if page is in active list.
PG_slab	Used to indicate that the page is managed by slab allocator.
PG_reserved	Used to indicate reserved pages which are not swappable.
PG_private	Used to indicate that the page is used by a filesystem to hold its private data.
PG_writeback	Set while commencing write-back operation on a file-backed page
PG_head	Used to indicate head page of a compound page.
PG_swapcache	Used to indicate if page is in swapcache.
PG_mappedtodisk	Used to indicate that page is mapped to *blocks* on storage.
PG_swapbacked	Page is backed by swap.
PG_unevictable	Used to indicate that page is in unevictable list; generally, this bit is set for pages owned by ramfs and SHM_LOCKed shared memory pages.
PG_mlocked	Used to indicate that VMA lock is enabled on the page.

A number of macros exist to check, set, and clear individual page bits; these operations are guaranteed to be atomic and are declared in kernel header /include/linux/page-flags.h. They are invoked to manipulate page flags from various kernel code paths:

```
/*Macros to create function definitions for page flags */
#define TESTPAGEFLAG(uname, lname, policy) \
static __always_inline int Page##uname(struct page *page) \
{ return test_bit(PG_##lname, &policy(page, 0)->flags); }

#define SETPAGEFLAG(uname, lname, policy) \
static __always_inline void SetPage##uname(struct page *page) \
{ set_bit(PG_##lname, &policy(page, 1)->flags); }

#define CLEARPAGEFLAG(uname, lname, policy) \
static __always_inline void ClearPage##uname(struct page *page) \
{ clear_bit(PG_##lname, &policy(page, 1)->flags); }

#define __SETPAGEFLAG(uname, lname, policy) \
static __always_inline void __SetPage##uname(struct page *page) \
{ __set_bit(PG_##lname, &policy(page, 1)->flags); }

#define __CLEARPAGEFLAG(uname, lname, policy) \
```

```
static __always_inline void __ClearPage##uname(struct page *page) \
{ __clear_bit(PG_##lname, &policy(page, 1)->flags); }

#define TESTSETFLAG(uname, lname, policy) \
static __always_inline int TestSetPage##uname(struct page *page) \
{ return test_and_set_bit(PG_##lname, &policy(page, 1)->flags); }

#define TESTCLEARFLAG(uname, lname, policy) \
static __always_inline int TestClearPage##uname(struct page *page) \
{ return test_and_clear_bit(PG_##lname, &policy(page, 1)->flags); }

. . . .
. . . .
```

Mapping

Another important element of the page descriptor is a pointer `*mapping` of type `struct address_space`. However, this is one of the tricky pointers which might either refer to an instance of `struct address_space`, or to an instance of `struct anon_vma`. Before we get into details of how this is achieved, let's first understand the importance of those structures and the resources they represent.

Filesystems engage free pages(from page cache) to cache data of recently accessed disk files. This mechanism helps minimize disk I/O operations: when file data in the cache is modified, the appropriate page is marked dirty by setting the `PG_dirty` bit; all dirty pages are written to the corresponding disk block by scheduling disk I/O at strategic intervals. `struct address_space` is an abstraction that represents a set of pages engaged for a file cache. Free pages of the page cache can also be **mapped** to a process or process group for dynamic allocations, pages mapped for such allocations are referred to as **anonymous** page mappings. An instance of `struct anon_vma` represents a memory block created with anonymous pages, that are mapped to the virtual address space (through VMA instance) of a process or processes.

The tricky dynamic initialization of the pointer with address to either of the data structures is achieved by bit manipulations. If low bit of pointer `*mapping` is clear, then it is an indication that the page is mapped to an `inode` and the pointer refers to `struct address_space`. If low bit is set, it is an indication for anonymous mapping, which means the pointer refers to an instance of `struct anon_vma`. This is made possible by ensuring allocation of `address_space` instances aligned to `sizeof(long)`, which makes the least significant bit of a pointer to `address_space` be unset (that is, set to 0).

Zones and nodes

Principal data structures that are elementary for entire memory management framework are **zones** and **nodes**. Let's familiarize ourselves with core concepts behind these data structures.

Memory zones

For efficient management of memory allocations, physical pages are organized into groups called **zones.** Pages in each *zone* are utilized for specific needs like DMA, high memory, and other regular allocation needs. An `enum` in kernel header `mmzone.h` declares *zone* constants:

```
/* include/linux/mmzone.h */
enum zone_type {
#ifdef CONFIG_ZONE_DMA
ZONE_DMA,
#endif
#ifdef CONFIG_ZONE_DMA32
  ZONE_DMA32,
#endif
#ifdef CONFIG_HIGHMEM
  ZONE_HIGHMEM,
#endif
  ZONE_MOVABLE,
#ifdef CONFIG_ZONE_DEVICE
  ZONE_DEVICE,
#endif
  __MAX_NR_ZONES
};
```

`ZONE_DMA:`
Pages in this *zone* are reserved for devices which cannot initiate DMA on all addressable memory. Size of this *zone* is architecture specific:

Architecture	Limit
parsic, ia64, sparc	<4G
s390	<2G
ARM	variable
alpha	unlimited or <16MB
alpha, i386, x86-64	<16MB

`ZONE_DMA32`: This *zone* is used for supporting 32-bit devices which can perform DMA on <4G of memory. This *zone* is only present on x86-64 platforms.

`ZONE_NORMAL`: All addressable memory is considered to be normal *zone*. DMA operations can be initiated on these pages, provided DMA devices support all addressable memory.

`ZONE_HIGHMEM`: This *zone* contains pages that are only accessible by kernel through explicit mapping into its address space; in other words, all physical memory pages beyond kernel segment fall into this *zone*. This *zone* exists only for 32-bit platforms with 3:1 virtual address split (3G for user mode and 1G address space for kernel); for instance on i386, allowing the kernel to address memory beyond 900 MB will require setting up special mappings (page table entries) for each page that the kernel needs to access.

`ZONE_MOVABLE`: Memory fragmentation is one of the challenges for modern operating systems to handle, and Linux is no exception to this. Right from the moment kernel boots, throughout its runtime, pages are allocated and deallocated for an array of tasks, resulting in small regions of memory with physically contiguous pages. Considering Linux support for virtual addressing, fragmentation might not be an obstacle for smooth execution of various processes, since physically scattered memory can always be mapped to virtually contiguous address space through page tables. Yet, there are a few scenarios like DMA allocations and setting up caches for kernel data structures that have a stringent need for physically contiguous regions.

Over the years, kernel developers have been evolving numerous anti-fragmentation techniques to alleviate **fragmentation**. Introduction of `ZONE_MOVABLE` is one of those attempts. The core idea here is to track *movable* pages in each *zone* and represent them under this pseudo *zone*, which helps prevent fragmentation (we discuss more on this in the next section on the buddy system).

The size of this *zone* is to be configured at boot time through one of the kernel parameters `kernelcore`; note that the value assigned specifies the amount of memory considered *non-movable,* and the rest, *movable*. As a general rule, the memory manager is configured to consider migration of pages from the highest populated *zone* to `ZONE_MOVABLE`, which is probably going to be `ZONE_HIGHMEM` for x86 32-bit machines and `ZONE_DMA32` on x86_64.

ZONE_DEVICE: This *zone* has been carved out to support hotplug memories, like large capacity *persistent-memory arrays*. **Persistent memories** are very similar to DRAM in many ways; specifically, CPUs can directly address them at byte level. However, characteristics such as persistence, performance (slower writes), and size (usually measured in terabytes) separate them from normal memory. For the kernel to support such memories with 4 KB page size, it would need to enumerate billions of page structures, which would consume significant percent of main memory or not be fit at all. As a result, it was chosen by kernel developers to consider persistent memory a **device**, rather than like **memory**; which means that the kernel can fall back on appropriate **drivers** to manage such memories.

```
void *devm_memremap_pages(struct device *dev, struct resource *res,
                      struct percpu_ref *ref, struct vmem_altmap
    *altmap);
```

The devm_memremap_pages() routine of the persistent memory driver maps a region of persistent memory into kernel's address space with relevant page structures set up in persistent device memory. All pages under these mappings are grouped under ZONE_DEVICE. Having a distinct *zone* to tag such pages allows the memory manager to distinguish them from regular uniform memory pages.

Memory nodes

Linux kernel is implemented to support multi-processor machine architectures for a long time now. Kernel implements various resources such as per-CPU data caches, mutual exclusion locks, and atomic operation macros, which are used across various SMP-aware subsystems, such as process scheduler and device management, among others. In particular, the role of memory management subsystem is crucial for kernel to tick on such architectures, since it needs to virtualize memory as viewed by each processor. Multi-processor machine architectures are broadly categorized into two types based on each processor's perception, and access latency to memory on the system.

Uniform Memory Access Architecture (UMA): These are multi-processor architecture machines, where processors are joined through an interconnect and share physical memory and I/O ports. They are named as UMA systems due to memory access latency, which is uniform and fixed irrespective of the processor from which they were initiated. Most symmetric multi-processor systems are UMA.

Non-Uniform Memory Access Architecture (NUMA): These are multi-processor machines with a contrasting design to that of UMA. These systems are designed with dedicated memory for each processor with fixed time access latencies. However, processors can initiate access operations on local memory of other processors through appropriate interconnects, and such operations render variable time access latencies.
Machines of this model are appropriately named **NUMA** due to non-uniform (non-contiguous) view of systems memory for each processor:

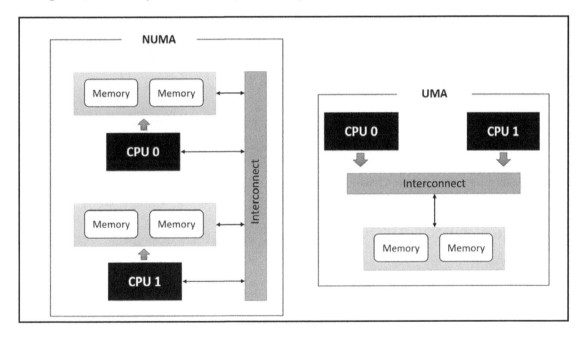

To extend support for NUMA machines, kernel views each non uniform memory partition (local memory) as a `node`. Each node is identified by a descriptor of `type pg_data_t`, which refers to pages under that node as per zoning policy, discussed earlier. Each *zone* is represented through an instance of `struct zone`. UMA machines would contain one node descriptor under which the entire memory is represented, and on NUMA machines, a list of node descriptors are enumerated, each representing a contiguous memory node. The following diagram illustrates the relationship between these data structures:

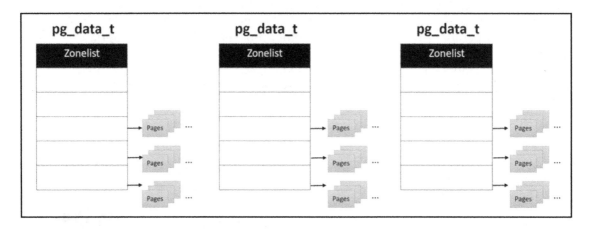

We shall follow on with *node* and *zone* descriptor data structure definitions. Note that we do not intend to describe every element of these structures as they are related to various aspects of memory management which are out of scope of this chapter.

Node descriptor structure

Node descriptor structure `pg_data_t` is declared in kernel header `mmzone.h`:

```
/* include/linux/mmzone.h */

typedef struct pglist_data {
  struct zone node_zones[MAX_NR_ZONES];
  struct zonelist node_zonelists[MAX_ZONELISTS];
  int nr_zones;

#ifdef CONFIG_FLAT_NODE_MEM_MAP /* means !SPARSEMEM */
  struct page *node_mem_map;
#ifdef CONFIG_PAGE_EXTENSION
  struct page_ext *node_page_ext;
#endif
#endif
```

```
#ifndef CONFIG_NO_BOOTMEM
  struct bootmem_data *bdata;
#endif
#ifdef CONFIG_MEMORY_HOTPLUG
 spinlock_t node_size_lock;
#endif
 unsigned long node_start_pfn;
 unsigned long node_present_pages; /* total number of physical pages */
 unsigned long node_spanned_pages;
 int node_id;
 wait_queue_head_t kswapd_wait;
 wait_queue_head_t pfmemalloc_wait;
 struct task_struct *kswapd;
 int kswapd_order;
 enum zone_type kswapd_classzone_idx;

#ifdef CONFIG_COMPACTION
 int kcompactd_max_order;
 enum zone_type kcompactd_classzone_idx;
 wait_queue_head_t kcompactd_wait;
 struct task_struct *kcompactd;
#endif
#ifdef CONFIG_NUMA_BALANCING
 spinlock_t numabalancing_migrate_lock;
 unsigned long numabalancing_migrate_next_window;
 unsigned long numabalancing_migrate_nr_pages;
#endif
 unsigned long totalreserve_pages;

#ifdef CONFIG_NUMA
 unsigned long min_unmapped_pages;
 unsigned long min_slab_pages;
#endif /* CONFIG_NUMA */

 ZONE_PADDING(_pad1_)
 spinlock_t lru_lock;

#ifdef CONFIG_DEFERRED_STRUCT_PAGE_INIT
 unsigned long first_deferred_pfn;
#endif /* CONFIG_DEFERRED_STRUCT_PAGE_INIT */

#ifdef CONFIG_TRANSPARENT_HUGEPAGE
 spinlock_t split_queue_lock;
 struct list_head split_queue;
 unsigned long split_queue_len;
#endif
 unsigned int inactive_ratio;
 unsigned long flags;
```

```
    ZONE_PADDING(_pad2_)
    struct per_cpu_nodestat __percpu *per_cpu_nodestats;
    atomic_long_t vm_stat[NR_VM_NODE_STAT_ITEMS];
} pg_data_t;
```

Depending on the type of machine and kernel configuration chosen, various elements are compiled into this structure. We'll look at few important elements:

Field	Description
node_zones	An array that holds *zone* instances for pages in this node.
node_zonelists	An array that specifies preferred allocation order for zones in the node.
nr_zones	Count of zones in the current node.
node_mem_map	Pointer to list of page descriptors in the current node.
bdata	Pointer to boot memory descriptor (discussed in later section)
node_start_pfn	Holds frame number of the first physical page in this node; this value would be *zero* for UMA systems.
node_present_pages	Total count of pages in the node
node_spanned_pages	Total size of physical page range, including holes if any.
node_id	Holds unique node identifier (nodes are numbered from zero)
kswapd_wait	Wait queue of kswapd kernel thread
kswapd	Pointer to task structure of kswapd kernel thread
totalreserve_pages	Count of reserve pages not used for user space allocations

Zone descriptor structure

The mmzone.h header also declares struct zone, which serves as *zone* descriptor. Following is a code snippet of structure definition and is well commented. We shall follow on with descriptions of a few important fields:

```
struct zone {
  /* Read-mostly fields */

  /* zone watermarks, access with *_wmark_pages(zone) macros */
  unsigned long watermark[NR_WMARK];
```

```
unsigned long nr_reserved_highatomic;

/*
 * We don't know if the memory that we're going to allocate will be
 * freeable or/and it will be released eventually, so to avoid totally
 * wasting several GB of ram we must reserve some of the lower zone
 * memory (otherwise we risk to run OOM on the lower zones despite
 * there being tons of freeable ram on the higher zones). This array is
 * recalculated at runtime if the sysctl_lowmem_reserve_ratio sysctl
 * changes.
 */
long lowmem_reserve[MAX_NR_ZONES];

#ifdef CONFIG_NUMA
 int node;
#endif
 struct pglist_data *zone_pgdat;
 struct per_cpu_pageset __percpu *pageset;

#ifndef CONFIG_SPARSEMEM
 /*
 * Flags for a pageblock_nr_pages block. See pageblock-flags.h.
 * In SPARSEMEM, this map is stored in struct mem_section
 */
 unsigned long *pageblock_flags;
#endif /* CONFIG_SPARSEMEM */

 /* zone_start_pfn == zone_start_paddr >> PAGE_SHIFT */
 unsigned long zone_start_pfn;

 /*
 * spanned_pages is the total pages spanned by the zone, including
 * holes, which is calculated as:
 * spanned_pages = zone_end_pfn - zone_start_pfn;
 *
 * present_pages is physical pages existing within the zone, which
 * is calculated as:
 * present_pages = spanned_pages - absent_pages(pages in holes);
 *
 * managed_pages is present pages managed by the buddy system, which
 * is calculated as (reserved_pages includes pages allocated by the
 * bootmem allocator):
 * managed_pages = present_pages - reserved_pages;
 *
 * So present_pages may be used by memory hotplug or memory power
 * management logic to figure out unmanaged pages by checking
 * (present_pages - managed_pages). And managed_pages should be used
 * by page allocator and vm scanner to calculate all kinds of watermarks
```

```
 * and thresholds.
 *
 * Locking rules:
 *
 * zone_start_pfn and spanned_pages are protected by span_seqlock.
 * It is a seqlock because it has to be read outside of zone->lock,
 * and it is done in the main allocator path. But, it is written
 * quite infrequently.
 *
 * The span_seq lock is declared along with zone->lock because it is
 * frequently read in proximity to zone->lock. It's good to
 * give them a chance of being in the same cacheline.
 *
 * Write access to present_pages at runtime should be protected by
 * mem_hotplug_begin/end(). Any reader who can't tolerant drift of
 * present_pages should get_online_mems() to get a stable value.
 *
 * Read access to managed_pages should be safe because it's unsigned
 * long. Write access to zone->managed_pages and totalram_pages are
 * protected by managed_page_count_lock at runtime. Idealy only
 * adjust_managed_page_count() should be used instead of directly
 * touching zone->managed_pages and totalram_pages.
 */
unsigned long managed_pages;
unsigned long spanned_pages;
unsigned long present_pages;

const char *name;// name of this zone

#ifdef CONFIG_MEMORY_ISOLATION
 /*
 * Number of isolated pageblock. It is used to solve incorrect
 * freepage counting problem due to racy retrieving migratetype
 * of pageblock. Protected by zone->lock.
 */
unsigned long nr_isolate_pageblock;
#endif

#ifdef CONFIG_MEMORY_HOTPLUG
 /* see spanned/present_pages for more description */
 seqlock_t span_seqlock;
#endif

 int initialized;

 /* Write-intensive fields used from the page allocator */
 ZONE_PADDING(_pad1_)
```

```
 /* free areas of different sizes */
struct free_area free_area[MAX_ORDER];

 /* zone flags, see below */
unsigned long flags;

 /* Primarily protects free_area */
spinlock_t lock;

 /* Write-intensive fields used by compaction and vmstats. */
ZONE_PADDING(_pad2_)

 /*
 * When free pages are below this point, additional steps are taken
 * when reading the number of free pages to avoid per-CPU counter
 * drift allowing watermarks to be breached
 */
unsigned long percpu_drift_mark;

#if defined CONFIG_COMPACTION || defined CONFIG_CMA
 /* pfn where compaction free scanner should start */
unsigned long compact_cached_free_pfn;
 /* pfn where async and sync compaction migration scanner should start */
unsigned long compact_cached_migrate_pfn[2];
#endif

#ifdef CONFIG_COMPACTION
 /*
 * On compaction failure, 1<<compact_defer_shift compactions
 * are skipped before trying again. The number attempted since
 * last failure is tracked with compact_considered.
 */
unsigned int compact_considered;
unsigned int compact_defer_shift;
int compact_order_failed;
#endif

#if defined CONFIG_COMPACTION || defined CONFIG_CMA
 /* Set to true when the PG_migrate_skip bits should be cleared */
bool compact_blockskip_flush;
#endif

 bool contiguous;

 ZONE_PADDING(_pad3_)
 /* Zone statistics */
 atomic_long_t vm_stat[NR_VM_ZONE_STAT_ITEMS];
} ____cacheline_internodealigned_in_smp;
```

Following is the summarized table of important fields, with short descriptions for each of them:

Field	Description
`watermark`	An array of unsigned long with `WRMARK_MIN`, `WRMARK_LOW`, and `WRMARK_HIGH` offsets. Values in these offsets impact swap operations carried out by `kswapd` kernel thread.
`nr_reserved_highatomic`	Holds count of reserved high order atomic pages
`lowmem_reserve`	Array that specifies count of pages for each *zone* that are reserved for critical allocations
`zone_pgdat`	Pointer to node descriptor for this *zone*.
`pageset`	Pointer to per-CPU hot-and-cold page lists.
`free_area`	An array of instances of type `struct free_area`, each abstracting contiguous free pages made available for buddy allocator. More on buddy allocator in a later section.
`flags`	Unsigned long variable used to store current status of the *zone*.
`zone_start_pfn`	Index of first page frame in the *zone*
`vm_stat`	Statistical information of the *zone*

Memory allocators

Having looked at how physical memory is organized, and represented through core data structures, we will now shift our attention to management of physical memory for processing allocation and deallocation requests. Memory allocation requests can be raised by various entities in the system, such as usermode process, drivers, and filesystems. Depending on the type of entity and context from which allocation is being requested, allocations returned might need to meet certain characteristics, such as page-aligned physically contiguous large blocks or physically contiguous small blocks, hardware cache aligned memory, or physically fragmented blocks that are mapped to virtually contiguous address space.

To efficiently manage physical memory, and cater to memory as per chosen priority and pattern, the kernel engages with a group of memory allocators. Each allocator has a distinct set of interface routines, which are backed by precisely designed algorithms optimized for a specific allocation pattern.

Page frame allocator

Also called the zoned page frame allocator, this serves as an interface for physically contiguous allocations in multiples of page size. Allocation operations are carried out by looking into appropriate zones for free pages. Physical pages in each *zone* are managed by **Buddy System**, which serves as the backend algorithm for the page frame allocator:

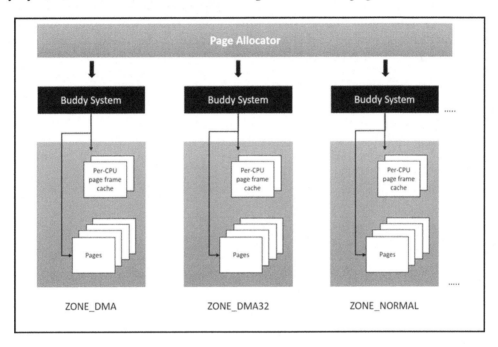

Kernel code can initiate memory allocation/deallocation operations on this algorithm through interface inline functions and macros provided in the kernel header `linux/include/gfp.h`:

```
static inline struct page *alloc_pages(gfp_t gfp_mask, unsigned int order);
```

The first parameter `gfp_mask` serves as a means to specify attributes as per which allocations are to be fulfilled; we will look into details of the attribute flags in coming sections. The second parameter `order` is used to specify size of the allocation; the value assigned is considered 2^{order}. On success, it returns the address of the first page structure, and NULL on failure. For single page allocations an alternate macro is made available, which again falls back on `alloc_pages()`:

```
#define alloc_page(gfp_mask) alloc_pages(gfp_mask, 0);
```

Allocated page(s) are mapped on to contiguous kernel address space, through appropriate page table entries (for paged address translation during access operations). Addresses generated after page table mapping, for use in kernel code, are referred to as **linear addresses**. Through another function interface `page_address()`, the caller code can retrieve the start linear address of the allocated block.

Allocations can also be initiated through a set of **wrapper** routines and macros to `alloc_pages()`, which marginally extend functionality and return the start linear address for the allocated chunk, instead of pointer to page structure. The following code snippet shows a list of wrapper functions and macros:

```
/* allocates 2^order pages and returns start linear address */
unsigned long __get_free_pages(gfp_t gfp_mask, unsigned int order)
{
struct page *page;
/*
* __get_free_pages() returns a 32-bit address, which cannot represent
* a highmem page
*/
VM_BUG_ON((gfp_mask & __GFP_HIGHMEM) != 0);

page = alloc_pages(gfp_mask, order);
if (!page)
return 0;
return (unsigned long) page_address(page);
}


/* Returns start linear address to zero initialized page */
unsigned long get_zeroed_page(gfp_t gfp_mask)
{
return __get_free_pages(gfp_mask | __GFP_ZERO, 0);
}


/* Allocates a page */
#define __get_free_page(gfp_mask) \
__get_free_pages((gfp_mask), 0)


/* Allocate page/pages from DMA zone */
#define __get_dma_pages(gfp_mask, order) \
 __get_free_pages((gfp_mask) | GFP_DMA, (order))
```

Following are the interfaces for releasing memory back to the system. We need to invoke an appropriate one that matches the allocation routine; passing an incorrect address will cause corruption:

```
void __free_pages(struct page *page, unsigned int order);
void free_pages(unsigned long addr, unsigned int order);
void free_page(addr);
```

Buddy system

While the page allocator serves as an interface for memory allocations (in multiples of page size), the buddy system operates at the back-end to administer physical page management. This algorithm manages all physical pages for each *zone*. It is optimized to accomplish allocations of large physically contiguous blocks (pages), by minimizing external fragmentation. Let's explore its operational details.

The *zone* descriptor structure contains an array of `struct free_area`, and the size of the array is defined through a kernel macro `MAX_ORDER` whose default value is `11`:

```
struct zone {
        ...
        ...
        struct free_area[MAX_ORDER];
        ...
        ...
};
```

Each offset contains an instance of `free_area` structure. All free pages are split into 11 (`MAX_ORDER`) lists, each containing a list of blocks of 2^{order} pages, with order values in the range of 0 to 11 (that is, a list of of 2^2 would contain 16 KB sized blocks, and 2^3 to be 32 KB sized blocks, and so on). This strategy ensures each block to be naturally aligned. Blocks in each list are exactly double in size to that of blocks in lower lists, resulting in faster allocation and deallocation operations. It also provides the allocator with the capability to handle contiguous allocations, of upto 8 MB block size (2^{11} list):

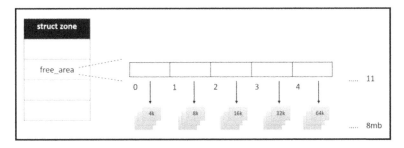

When an allocation request is made for a particular size, the *buddy system* looks into the appropriate list for a free block, and returns its address, if available. However, if it cannot find a free block, it moves to check in the next high-order list for a larger block, which if available it splits the higher-order block into equal parts called *buddies*, returns one for the allocator, and queues the second into a lower-order list. When both buddy blocks become free at some future time, they are coalesced to create a larger block. Algorithm can identify buddy blocks through their aligned address, which makes it possible to coalesce them.

Let's consider an example to comprehend this better, assuming there were a request to allocate an 8k block (through page allocator routines). Buddy system looks for free blocks in an 8k list of the `free_pages` array(first offset containing 2^1 sized blocks), and returns the start linear address of the block if available; however, if there are no free blocks in the 8k list, it moves on to the next higher-order list, which is of 16k blocks (second offset of the `free_pages` array) to find a free block. Let's further assume that there were no free block in this list as well. It then moves ahead into the next high-order list of size 32k(third offset in the *free_pages* array) to find a free block; if available, it splits the 32k block into two equal halves of 16k each (*buddies*). The first 16k chunk is further split into two halves of 8k (*buddies*) of which one is allocated for the caller and other is put into the 8k list. The second chunk of 16k is put into the 16k free list, when lower order (8k) buddies become free at some future time, they are coalesced to form a higher-order 16k block. When both 16k buddies become free, they are again coalesced to arrive at a 32k block which is put back into the free list.

When a request for allocation from a desired *zone* cannot be processed, the buddy system uses a fallback mechanism to look for other zones and nodes:

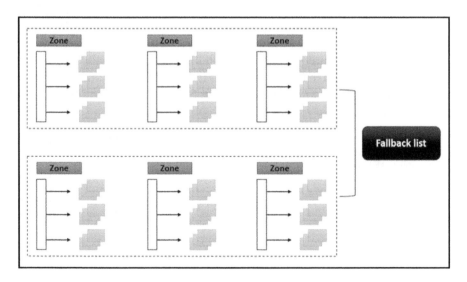

The buddy system has a long history with extensive implementations across various *nix operating systems with appropriate optimizations. As discussed earlier, it helps faster memory allocation and deallocations, and it also minimizes external fragmentation to some degree. With the advent of *huge pages,* which provide much-needed performance benefits, it has become all the more important to further efforts toward anti-fragmentation. To accomplish this, the Linux kernel's implementation of the buddy system is equipped with anti-fragmentation capability through page migration.

Page migration is a process of *moving* data of a virtual page from one physical memory region to another. This mechanism helps create larger blocks with contiguous pages. To realize this, pages are categorized into the following types:

1. Unmovable pages: Physical pages which are pinned and reserved for a specific allocation are considered unmovable. Pages pinned for the core kernel fall into this category. These pages are non reclaimable.

2. Reclaimable pages: Physical pages mapped to a dynamic allocation that can be evicted to a backstore, and those which can be regenerated are considered *reclaimable*. Pages held for file caching, anonymous page mappings, and those held by the kernel's slab caches fall into this category. Reclaim operations are carried out in two modes: periodic and direct reclaim, the former is achieved through a kthread called `kswapd`. When system runs exceedingly short of memory, kernel enters into *direct reclaim.*

3. Movable pages: Physical pages that can be *moved to* different regions through page migration mechanism. Pages mapped to virtual address space of user-mode *process* are considered movable, since all the VM subsystem needs to do is copy data and change relevant page table entries. This works, considering all access operations from the user mode *process* are put through page table translations.

The buddy system groups pages on the basis of *movability* into independent lists, and uses them for appropriate allocations. This is achieved by organizing each 2^n list in `struct free_area` as a group of autonomous lists based on mobility of pages. Each `free_area` instance holds an array of lists of size `MIGRATE_TYPES`. Each offset holds `list_head` of a respective group of pages:

```
struct free_area {
        struct list_head free_list[MIGRATE_TYPES];
        unsigned long nr_free;
};
```

`nr_free` is a counter that holds the total number of free pages for this `free_area` (all migration lists put together). The following diagram depicts free lists for each migration type:

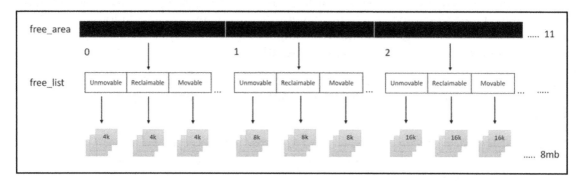

The following enum defines page migration types:

```
enum {
 MIGRATE_UNMOVABLE,
 MIGRATE_MOVABLE,
 MIGRATE_RECLAIMABLE,
 MIGRATE_PCPTYPES, /* the number of types on the pcp lists */
 MIGRATE_HIGHATOMIC = MIGRATE_PCPTYPES,
#ifdef CONFIG_CMA
 MIGRATE_CMA,
#endif
#ifdef CONFIG_MEMORY_ISOLATION
 MIGRATE_ISOLATE, /* can't allocate from here */
#endif
 MIGRATE_TYPES
};
```

We have discussed key migration types `MIGRATE_MOVABLE`, `MIGRATE_UNMOVABLE`, and `MIGRATE_RECLAIMABLE` types. `MIGRATE_PCPTYPES` is a special type introduced to improve systems performance; each *zone* maintains a list of cache-hot pages in a per-CPU page cache. These pages are used to serve allocation requests raised by the local CPU. The *zone* descriptor structures `pageset` element points to pages in the per-CPU cache:

```
/* include/linux/mmzone.h */

struct per_cpu_pages {
  int count; /* number of pages in the list */
  int high; /* high watermark, emptying needed */
  int batch; /* chunk size for buddy add/remove */
```

```
    /* Lists of pages, one per migrate type stored on the pcp-lists */
    struct list_head lists[MIGRATE_PCPTYPES];
};

struct per_cpu_pageset {
    struct per_cpu_pages pcp;
#ifdef CONFIG_NUMA
    s8 expire;
#endif
#ifdef CONFIG_SMP
    s8 stat_threshold;
    s8 vm_stat_diff[NR_VM_ZONE_STAT_ITEMS];
#endif
};

struct zone {
    ...
    ...
    struct per_cpu_pageset __percpu *pageset;
    ...
    ...
};
```

struct per_cpu_pageset is an abstraction that represents *unmovable, reclaimable,* and *movable* page lists. MIGRATE_PCPTYPES is a count of per-CPU page lists sorted as per page *mobility*. MIGRATE_CMA is list of pages for the contiguous memory allocator, which we shall discuss in further sections:

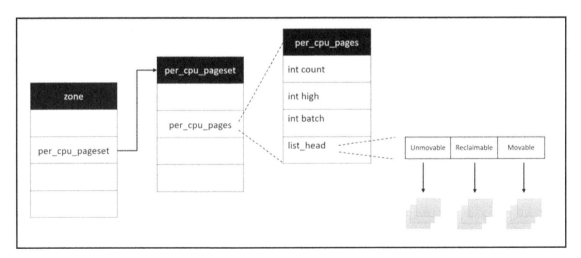

The buddy system is implemented to *fall back* on the alternate list, to process an allocation request when pages of desired mobility are not available. The following array defines the fallback order for various migration types; we will not go into further elaboration as it is self explanatory:

```
static int fallbacks[MIGRATE_TYPES][4] = {
  [MIGRATE_UNMOVABLE] = { MIGRATE_RECLAIMABLE, MIGRATE_MOVABLE,
MIGRATE_TYPES },
  [MIGRATE_RECLAIMABLE] = { MIGRATE_UNMOVABLE, MIGRATE_MOVABLE,
MIGRATE_TYPES },
  [MIGRATE_MOVABLE] = { MIGRATE_RECLAIMABLE, MIGRATE_UNMOVABLE,
MIGRATE_TYPES },
#ifdef CONFIG_CMA
  [MIGRATE_CMA] = { MIGRATE_TYPES }, /* Never used */
#endif
#ifdef CONFIG_MEMORY_ISOLATION
  [MIGRATE_ISOLATE] = { MIGRATE_TYPES }, /* Never used */
#endif
};
```

GFP mask

Page allocator and other allocator routines (which we'll discuss in the following sections) need the gfp_mask flag as an argument, which is of type gfp_t:

```
typedef unsigned __bitwise__ gfp_t;
```

Gfp flags are used to supply two vital attributes for the allocator functions: the first is the **mode** of the allocation, which controls the behavior of the allocator function, and the second is the *source* of the allocation, which indicates the *zone* or list of *zones* from which memory can be sourced. The kernel header gfp.h defines various flag constants that are categorized into distinct groups, called **zone modifiers, mobility and placement flags, watermark modifiers, reclaim modifiers,** and **action modifiers.**

Zone modifiers

Following is a summarized list of modifiers used to specify the *zone* from which memory is to be sourced. Recall our discussions on *zones* in an earlier section; for each of them, a `gfp` flag is defined:

```
#define __GFP_DMA ((__force gfp_t)___GFP_DMA)
#define __GFP_HIGHMEM ((__force gfp_t)___GFP_HIGHMEM)
#define __GFP_DMA32 ((__force gfp_t)___GFP_DMA32)
#define __GFP_MOVABLE ((__force gfp_t)___GFP_MOVABLE) /* ZONE_MOVABLE
allowed */
```

Page mobility and placement

The following code snippet defines page mobility and placement flags:

```
#define __GFP_RECLAIMABLE ((__force gfp_t)___GFP_RECLAIMABLE)
#define __GFP_WRITE ((__force gfp_t)___GFP_WRITE)
#define __GFP_HARDWALL ((__force gfp_t)___GFP_HARDWALL)
#define __GFP_THISNODE ((__force gfp_t)___GFP_THISNODE)
#define __GFP_ACCOUNT ((__force gfp_t)___GFP_ACCOUNT)
```

Following is a list of page mobility and placement flags:

- `__GFP_RECLAIMABLE`: Most kernel subsystems are designed to engage *memory caches* for caching frequently needed resources such as data structures, memory blocks, persistent file data, and so on. The memory manager maintains such caches and allows them to dynamically expand on demand. However, such caches cannot be allowed to expand boundlessly, or they will eventually consume all memory. The memory manager handles this issue through the **shrinker** interface, a mechanism by which the memory manager can shrink a cache, and reclaim pages when needed. Enabling this flag while allocating pages (for the cache) is an indication to the shrinker that the page is *reclaimable.* This flag is used by the slab allocator, which is discussed in a later section.

- `__GFP_WRITE`: When this flag is used, it indicates to the kernel that the caller intends to dirty the page. The memory manager allocates the appropriate page as per the fair-zone allocation policy, which round-robins the allocation of such pages across local *zones* of the node to avoid all the dirty pages being in one *zone*.

- `__GFP_HARDWALL`: This flag ensures that allocation is carried out on same node or nodes to which the caller is bound; in other words, it enforces the CPUSET memory allocation policy.
- `__GFP_THISNODE`: This flag forces the allocation to be satisfied from the requested node with no fallbacks or placement policy enforcements.
- `__GFP_ACCOUNT`: This flag causes allocations to be accounted for the kmem control group.

Watermark modifiers

The following code snippet defines the watermark modifiers:

```
#define __GFP_ATOMIC ((__force gfp_t)___GFP_ATOMIC)
#define __GFP_HIGH ((__force gfp_t)___GFP_HIGH)
#define __GFP_MEMALLOC ((__force gfp_t)___GFP_MEMALLOC)
#define __GFP_NOMEMALLOC ((__force gfp_t)___GFP_NOMEMALLOC)
```

Following is list of watermark modifiers, which provide control over emergency reserve pools of memory:

- `__GFP_ATOMIC`: This flag indicates that allocation is high priority and the caller context cannot be put into wait.
- `__GFP_HIGH`: This flag indicates that the caller is high priority and granting allocation request is necessary for the system to make progress. Setting this flag will cause the allocator to access the emergency pool.
- `__GFP_MEMALLOC`: This flag allows access to all memory. This should only be used when the caller guarantees the allocation will allow more memory to be freed very shortly, for example, process exiting or swapping.
- `__GFP_NOMEMALLOC`: This flag is used to forbid access to all reserved emergency pools.

Page reclaim modifiers

As systems load increases, the amount of free memory in *zones* might fall below the *low watermark,* resulting in memory crunch that will acutely impact overall performance of the system. To handle such eventuality, the memory manager is equipped with **page reclaim algorithms,** which are implemented to identify and reclaim pages. Kernel memory allocator routines, engage reclaim algorithms when invoked with appropriate GFP constants called **page reclaim modifiers**:

```
#define __GFP_IO ((__force gfp_t)___GFP_IO)
#define __GFP_FS ((__force gfp_t)___GFP_FS)
#define __GFP_DIRECT_RECLAIM ((__force gfp_t)___GFP_DIRECT_RECLAIM) /*
Caller can reclaim */
#define __GFP_KSWAPD_RECLAIM ((__force gfp_t)___GFP_KSWAPD_RECLAIM) /*
kswapd can wake */
#define __GFP_RECLAIM ((__force
gfp_t)(___GFP_DIRECT_RECLAIM|___GFP_KSWAPD_RECLAIM))
#define __GFP_REPEAT ((__force gfp_t)___GFP_REPEAT)
#define __GFP_NOFAIL ((__force gfp_t)___GFP_NOFAIL)
#define __GFP_NORETRY ((__force gfp_t)___GFP_NORETRY)
```

Following is a list of reclaim modifiers that can be passed as arguments to allocation routines; each flag enables reclaim operations on a specific region of memory:

- __GFP_IO: This flag indicates that the allocator can start physical I/O (swap) to reclaim memory.

- __GFP_FS: This flag indicates that the allocator may call down to the low-level FS for reclaim.

- __GFP_DIRECT_RECLAIM: This flag indicates that the caller is willing to enter direct reclaim. This might cause the caller to block.

- __GFP_KSWAPD_RECLAIM: This flag indicates that the allocator can wake the kswapd kernel thread to initiate reclaim, when the low watermark is reached.

- __GFP_RECLAIM: This flag is used to enable direct and kswapd reclaim.

- __GFP_REPEAT: This flag indicates to try hard to allocate the memory, but the allocation attempt might fail.

- __GFP_NOFAIL: This flag forces the virtual memory manager to *retry* until the allocation request. succeeds. This might cause the VM to trigger the OOM killer to reclaim memory.

- __GFP_NORETRY: This flag will cause the allocator to return appropriate failure status when the request cannot be served.

Action modifiers

The following code snippet defines action modifiers:

```
#define __GFP_COLD ((__force gfp_t)___GFP_COLD)
#define __GFP_NOWARN ((__force gfp_t)___GFP_NOWARN)
#define __GFP_COMP ((__force gfp_t)___GFP_COMP)
#define __GFP_ZERO ((__force gfp_t)___GFP_ZERO)
#define __GFP_NOTRACK ((__force gfp_t)___GFP_NOTRACK)
#define __GFP_NOTRACK_FALSE_POSITIVE (__GFP_NOTRACK)
#define __GFP_OTHER_NODE ((__force gfp_t)___GFP_OTHER_NODE)
```

Following is a list of action modifier flags; these flags specify additional attributes to be considered by the allocator routines while processing a request:

- `__GFP_COLD`: To enable quick access, a few pages in each *zone* are cached into per-CPU caches; pages held in cache are referred to as **hot**, and uncached pages are referred to as **cold.** This flag indicates that the allocator should serve memory requests through cache cold page(s).

- `__GFP_NOWARN`: This flag causes the allocator to run in silent mode, which results in warning and error conditions to go unreported.

- `__GFP_COMP`: This flag is used to allocate a compound page with appropriate metadata. A compound page is a group of two or more physically contiguous pages, which are treated as a single large page. Metadata makes a compound page distinct from other physically contiguous pages. The first physical page of a compound page is called the **head page** with the `PG_head` flag set in its page descriptor, and the rest of the pages are referred to as **tail pages**.

- `__GFP_ZERO`: This flag causes the allocator to return zero filled page(s).

- `__GFP_NOTRACK`: kmemcheck is one of the in-kernel debuggers which is used detect and warn about uninitialized memory access. Nonetheless, such checks cause memory access operations to be delayed. When performance is a criteria, the caller might want to allocate memory which is not tracked by kmemcheck. This flag causes the allocator to return such memory.

- `__GFP_NOTRACK_FALSE_POSITIVE`: This flag is an alias of `__GFP_NOTRACK`.

- `__GFP_OTHER_NODE`: This flag is used for allocation of transparent huge pages (THP).

Type flags

With so many categories of modifier flags (each addressing different attributes), programmers exercise extreme care when choosing flags for corresponding allocations. To make the process easier and quicker, type flags were introduced, which enable programmers to make quick allocation choices. **Type flags** are derived from combinations of various modifier constants (listed previously) for specific allocation use cases. Programmers however can further customize type flags if required:

```
#define GFP_ATOMIC (__GFP_HIGH|__GFP_ATOMIC|__GFP_KSWAPD_RECLAIM)
#define GFP_KERNEL (__GFP_RECLAIM | __GFP_IO | __GFP_FS)
#define GFP_KERNEL_ACCOUNT (GFP_KERNEL | __GFP_ACCOUNT)
#define GFP_NOWAIT (__GFP_KSWAPD_RECLAIM)
#define GFP_NOIO (__GFP_RECLAIM)
#define GFP_NOFS (__GFP_RECLAIM | __GFP_IO)
#define GFP_TEMPORARY (__GFP_RECLAIM | __GFP_IO | __GFP_FS |
__GFP_RECLAIMABLE)
#define GFP_USER (__GFP_RECLAIM | __GFP_IO | __GFP_FS | __GFP_HARDWALL)
#define GFP_DMA __GFP_DMA
#define GFP_DMA32 __GFP_DMA32
#define GFP_HIGHUSER (GFP_USER | __GFP_HIGHMEM)
#define GFP_HIGHUSER_MOVABLE (GFP_HIGHUSER | __GFP_MOVABLE)
#define GFP_TRANSHUGE_LIGHT ((GFP_HIGHUSER_MOVABLE | __GFP_COMP |
__GFP_NOMEMALLOC | \ __GFP_NOWARN) & ~__GFP_RECLAIM)
#define GFP_TRANSHUGE (GFP_TRANSHUGE_LIGHT | __GFP_DIRECT_RECLAIM)
```

The following is the list of type flags:

- `GFP_ATOMIC`: This flag is specified for non blocking allocations that cannot fail. This flag will cause allocations from emergency reserves. This is generally used while invoking the allocator from an atomic context.
- `GFP_KERNEL`: This flag is used while allocating memory for kernel use. These requests are processed from normal *zone*. This flag might cause the allocator to enter direct reclaim.
- `GFP_KERNEL_ACCOUNT`: Same as `GFP_KERNEL` with an addition that allocation is tracked by the kmem control group.
- `GFP_NOWAIT`: This flag is used for kernel allocations that are non-blocking.
- `GFP_NOIO`: This flag allows the allocator to begin direct reclaim on clean pages that do not require physical I/O(swap).
- `GFP_NOFS`: This flag allows the allocator to begin direct reclaim but prevents invocation of filesystem interfaces.

- `GFP_TEMPORARY`: This flag is used while allocating pages for kernel caches, which are reclaimable through the appropriate shrinker interface. This flag sets the `__GFP_RECLAIMABLE` flag we discussed earlier.
- `GFP_USER`: This flag is used for user-space allocations. Memory allocated is mapped to a user process and can also be accessed by kernel services or hardware for DMA transfers from device into buffer or vice versa.
- `GFP_DMA`: This flag causes allocation from the lowest *zone*, called `ZONE_DMA`. This flag is still supported for backward compatibility.
- `GFP_DMA32`: This flag causes allocation to be processed from `ZONE_DMA32` which contains pages in < 4G memory.
- `GFP_HIGHUSER`: This flag is used for user space allocations from `ZONE_HIGHMEM` (relevant only on 32-bit platforms).
- `GFP_HIGHUSER_MOVABLE`: This flag is similar to `GFP_HIGHUSER`, with an addition that allocations are carried out from movable pages, which enables page migration and reclaim.
- `GFP_TRANSHUGE_LIGHT`: This causes the allocation of transparent huge allocations (THP), which are compound allocations. This type flag sets `__GFP_COMP`, which we discussed earlier.

Slab allocator

As discussed in earlier sections, the page allocator (in coordination with buddy system) does an efficient job of handling memory allocation requests in multiples of page size. However, most allocation requests initiated by kernel code for its internal use are for smaller blocks (usually less than a page); engaging the page allocator for such allocations results in *internal fragmentation*, causing wastage of memory. The slab allocator is implemented precisely to address this; it is built on top of the buddy system and is used to allocate small memory blocks, to hold structure objects or data used by kernel services.

Design of the slab allocator is based on an idea of *object cache*. The concept of an **object cache** is quite simple: it involves reserving a set of free page frames, dividing and organize them into independent free lists (with each list containing a few free pages) called **slab caches**, and using each list for allocation of a pool of objects or memory blocks of a fixed size, called a **unit**. This way, each list is assigned a unique *unit* size, and would contain a pool of objects or memory blocks of that size. When an allocation request arrives for a block of memory of a given size, the allocator algorithm selects an appropriate *slab cache* whose *unit* size is the best fit for the requested size, and returns the address of a free block.

However, at a low level, there is fair bit of complexity involved in terms of initialization and management of slab caches. The algorithm needs to consider various issues such as object tracking, dynamic expansion, and safe reclaim through the shrinker interface. Addressing all these issues and achieving a proper balance between enhanced performance and optimum memory footprint is quite a challenge. We shall explore more on these challenges in subsequent sections, but for now we will continue our discussion with allocator function interfaces.

Kmalloc caches

Slab allocator maintains a set of generic slab caches to cache memory blocks of *unit* sizes in multiples of 8. It maintains two sets of slab caches for each *unit* size, one to maintain a pool of memory blocks allocated from ZONE_NORMAL pages and another from ZONE_DMA pages. These caches are global and shared by all kernel code. Users can track the status of these caches through a special file /proc/slabinfo. Kernel services can allocate and release memory blocks from these caches through the kmalloc family of routines. They are referred to as kmalloc caches:

```
#cat /proc/slabinfo
slabinfo - version: 2.1
# name <active_objs> <num_objs> <objsize> <objperslab> <pagesperslab> :
tunables <limit> <batchcount> <sharedfactor> : slabdata <active_slabs>
<num_slabs> <sharedavail>
dma-kmalloc-8192 0 0 8192 4 8 : tunables 0 0 0 : slabdata 0 0 0
dma-kmalloc-4096 0 0 4096 8 8 : tunables 0 0 0 : slabdata 0 0 0
dma-kmalloc-2048 0 0 2048 16 8 : tunables 0 0 0 : slabdata 0 0 0
dma-kmalloc-1024 0 0 1024 16 4 : tunables 0 0 0 : slabdata 0 0 0
dma-kmalloc-512 0 0 512 16 2 : tunables 0 0 0 : slabdata 0 0 0
dma-kmalloc-256 0 0 256 16 1 : tunables 0 0 0 : slabdata 0 0 0
dma-kmalloc-128 0 0 128 32 1 : tunables 0 0 0 : slabdata 0 0 0
dma-kmalloc-64 0 0 64 64 1 : tunables 0 0 0 : slabdata 0 0 0
dma-kmalloc-32 0 0 32 128 1 : tunables 0 0 0 : slabdata 0 0 0
dma-kmalloc-16 0 0 16 256 1 : tunables 0 0 0 : slabdata 0 0 0
dma-kmalloc-8 0 0 8 512 1 : tunables 0 0 0 : slabdata 0 0 0
dma-kmalloc-192 0 0 192 21 1 : tunables 0 0 0 : slabdata 0 0 0
dma-kmalloc-96 0 0 96 42 1 : tunables 0 0 0 : slabdata 0 0 0
kmalloc-8192 156 156 8192 4 8 : tunables 0 0 0 : slabdata 39 39 0
kmalloc-4096 325 352 4096 8 8 : tunables 0 0 0 : slabdata 44 44 0
kmalloc-2048 1105 1184 2048 16 8 : tunables 0 0 0 : slabdata 74 74 0
kmalloc-1024 2374 2448 1024 16 4 : tunables 0 0 0 : slabdata 153 153 0
kmalloc-512 1445 1520 512 16 2 : tunables 0 0 0 : slabdata 95 95 0
kmalloc-256 9988 10400 256 16 1 : tunables 0 0 0 : slabdata 650 650 0
kmalloc-192 3561 4053 192 21 1 : tunables 0 0 0 : slabdata 193 193 0
kmalloc-128 3588 5728 128 32 1 : tunables 0 0 0 : slabdata 179 179 0
```

```
kmalloc-96 3402 3402 96 42 1 : tunables 0 0 0 : slabdata 81 81 0
kmalloc-64 42672 45184 64 64 1 : tunables 0 0 0 : slabdata 706 706 0
kmalloc-32 15095 16000 32 128 1 : tunables 0 0 0 : slabdata 125 125 0
kmalloc-16 6400 6400 16 256 1 : tunables 0 0 0 : slabdata 25 25 0
kmalloc-8 6144 6144 8 512 1 : tunables 0 0 0 : slabdata 12 12 0
```

`kmalloc-96` and `kmalloc-192` are caches used to maintain memory blocks aligned with the level 1 hardware cache. For allocations above 8k (large blocks), the slab allocator falls back on buddy system.

Following are the kmalloc family of allocator routines; all of these need appropriate GFP flags:

```
/**
 * kmalloc - allocate memory.
 * @size: bytes of memory required.
 * @flags: the type of memory to allocate.
 */
void *kmalloc(size_t size, gfp_t flags)

/**
 * kzalloc - allocate memory. The memory is set to zero.
 * @size: bytes of memory required.
 * @flags: the type of memory to allocate.
 */
inline void *kzalloc(size_t size, gfp_t flags)

/**
 * kmalloc_array - allocate memory for an array.
 * @n: number of elements.
 * @size: element size.
 * @flags: the type of memory to allocate (see kmalloc).
 */
inline void *kmalloc_array(size_t n, size_t size, gfp_t flags)


/**
 * kcalloc - allocate memory for an array. The memory is set to zero.
 * @n: number of elements.
 * @size: element size.
 * @flags: the type of memory to allocate (see kmalloc).
 */
inline void *kcalloc(size_t n, size_t size, gfp_t flags)

/**
 * krealloc - reallocate memory. The contents will remain unchanged.
 * @p: object to reallocate memory for.
 * @new_size: bytes of memory are required.
```

```
 * @flags: the type of memory to allocate.
 *
 * The contents of the object pointed to are preserved up to the
 * lesser of the new and old sizes. If @p is %NULL, krealloc()
 * behaves exactly like kmalloc(). If @new_size is 0 and @p is not a
 * %NULL pointer, the object pointed to is freed
 */
void *krealloc(const void *p, size_t new_size, gfp_t flags)


/**
 * kmalloc_node - allocate memory from a particular memory node.
 * @size: bytes of memory are required.
 * @flags: the type of memory to allocate.
 * @node: memory node from which to allocate
 */
void *kmalloc_node(size_t size, gfp_t flags, int node)


/**
 * kzalloc_node - allocate zeroed memory from a particular memory node.
 * @size: how many bytes of memory are required.
 * @flags: the type of memory to allocate (see kmalloc).
 * @node: memory node from which to allocate
 */
void *kzalloc_node(size_t size, gfp_t flags, int node)
```

Following routines return the allocated block to the free pool. Callers need to ensure that address passed as argument is of a valid allocated block:

```
/**
 * kfree - free previously allocated memory
 * @objp: pointer returned by kmalloc.
 *
 * If @objp is NULL, no operation is performed.
 *
 * Don't free memory not originally allocated by kmalloc()
 * or you will run into trouble.
 */
void kfree(const void *objp)

/**
 * kzfree - like kfree but zero memory
 * @p: object to free memory of
 *
 * The memory of the object @p points to is zeroed before freed.
 * If @p is %NULL, kzfree() does nothing.
 *
 * Note: this function zeroes the whole allocated buffer which can be a
```

```
good
 * deal bigger than the requested buffer size passed to kmalloc(). So be
 * careful when using this function in performance sensitive code.
 */
void kzfree(const void *p)
```

Object caches

The slab allocator provides function interfaces for setting up slab caches, which can be owned by a kernel service or a subsystem. Such caches are considered private since they are local to kernel services (or a kernel subsystem) like device drivers, file systems, process scheduler, and so on. This facility is used by most kernel subsystems to set up object caches and pool intermittently needed data structures. Most data structures we've encountered so far (since Chapter 1, *Comprehending Processes, Address Space, and Threads*) including process descriptor, signal descriptor, page descriptor, and so on are maintained in such object pools. The pseudo file /proc/slabinfo shows the status of object caches:

```
# cat /proc/slabinfo
slabinfo - version: 2.1
# name <active_objs> <num_objs> <objsize> <objperslab> <pagesperslab> :
tunables <limit> <batchcount> <sharedfactor> : slabdata <active_slabs>
<num_slabs> <sharedavail>
sigqueue 100 100 160 25 1 : tunables 0 0 0 : slabdata 4 4 0
bdev_cache 76 76 832 19 4 : tunables 0 0 0 : slabdata 4 4 0
kernfs_node_cache 28594 28594 120 34 1 : tunables 0 0 0 : slabdata 841 841
0
mnt_cache 489 588 384 21 2 : tunables 0 0 0 : slabdata 28 28 0
inode_cache 15932 15932 568 28 4 : tunables 0 0 0 : slabdata 569 569 0
dentry 89541 89817 192 21 1 : tunables 0 0 0 : slabdata 4277 4277 0
iint_cache 0 0 72 56 1 : tunables 0 0 0 : slabdata 0 0 0
buffer_head 53079 53430 104 39 1 : tunables 0 0 0 : slabdata 1370 1370 0
vm_area_struct 41287 42400 200 20 1 : tunables 0 0 0 : slabdata 2120 2120 0
files_cache 207 207 704 23 4 : tunables 0 0 0 : slabdata 9 9 0
signal_cache 420 420 1088 30 8 : tunables 0 0 0 : slabdata 14 14 0
sighand_cache 289 315 2112 15 8 : tunables 0 0 0 : slabdata 21 21 0
task_struct 750 801 3584 9 8 : tunables 0 0 0 : slabdata 89 89 0
```

The *kmem_cache_create()* routine sets up a new *cache* as per the parameter passed. On success, it returns the address to the cache descriptor structure of type *kmem_cache*:

```
/*
 * kmem_cache_create - Create a cache.
 * @name: A string which is used in /proc/slabinfo to identify this cache.
 * @size: The size of objects to be created in this cache.
 * @align: The required alignment for the objects.
 * @flags: SLAB flags
```

```
 * @ctor: A constructor for the objects.
 *
 * Returns a ptr to the cache on success, NULL on failure.
 * Cannot be called within a interrupt, but can be interrupted.
 * The @ctor is run when new pages are allocated by the cache.
 *
 */
struct kmem_cache * kmem_cache_create(const char *name, size_t size, size_t
align,
                                      unsigned long flags, void
(*ctor)(void *))
```

The cache is created by allocating free page frames (from buddy system), and data objects of *size* specified (second argument) are populated. Though each cache starts by hosting a fixed number of data objects during creation, they can grow dynamically when required to accommodate more number of data objects. Data structures can be complicated (we have encountered a few), and can contain varied elements such as list headers, sub-objects, arrays, atomic counters, bit-fields, and so on. Setting up each object might require all its fields to be initialized to the default state; this can be achieved through an initializer routine assigned to a *ctor function pointer (last argument). The initializer is called for each new object allocated, both during cache creation and when it grows to add more free objects. However, for simple objects, a *cache* can be created without an initializer.

Following is a sample code snippet that shows the usage of kmem_cache_create():

```
/* net/core/skbuff.c */

struct kmem_cache *skbuff_head_cache;
skbuff_head_cache = kmem_cache_create("skbuff_head_cache",sizeof(struct
sk_buff), 0,
                                      SLAB_HWCACHE_ALIGN|SLAB_PANIC,
NULL);
```

Flags are used to enable debug checks, and enhance the performance of access operations on cache by aligning objects with the hardware cache. The following flag constants are supported:

```
SLAB_CONSISTENCY_CHECKS /* DEBUG: Perform (expensive) checks o alloc/free
*/
SLAB_RED_ZONE /* DEBUG: Red zone objs in a cache */
SLAB_POISON /* DEBUG: Poison objects */
SLAB_HWCACHE_ALIGN  /* Align objs on cache lines */
SLAB_CACHE_DMA  /* Use GFP_DMA memory */
SLAB_STORE_USER  /* DEBUG: Store the last owner for bug hunting */
SLAB_PANIC  /* Panic if kmem_cache_create() fails */
```

Subsequently, *objects* can be allocated and released through relevant functions. Upon release, *objects* are put back into the free list of the *cache*, making them available for reuse; this results in a possible performance boost, particularly when *objects* are cache hot:

```
/**
 * kmem_cache_alloc - Allocate an object
 * @cachep: The cache to allocate from.
 * @flags: GFP mask.
 *
 * Allocate an object from this cache. The flags are only relevant
 * if the cache has no available objects.
 */
void *kmem_cache_alloc(struct kmem_cache *cachep, gfp_t flags);

/**
 * kmem_cache_alloc_node - Allocate an object on the specified node
 * @cachep: The cache to allocate from.
 * @flags: GFP mask.
 * @nodeid: node number of the target node.
 *
 * Identical to kmem_cache_alloc but it will allocate memory on the given
 * node, which can improve the performance for cpu bound structures.
 *
 * Fallback to other node is possible if __GFP_THISNODE is not set.
 */
void *kmem_cache_alloc_node(struct kmem_cache *cachep, gfp_t flags, int
nodeid);

/**
 * kmem_cache_free - Deallocate an object
 * @cachep: The cache the allocation was from.
 * @objp: The previously allocated object.
 *
 * Free an object which was previously allocated from this
 * cache.
 */
void kmem_cache_free(struct kmem_cache *cachep, void *objp);
```

kmem caches can be destroyed when all hosted data objects are *free* (not in use), by calling `kmem_cache_destroy()`.

Cache management

All slab caches are managed internally by **slab core**, which is a low-level algorithm. It defines various control structures that describe the physical layout for each **cache list**, and implements core cache-management operations which are invoked by interface routines. The slab allocator was originally implemented in Solaris 2.4 kernels, and used by most other *nix kernels, based on a paper by Bonwick.

Traditionally, Linux was used on uniprocessor desktop and server systems with moderate memories, and the kernel adopted the classic model of Bonwick with appropriate performance improvements. Over the years, due to diversity of the platforms with distinct priorities for which the Linux kernel is ported and used, it turns out that the classic implementation of the slab core algorithm is inefficient to cater to all the needs. While memory-constrained embedded platforms cannot afford the higher footprint of the allocator (space used to manage metadata and density of allocator operations), SMP systems with huge memories need consistent performance, scalability, and better mechanisms to generate trace and debug information on allocations.

To cater to these dissimilar requirements, current versions of the kernel provide three distinct implementations of the slab algorithm: **slob**, a classic K&R type list allocator, designed for low-memory systems with scarce allocation needs, and was default object allocator for Linux during its initial years(1991-1999); **slab**, a classic Solaris-style slab allocator that has been around in Linux since 1999; and **slub**, improved for current generation SMP hardware with huge memories, and delivers consistent performance with better control and debug mechanisms. The default kernel configuration for most architectures enables **slub** as default slab allocator; this can be changed during kernel build through kernel configuration options.

> CONFIG_SLAB: The regular slab allocator that is established and known to work well in all environments. It organizes cache hot objects in per-CPU and per node queues.

> CONFIG_SLUB: **SLUB** is a slab allocator that minimizes cache line usage instead of managing queues of cached objects (SLAB approach). per-CPU caching is realized using slabs of objects instead of queues of objects. SLUB can use memory efficiently and has enhanced diagnostics. SLUB is the default choice for a slab allocator.

> CONFIG_SLOB: **SLOB** replaces the stock allocator with a drastically simpler allocator. SLOB is generally more space efficient but does not perform as well on large systems.

Irrespective of the type of allocator chosen, the programming interface remains unchanged. In fact, at low level, all three allocators share some common code base:

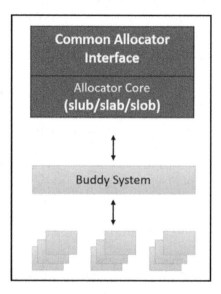

We shall now look into physical layout of a *cache* and its control structures.

Cache layout - generic

Each cache is represented by a cache descriptor structure `kmem_cache`; this structure contains all crucial metadata of the cache. It includes a list of slab descriptors, each hosting a page or a group of page frames. Pages under slabs contain objects or memory blocks, which are the allocation *units* of the cache. The **slab descriptor** points to a list of objects contained in the pages and tracks their state. A slab may be in one of three possible states--full, partial or empty--based on the state of the objects it is hosting. A *slab* is considered *full* when all its objects are *in use* with no *free* objects left for allocation. *A slab* with at least one free object is considered to be in *partial* state, and those with all objects in *free* state are considered *empty*.

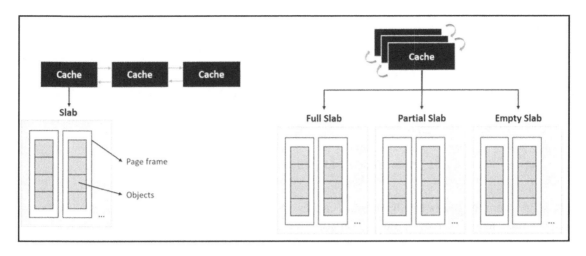

This arrangement enables quick object allocations, since allocator routines can look up to the *partial* slab for a free object, and possibly move on to an *empty* slab if required. It also helps easier expansion of the cache with new page frames to accommodate more objects (when required), and facilitates safe and quick reclaims (slabs in *empty* state can be reclaimed).

Slub data structures

Having looked at the layout of a cache and descriptors involved at a generic level, let's push further to view specific data structures used by the **slub** allocator and explore the management of free lists. A **slub** defines its version of cache descriptor, struct kmem_cache, in kernel header /include/linux/slub-def.h:

```
struct kmem_cache {
  struct kmem_cache_cpu __percpu *cpu_slab;
  /* Used for retriving partial slabs etc */
  unsigned long flags;
  unsigned long min_partial;
  int size; /* The size of an object including meta data */
  int object_size; /* The size of an object without meta data */
  int offset; /* Free pointer offset. */
  int cpu_partial; /* Number of per cpu partial objects to keep around */
  struct kmem_cache_order_objects oo;

  /* Allocation and freeing of slabs */
  struct kmem_cache_order_objects max;
  struct kmem_cache_order_objects min;
  gfp_t allocflags; /* gfp flags to use on each alloc */
  int refcount; /* Refcount for slab cache destroy */
```

```
    void (*ctor)(void *);
    int inuse; /* Offset to metadata */
    int align; /* Alignment */
    int reserved; /* Reserved bytes at the end of slabs */
    const char *name; /* Name (only for display!) */
    struct list_head list; /* List of slab caches */
    int red_left_pad; /* Left redzone padding size */
    ...
    ...
    ...
    struct kmem_cache_node *node[MAX_NUMNODES];
};
```

The list element refers to a list of slab caches. When a new slab is allocated, it is stored on a list in the cache descriptor, and is considered *empty*, since all its objects are *free* and available. Upon allocation of an object, the slab turns into *partial* state. Partial slabs are the only type of slabs that the allocator needs to keep track of and are connected in a list inside the kmem_cache structure. The **SLUB** allocator has no interest in tracking *full* slabs whose objects have all been allocated, or *empty* slabs whose objects are *free*. **SLUB** tracks partial slabs for each node through an array of pointers of type struct kmem_cache_node[MAX_NUMNODES], which encapsulates a list of *partial* slabs:

```
struct kmem_cache_node {
 spinlock_t list_lock;
 ...
 ...
#ifdef CONFIG_SLUB
 unsigned long nr_partial;
 struct list_head partial;
#ifdef CONFIG_SLUB_DEBUG
 atomic_long_t nr_slabs;
 atomic_long_t total_objects;
 struct list_head full;
#endif
#endif
};
```

All *free* objects in a slab form a linked list; when allocation requests arrive, the first free object is removed from the list and its address is returned to the caller. Tracking free objects through a linked list requires significant metadata; while the traditional **SLAB** allocator maintained metadata for all pages of a slab within the slab header (causing data alignment issues), **SLUB** maintains per-page metadata for pages in a slab by cramming more fields into the page descriptor structure, thereby eliminating metadata from the slab head. **SLUB** metadata elements in the page descriptor are only valid when the corresponding page is part of a slab. Pages engaged for slab allocations have the PG_slab flag set.

The following are fields of the page descriptor relevant to SLUB:

```
struct page {
      ...
      ...
   union {
     pgoff_t index; /* Our offset within mapping. */
     void *freelist; /* sl[aou]b first free object */
   };
      ...
      ...
   struct {
         union {
                  ...
                  struct { /* SLUB */
                        unsigned inuse:16;
                        unsigned objects:15;
                        unsigned frozen:1;
                     };
                  ...
               };
               ...
         };
   ...
   ...
   union {
            ...
            ...
            struct kmem_cache *slab_cache; /* SL[AU]B: Pointer to slab */
      };
   ...
   ...
};
```

The `freelist` pointer refers to the first free object in the list. Each free object is composed of a metadata area that contain a pointer to the next free object in the list. `index` holds the offset to the metadata area of the first free object (contains a pointer to next free object). The metadata area of last free object would contain the next free object pointer set to NULL. `inuse` contains the total count of allocated objects, and `objects` contains the total number of objects. `frozen` is a flag that is used as a page lock: if a page has been frozen by a CPU core, only that core can retrieve free objects from the page. `slab_cache` is a pointer to the kmem cache currently using this page:

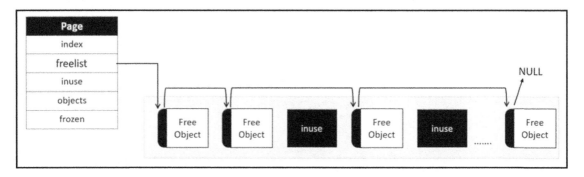

When an allocation request arrives, the first free object is located through the `freelist` pointer, and is removed from the list by returning its address to the caller. The `inuse` counter is also incremented to indicate an increase in the number of allocated objects. The `freelist` pointer is then updated with the address of the next free object in the list.

For achieving enhanced allocation efficiency, each CPU is assigned a private active-slab list, which comprises a partial/free slab list for each object type. These slabs are referred to as CPU local slabs, and are tracked by struct `kmem_cache_cpu`:

```
struct kmem_cache_cpu {
    void **freelist; /* Pointer to next available object */
    unsigned long tid; /* Globally unique transaction id */
    struct page *page; /* The slab from which we are allocating */
    struct page *partial; /* Partially allocated frozen slabs */
    #ifdef CONFIG_SLUB_STATS
        unsigned stat[NR_SLUB_STAT_ITEMS];
    #endif
};
```

When an allocation request arrives, the allocator takes the fast path and looks into the `freelist` of the per-CPU cache, and it then returns free objects. This is referred as the fast path since allocations are carried out through interrupt-safe atomic instructions that does not require lock contention. When the fast path fails, the allocator takes the slow path and looks through *page* and *partial* lists of the cpu cache sequentially. If no free objects are found, the allocator moves into the *partial* lists of nodes; this operation requires the allocator to contend for appropriate exclusion lock. On failure, the allocator gets a new slab from the buddy system. Fetching from either node lists or acquiring a new slab from buddy system are considered very slow paths, since both of these operations are not deterministic.

The following diagram depicts the relationship between slub data structures and free lists:

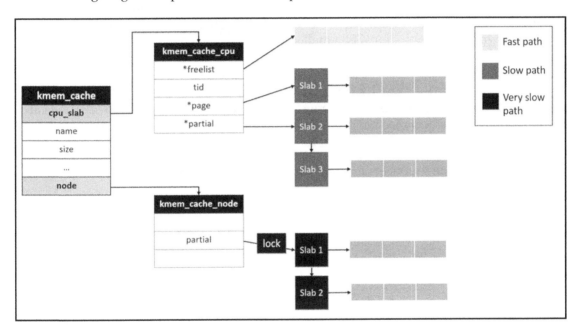

Vmalloc

Page and slab allocators both allocate physically contiguous blocks of memory, mapped to contiguous kernel address space. Most of the time, kernel services and subsystems prefer to allocate physically contiguous blocks for exploiting caching, address translation, and other performance-related benefits. Nonetheless, allocation requests for very large blocks might fail due to fragmentation of physical memory, and there are few situations that necessitate allocation of large blocks, such as support for dynamically loadable modules, swap management operations, large file caches and so on.

As a solution, the kernel provides **vmalloc**, a fragmented memory allocator that attempts to allocate memory, by joining physically scattered memory regions through virtually contiguous address space. A range of virtual addresses within the kernel segment are reserved for vmalloc mappings, called vmalloc address space. Total memory that can be mapped through the vmalloc interface depends on the size of the vmalloc address space, which is defined by architecture-specific kernel macros VMALLOC_START and VMALLOC_END; for x86-64 systems, the total range of vmalloc address space is a staggering 32 TB. However, on the flip side, this range is too little for most 32-bit architectures (a mere 12o MB). Recent kernel versions use the vmalloc range for setting up a virtually mapped kernel stack (x86-64 only), which we discussed in the first chapter.

Following are interface routines for vmalloc allocations and deallocations:

```
/**
 * vmalloc  -  allocate virtually contiguous memory
 * @size:   -  allocation size
 * Allocate enough pages to cover @size from the page level
 * allocator and map them into contiguous kernel virtual space.
 *
 */
    void *vmalloc(unsigned long size)

/**
 * vzalloc - allocate virtually contiguous memory with zero fill
 * @size:   allocation size
 * Allocate enough pages to cover @size from the page level
 * allocator and map them into contiguous kernel virtual space.
 * The memory allocated is set to zero.
 *
 */
    void *vzalloc(unsigned long size)

/**
 * vmalloc_user - allocate zeroed virtually contiguous memory for
userspace
```

```
 * @size: allocation size
 * The resulting memory area is zeroed so it can be mapped to userspace
 * without leaking data.
 */
   void *vmalloc_user(unsigned long size)

/**
 * vmalloc_node  -  allocate memory on a specific node
 * @size:           allocation size
 * @node:           numa node
 * Allocate enough pages to cover @size from the page level
 * allocator and map them into contiguous kernel virtual space.
 *
 */
   void *vmalloc_node(unsigned long size, int node)

/**
 * vfree  -  release memory allocated by vmalloc()
 * @addr:           memory base address
 * Free the virtually continuous memory area starting at @addr, as
 * obtained from vmalloc(), vmalloc_32() or __vmalloc(). If @addr is
 * NULL, no operation is performed.
 */
   void vfree(const void *addr)


/**
 * vfree_atomic  -  release memory allocated by vmalloc()
 * @addr:           memory base address
 * This one is just like vfree() but can be called in any atomic context
except NMIs.
 */
   void vfree_atomic(const void *addr)
```

Most kernel developers avoid vmalloc allocations due to allocation overheads (since those are not identity mapped and require specific page table tweaks, resulting in TLB flushes) and performance penalties involved during access operations.

Contiguous Memory Allocator (CMA)

Albeit with significant overheads, virtually mapped allocations solve the problem of large memory allocations to a greater extent. However, there are a few scenarios that mandate the allocation of physically contiguous buffers. DMA transfers are one such case. Device drivers often find a stringent need for physically contiguous buffer allocations (for setting up DMA transfers), which are carried out through any of the physically contiguous allocators discussed earlier.

However, drivers dealing with specific classes of devices such as multimedia often find themselves searching for huge blocks of contiguous memory. To meet this end, over the years, such drivers have been *reserving* memory during system boot through the kernel parameter mem, which allows setting aside enough contiguous memory at boot, which can be *remapped* into linear address space during driver runtime. Though valuable, this strategy has its limitations: first, such reserved memories lie momentarily unused when the corresponding device is not initiating access operations, and second, depending on the number of devices to be supported, the size of reserved memories might increase substantially, which might severely impact system performance due to cramped physical memory.

A **contiguous Memory Allocator** (**CMA**) is a kernel mechanism introduced to effectively manage *reserved* memories. The crux of *CMA* is to bring in *reserved* memories under the allocator algorithm, and such memory is referred to as *CMA area*. *CMA* allows allocations from the *CMA area* for both devices' and system's use. This is achieved by building a page descriptor list for pages in reserve memory, and enumerating it into the buddy system, which enables allocation of *CMA pages* through the page allocator for regular needs (kernel subsystems) and through DMA allocation routines for device drivers.

However, it must be ensured that DMA allocations do not fail due to the usage of *CMA pages* for other purposes, and this is taken care through the migratetype attribute, which we discussed earlier. Pages enumerated by CMA into buddy system are assigned the MIGRATE_CMA property, which indicates that pages are movable. While allocating memory for non-DMA purposes , the page allocator can use CMA pages only for movable allocations (recall that such allocations can be made through the __GFP_MOVABLE flag). When a DMA allocation request arrives, CMA pages held by kernel allocations are *moved* out of the reserved region (through a page-migration mechanism), resulting in the availability of memory for the device driver's use. Further, when pages are allocated for DMA, their *migratetype* is changed from MIGRATE_CMA to MIGRATE_ISOLATE, making them invisible to the buddy system.

The size of the *CMA area* can be chosen during kernel build through its configuration interface; optionally, it can also be passed through the kernel parameter cma=.

Summary

We have traversed through one of the most crucial aspects of the Linux kernel, comprehending various nuances of memory representations and allocations. By understanding this subsystem, we have also succinctly captured the design acumen and implementation efficiency of the kernel, and more importantly understood the kernel's dynamism in accommodating finer and newer heuristics and mechanisms for continuous enhancements. Apart from the specifics of memory management, we also gauged the efficiency of the kernel in maximizing resource usage at minimal costs, ushering all classical mechanisms of code reuse and modular code structures.

Though the specifics of memory management may vary in correspondence to the underlying architecture, the generalities of design and implementation styles would mostly remain the same to achieve code stability and sensitivity to change.

In the next chapter, we will go further and look at another fundamental abstraction of the kernel: *files*. We will look through file I/O and explore its architecture and implementation details.

5
Filesystems and File I/O

Thus far we have traversed across the elemental resources of the kernel, such as address spaces, processor time, and physical memory. We have built an empirical understanding of *process management, CPU scheduling,* and *memory management* and the crucial abstractions they provide. We shall continue to build our understanding in this chapter by looking at another key abstraction provided by the kernel, the *file I/O architecture.* We will look in detail at aspects such as:

- Filesystem implementation
- File I/O
- VFS
- VFS data structures
- Special filesystems

Computing systems exist for the sole purpose of processing data. Most algorithms are designed and programmed to extract desired information from acquired data. Data which fuels this process must be stored persistently for continuous access, mandating storage systems to be engineered to contain information safely for longer periods of time. For users however it's the operating system which fetches data from these storage devices and makes it available for processing. The kernel's filesystem is the component that serves this purpose.

Filesystem - high-level view

Filesystems abstract the physical view of storage devices from users, and virtualize storage area on a disk for each valid user of the system through abstract containers called **files and directories**. **Files** serve as containers for user data and **directories** act as containers to a group of user files. In simple words, operating systems virtualize a view of a storage device for each user as a set of directories and files. Filesystem services implement routines to create, organize, store, and retrieve files, and these operations are invoked by user applications through appropriate system call interfaces.

We will begin this discussion by looking at the layout of a simple filesystem, designed to manage a standard magnetic storage disk. This discussion will help us comprehend key terms and concepts related to disk management in general. A typical filesystem implementation however involves appropriate data structures which describe the organization of file data on disk, and operations which enable applications to execute file I/O.

Metadata

A storage disk typically is composed of physical blocks of identical size called **sectors**; size of a sector is usually 512 bytes or in multiples, depending on type and capacity of storage. A sector is the minimal unit of I/O on the disk. When a disk is presented to the filesystem for management, it perceives storage area as an array of **blocks** of fixed size, where each block is identical to a sector or multiples of sector size. Typical default block size is 1024 bytes and can vary as per disk capacity and filesystem type. Block size is considered the minimal unit of I/O by a filesystem:

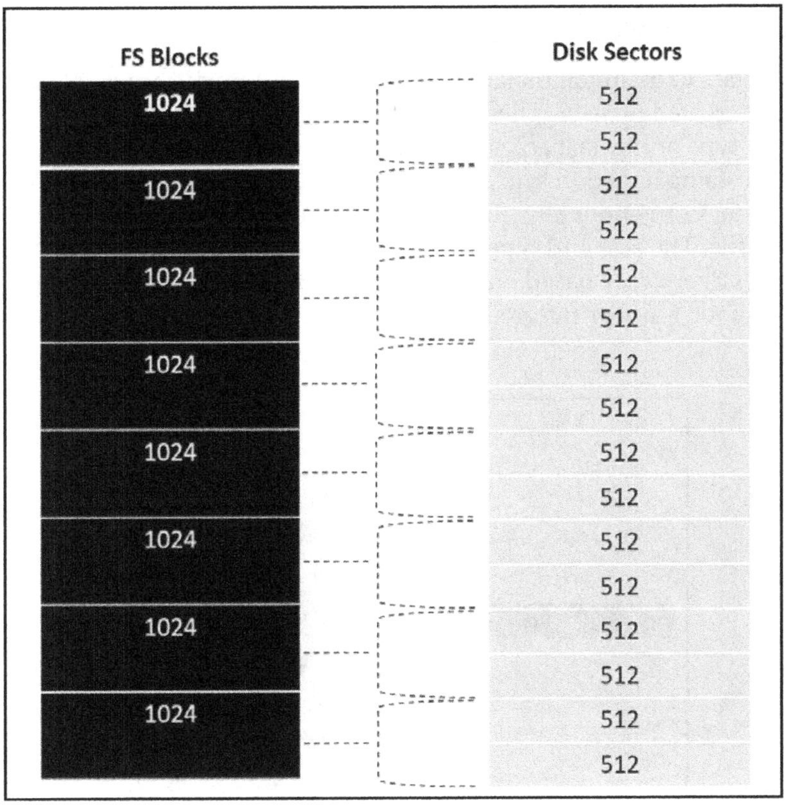
FS Blocks
Disk Sectors
1024
1024
1024
1024
1024
1024
1024
1024
512
512
512
512
512
512
512
512
512
512
512
512
512
512
512
512

Inode (index node)

The filesystem needs to maintain metadata to identify and track various attributes for each file and directory created by user. There are several elements of metadata that describe a file such as filename, type of file, last access timestamp, owner, access privileges, last modification timestamp, creation time, size of file data, and references to disk blocks containing file data. Conventionally, filesystems define a structure called inode to contain all metadata of a file. The size and type of information contained in inode is filesystem specific and may largely vary based on the functionalities it supports. Each inode is identified by a unique number referred to as an **index**, which is considered a low-level name of the file:

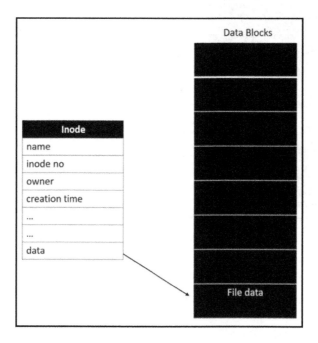

Filesystems reserve a few disk blocks for storing inode instances and the rest for storing corresponding file data. The number of blocks reserved for storing inodes depend on the storage capacity of the disk. The on-disk list of nodes held in inode blocks is referred to as the **inode table**. Filesystems would need to track the status of the inode and data blocks to identify free blocks. This is generally achieved through **bitmaps**, a bitmap for tracking free inodes and another to track free data blocks. The following diagram shows the typical layout with bitmap, inode, and data blocks:

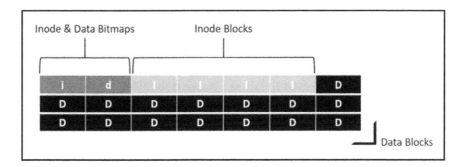

Data block map

As mentioned before, each inode should record the locations of data blocks in which corresponding file data is stored. Depending on the length of file data, each file might occupy *n* number of data blocks. There are various methods used to track data block details in an inode; the simplest being **direct references**, which involves the inode containing **direct pointers** to data blocks of the file. The number of such **direct pointers** would depend on filesystem design, and most implementations choose to engage fewer bytes for such pointers. This method is productive for small files which span across a few data blocks (usually < 16k), but lacks support for large files spread across numerous data blocks:

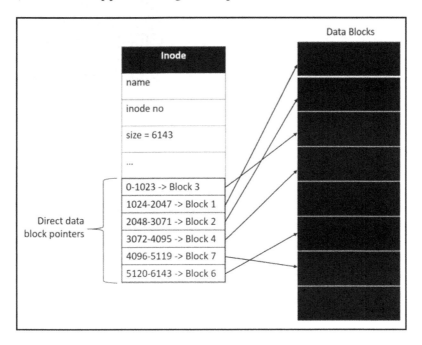

To support large files, filesystems engage an alternate method called **multi-level indexing** which involves indirect pointers. The simplest implementation would have an indirect pointer along with a few direct pointers in an inode structure. An **indirect pointer** refers to a block containing **direct pointers** to data blocks of the file. When a file grows too large to be referred through direct pointers of the inode, a free data block is engaged with direct pointers and the indirect pointer of the inode is referred to it. The data block referred to by an indirect pointer is called **indirect block**. The number of direct pointers in an indirect block can be determined by block size divided by the size of block addresses; for instance, on a 32-bit filesystem with 4-byte (32 bits) wide block addresses and 1024 block size, each indirect block can contain up to 256 entries, whereas in a 64-bit filesystem with 8-byte (64 bits) wide block addresses, each indirect block can contain up to 128 direct pointers:

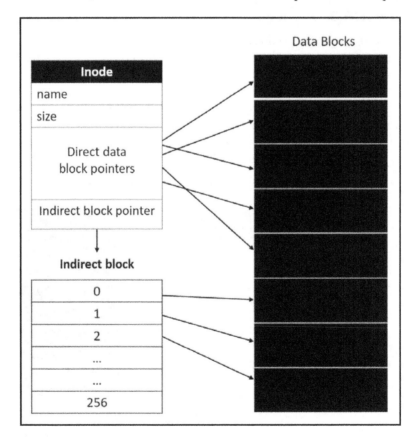

This technique can be furthered to support even larger files by engaging a **double-indirect pointer,** which refers to a block containing indirect pointers with each entry referring to a block containing direct pointers. Assuming a 64-bit filesystem with 1024 block size, with each block accommodating 128 entries, there would be 128 indirect pointers each pointing to a block holding 128 direct pointers; thus with this technique a filesystem can support a file that can span up to 16,384 (128 x 128) data blocks, which is 16 MB.

Further, this technique can be extended with a **triple-indirection pointer,** resulting in even more metadata to be managed by filesystems. However, despite of multi-level indexing, increasing filesystem block size with reduction in block address size is the most recommended and efficient solution to support larger files. Users will need to choose the appropriate block size while initializing a disk with a filesystem, to ensure proper support for larger files.

Some filesystems use a different approach called extents to store data block information in an inode. An **extent** is a pointer that refers to the start data block (similar to that of a direct pointer) with added length bits that specify the count of contiguous blocks where file data is stored. Depending on file size and disk fragmentation levels, a single extent might not be sufficient to refer to all data blocks of the file, and to handle such eventualities, filesystems build **extent lists** with each extent referring to the start address and length of one region of contiguous data blocks on disk.

The extents approach reduces metadata that filesystems need to manage to store data block maps by a significant volume, but this is realized at the cost of flexibility in filesystem operations. For instance, consider a read operation to be performed at a specific file position of a large file: to locate a data block of specified file offset position, the filesystem must begin with the first extent and scan through the list until it finds the extent that covers the required file offset.

Directories

Filesystems consider a directory as a special file. They represent a directory or a folder with an on-disk inode. They are differentiated from normal file inodes through the **type** field, which is marked as **directory**. Each directory is assigned data blocks where it holds information about files and subdirectories it contains. A directory maintains records of files, and each record includes the filename, which is a name string not exceeding a specific length as defined by the filesystem's naming policy, and the inode number associated with the file. For efficient management, filesystem implementations define the layout of file records contained in a directory through appropriate data structures such as binary trees, lists, radix trees, and hash tables:

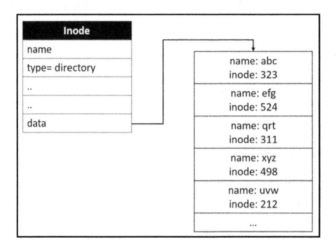

Superblock

Apart from storing inodes that captures metadata of individual files, filesystems also need to maintain metadata pertaining to disk volume as a whole, such as size of the volume, total block count, current state of filesystem, count of inode blocks, count of inodes, count of data blocks, start inode block number, and filesystem signature (magic number) for identity. These details are captured in a data structure called **superblock**. During initialization of filesystem on disk volume, the superblock is organized at start of disk storage. The following diagram illustrates the complete layout of disk storage with superblocks:

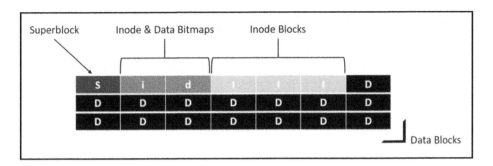

Operations

While **data structures** make up elementary constituents of a filesystem design, the operations possible on those data structures to render file access and manipulation operations makes the core feature set. The number of operations and type of functionalities supported are filesystem implementation specific. Following is a generic description of a few common operations that most filesystems provide.

Mount and unmount operations

Mount is an operation of enumerating an on-disk superblock and metadata into memory for the filesystem's use. This process creates in-memory data structures that describe file metadata and present the host operating system with a view of the directory and file layout in the volume. The mount operation is implemented to check consistency of disk volume. As discussed earlier, the **superblock** contains the state of the filesystem; it indicates whether the volume is *consistent* or *dirty*. If the volume is clean or consistent, a mount operation would succeed, and if the volume is marked as dirty or inconsistent, it returns with the appropriate failure status.

An abrupt shutdown causes filesystem state to be dirty, and requires consistency check before it can be marked for use again. Mechanisms adopted for consistency checks are complex and time consuming; such operations are filesystem implementation specific, and most simple ones provide specific tools for consistency and checks, and other modern implementations use journaling.

Unmount is an operation of flushing the in-memory state of filesystem data structures back to disk. This operation causes all metadata and file caches to be synchronized with disk blocks. Unmount marks the filesystem state in the superblock as consistent, indicating graceful shutdown. In other words, the on-disk superblock state remains dirty until unmount is executed.

File creation and deletion operations

Creation of a file is an operation that requires instantiation of a new inode with appropriate attributes. User programs invoke the file creation routine with chosen attributes such as filename, directory under which file is to be created, access permissions for various users, and file modes. This routine also initializes other specific fields of inode such as creation timestamp and file ownership information. This operation writes a new file record into the directory block, describing the filename and inode number.

When a user application initiates a `delete` operation on a valid file, the filesystem removes the corresponding file record from the directory and checks the file's reference count to determine the number of processes currently using the file. Deletion of a file record from a directory prevents other processes from opening the file that is marked for deletion. When all current references to a file are closed, all resources assigned to the file are released by returning its data blocks to the list of free data blocks, and inode to list of free inodes.

File open and close operations

When a user process attempts to open a file, it invokes the `open` operation of the filesystem with appropriate arguments, which include path and name of the file. The filesystem traverses through directories specified in the path until it reaches the immediate parent directory that contains the requested file's record. Lookup into the file record produces the inode number of the specified file. However, specific logic and efficiency of lookup operation depends on the data structure chosen by the particular filesystem implementation for organizing file records in a directory block.

Once the filesystem retrieves the related inode number of the file, it initiates appropriate sanity checks to enforce access control validation on the calling context. If the caller process is cleared for file access, the filesystem then instantiates an in-memory structure called **file descriptor** to maintain file access state and attributes. Upon successful completion, the open operation returns the reference of the file descriptor structure to the caller process, which serves as a handle to the file for the caller process to initiate other file operations such as `read`, `write`, and `close`.

Upon initiating a `close` operation, the file descriptor structure is destroyed and the file's reference count is decremented. The caller process will no longer be able to initiate any other file operation until it can open the file all over again.

File read and write operations

When user applications initiate *read* on a file with appropriate arguments, the underlying filesystem's `read` routine is invoked. Operations begin with a lookup into the file's data block map to locate the appropriate data disk sector to be read; it then allocates a page from the page cache and schedules disk I/O. On completion of I/O transfer, the filesystem moves requested data into the application's buffer and updates the file offset position in the caller's file descriptor structure.

Similarly, the `write` operation of the filesystem retrieves data passed from user buffer and writes it into the appropriate offset of file buffer in the page cache, and marks the page with the `PG_dirty` flag. However, when the `write` operation is invoked to append data at the end of the file, new data blocks might be required for the file to grow. The filesystem looks for free data blocks on disk, and allocates them for this file, before proceeding with *write*. Allocating new data blocks would need changes to the inode structure's data block map and allocation of new page(s) from page cache mapped to the new data blocks allocated.

Additional features

Though the fundamental components of a filesystem remain similar, the way data is organized and the heuristics to access data is implementation dependent. Designers consider factors such as **reliability**, **security**, **type** and **capacity of storage volume**, and **I/O efficiency** to identify and support features that enhance capabilities of a filesystem. Following are few extended features that are supported by modern filesystems.

Extended file attributes

General file attributes tracked by a filesystem implementation are maintained in an inode and interpreted by appropriate operations. Extended file attributes are a feature that enables users to define custom metadata for a file, which is not interpreted by the filesystem. Such attributes are often used to store various types of information which depend on the type of data the file contains. For instance, document files can define the author name and contact details, web files can specify URL of the file and other security-related attributes such as digital certificates and crypto hash keys. Similar to normal attributes, each extended attribute is identified by a **name** and a **value**. Ideally, most filesystems do not impose restrictions on the number of such extended attributes.

Some filesystems also provide a facility of **indexing** the attributes, which aids in quick lookup for required type of data without having to navigate file hierarchy. For instance, assume that files are assigned with an extended attribute called **Keywords**, which records keyword values that describe file data. With indexing, the user could issue queries to find the list of files matching specific keywords through appropriate scripts, regardless of the file's location. Thus, indexing offers a powerful alternative interface to the filesystem.

Filesystem consistency and crash recovery

Consistency of an on-disk image is critical for reliable functioning of a filesystem. While the filesystem is in the process of updating its on-disk structures, there is every possibility for a catastrophic error to occur (power down, OS crash, and so on), causing interruption of a partially committed critical update. This results in corruption of on-disk structures and leaves the filesystem in an inconsistent state. Dealing with such eventualities, by engaging an effective strategy for crash recovery, is one of the major challenges faced by most filesystem designers.

Some filesystems handle crash recovery through a specially designed filesystem consistency check tool like **fsck** (a widely used Unix tool). It is run at system boot before mount and scans through on-disk filesystem structures looking for inconsistencies, and fixes them when found. Once finished, the on-disk filesystem state is reverted to a consistent state and the system proceeds with the `mount` operation, thus making the disk accessible to users. The tool executes its operations in a number of phases, closely checking for consistency of each on-disk structure such as superblock, inode block, free blocks, checking individual inodes for valid state, directory checks, and bad block check in each phase. Though it provides much-needed crash recovery, it has its downsides: such phased operations can consume a lot of time to complete on a large disk volume, which directly impacts the system's boot time.

Journaling is another technique engaged by most modern filesystem implementations for quick and reliable crash recovery. This method is enforced by programming appropriate filesystem operations for crash recovery. The idea is to prepare a **log** (note) listing out changes to be committed to the on-disk image of the filesystem, and writing the log to a special disk block called a **journal block**, before beginning the actual update operation. This ensures that on a crash during actual update, the filesystem can easily detect inconsistencies and fix them by looking through information recorded in the log. Thus, an implementation of journaling filesystem eliminates the need for the tedious and expensive task of disk scan, by marginally extending work done during an update.

Access control lists (ACLs)

The default file and directory access permissions that specify access rights for the owner, the group to which owner belongs, and others users does not offer fine-grained control required in some situations. ACLs are a feature that enable an extended mechanism to specify file access permissions for various processes and users. This feature considers all files and directories as objects, and allows system administrators to define a list of access permissions for each. ACLs include operations valid on an object with access privileges, and restrictions for each user and system process on a specified object.

Filesystems in the Linux kernel

Now that we are familiar with fundamental concepts related to filesystem implementations, we will explore filesystem services supported by Linux systems. The kernel's filesystem branch has implementations of numerous filesystem services, which support diverse file types. Based on the type of files they manage, the kernel's filesystems can be broadly categorized into:

1. Storage filesystems
2. Special filesystems
3. Distributed filesystems or network filesystems

We shall discuss special filesystems in a later section of this chapter.

- **Storage filesystems**: Kernel supports various persistent storage filesystems, which can be broadly categorized into various groups based on the type of storage device they are designed to manage.
- **Disk filesystems**: This category includes various standard storage disk filesystems supported by the kernel, which includes the Linux native ext family of disk filesystems, such as Ext2, Ext3, Ext4, ReiserFS, and Btrfs; Unix variants such as the sysv filesystem, UFS, and MINIX filesystem; Microsoft filesystems such as MS-DOS, VFAT, and NTFS; other proprietary filesystems such as IBM's OS/2 (HPFS), Qnx based filesystems such as qnx4 and qnx6, Apple's Macintosh HFS and HFS2, Amiga's Fast Filesystem (AFFS), and Acorn Disk Filing System (ADFS); and journaling filesystems like IBM's JFS and SGI's XFS.

- **Removable media filesystems**: This category includes filesystems designed for CD, DVD, and other movable storage media devices, such as the ISO9660 CD-ROM filesystem and Universal Disk Format (UDF) DVD filesystem, and squashfs used in live CD images for Linux distributions.
- **Semiconductor storage filesystems**: This category includes filesystems designed and implemented for raw flash and other semiconductor storage devices that require support of wear-leveling and erase operations. The current set of filesystems supported include UBIFS, JFFS2, CRAMFS, and so on.

We shall discuss in brief a few native disk filesystems in the kernel, which are used across various distributions of Linux as default.

Ext family filesystems

The initial release of the Linux kernel used MINIX as the default native filesystem, which was designed for use in the Minix kernel for educational purposes and hence had many usage limitations. As the kernel matured, kernel developers built a new native filesystem for disk management called the **extended filesystem**. The design of *ext* was heavily influenced by the standard Unix filesystem UFS. Due to various implementation limitations and lack of efficiency, the original ext was short lived and was soon replaced by an improved, stable, and efficient version named **second extended filesystem (Ext2)**. The Ext2 filesystem continued to be the default native filesystem for quite a long period of time (until 2001, with the 2.4.15 release of the Linux kernel).

Later, rapid evolution in disk storage technologies led to a massive increase in storage capacity and efficiency of storage hardware. To exploit features provided by storage hardware, the kernel community evolved forks of *ext2* with appropriate design improvements and added features that are best suitable for a specific class of storage. Current versions of the Linux kernel contain three versions of extended filesystems, called Ext2, Ext3, and Ext4.

Ext2

The Ext2 filesystem was first introduced in kernel version 0.99.7 (1993). It retains the core design of classic UFS (Unix filesystem) with write-back caching, which enables short turnaround time and improved performance. Although it was implemented to support disk volumes in the range of 2 TB to 32 TB and file sizes in the range of 16 GB to 2 TB, its usage was restricted for up to 4 TB disk volumes and 2 GB max file sizes due to block device and application imposed restrictions in 2.4 kernels. It also includes support for ACLs, file memory maps, and crash recovery through the consistency checker tool fsck. Ext2 divides physical disk sectors into fixed-size block groups. A filesystem layout is constructed for each block group, with each having a complete superblock, free block bitmap, inode bitmap, inode, and data blocks. Thus, each block group appears as a miniature filesystem. This design assists *fsck* with faster consistency checks on a large disk.

Ext3

Also called **third extended filesystem**, it extends the functionality of Ext2 with journaling. It retains the entire structure of Ext2 with block groups, which enables seamless conversion of an Ext2 partition into an Ext3 type. As discussed earlier, journaling causes the filesystem to log details of an update operation into specific regions of disk called journal blocks; these logs help expedite crash recovery and ensure consistency and reliability of the filesystem. However, on journaling filesystems, disk update operations can turn expensive due to slower or variable-time write operations (due to journal log) which would directly impact performance of regular file I/O. As a solution, Ext3 provides journal configuration options through which system administrators or users can select specific types of information to be logged to a journal. These configuration options are referred to as **journaling modes**.

1. **Journal mode**: This mode causes the filesystem to record both file data and metadata changes into the journal. This results in maximized filesystem consistency with increased disk access, causing slower updates. This mode causes the journal to consume additional disk blocks and is the slowest Ext3 journaling mode.

2. **Ordered mode**: This mode records only filesystem metadata into the journal, but it guarantees that related file data is written to disk before associated metadata is committed to the journal block. This ensures that file data is valid; if a crash occurs while executing write to a file, the journal will indicate that the appended data has not been committed, resulting in a purge operation on such data by the cleanup process. This is the default journaling mode of Ext3.

3. **Writeback mode**: This is similar to ordered mode with only metadata journaling, but with an exception that the related file contents might be written to disk before or after the metadata is committed to journal. This can result in corruption of filedata. For example, consider a file being appended to may be marked in the journal as *committed* before actual file write: if a crash occurs during the file append operation, then the journal suggests the file being larger than it actually is. This mode is fastest but minimizes file data reliability. Many other journaling filesystems such as JFS uses this mode of journaling, but ensure that any *garbage* due to unwritten data is zeroed out on reboot.

All of these modes have a similar effect with respect to the consistency of metadata, but differ in consistency of file and directory data, with journal mode ensuring maximum safety with minimal chance of file data corruption, and writeback mode offering minimal safety with high risk of corruption. Administrators or users can tune the appropriate mode during mount operation on an Ext3 volume.

Ext4

Implemented as a replacement to Ext3 with enhanced features, Ext4 first appeared in kernel 2.6.28 (2008). It is fully backward compatible with Ext2 and Ext3, and a volume of either type can be mounted as Ext4. This is the default ext filesystem on most current Linux distributions. It extends journaling capabilities of Ext3 with **journal checksums** which increases its reliability. It also adds checksums for filesystem metadata and supports transparent encryption, resulting in enhanced filesystem integrity and security. Other features include support for extents, which help reduce fragmentation, persistent preallocation of disk blocks, which enables allocation of contiguous blocks for media files, and support for disk volumes with storage capacities up to 1 exbibyte (EiB) and files with sizes up to 16 tebibytes (TiB).

Common filesystem interface

Presence of diverse filesystems and storage partitions results in each filesystem maintaining its tree of files and data structures that are distinct from others. Upon mount, each filesystem will require to manage its in-memory file trees in isolation from others, resulting in an inconsistent view of the file tree for system users and applications. This complicates kernel support for various file operations such as open, read, write, copy, and move. As a solution, the Linux kernel (like many other Unix systems) engages an abstraction layer called **virtual file system (VFS)** that hides all filesystem implementations with a common interface.

The VFS layer builds a common file tree called **rootfs**, under which all filesystems can enumerate their directories and files. This enables all filesystem-specific subtrees with distinct on-disk representations to be unified and presented as a single filesystem. System users and applications have a consistent, homogeneous view of the file tree, resulting in flexibility for the kernel to define a simplified set of common system calls that applications can engage for file I/O, regardless of underlying filesystems and their representations. This model ensures simplicity in application design due to limited and flexible APIs and enables seamless copy or movement of files from one disk partition or filesystem tree to another, irrespective of underlying dissimilarities.

The following diagram depicts the virtual filesystem:

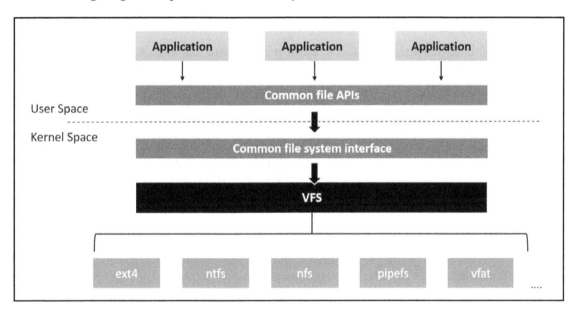

VFS defines two sets of functions: first, a set of generic filesystem-independent routines that serve as common entry functions for all file access and manipulation operations, and second, a set of abstract operation interfaces that are filesystem specific. Each filesystem defines its operations (as per its notion of files and directories) and maps them to an abstract interface provided, and with the virtual filesystem, this enables VFS to handle file I/O requests by dynamically switching into underlying filesystem-specific functions.

VFS structures and operations

Deciphering the key objects and data structures of VFS lets us gain clarity on how the VFS internally works with filesystems and enables the all-important abstraction. Following are four elemental data structures around which the entire web of abstraction is weaved:

- `struct super_block`--which contains information on specific filesystems that have been mounted
- `struct inode`--which represents a specific file
- `struct dentry`--representing a directory entry
- `struct file`--representing the file which has been opened and linked to a process

All of these data structures are bound to appropriate abstract operation interfaces that are defined by filesystems.

struct superblock

VFS defines a generic layout for the superblock through this structure. Each filesystem would need to instantiate an object of this structure to fill in its superblock details during mount. In other words, this structure abstracts the filesystem-specific superblock from the rest of the kernel, and helps VFS track all mounted filesystems through a list of `struct super_block`. Pseudo filesystems, which do not have persistent superblock structure, will dynamically generate superblocks. The superblock structure (`struct super_block`) is defined in `<linux/fs.h>`:

```
struct super_block {
        struct list_head        s_list;   /* Keep this first */
        dev_t                   s_dev;    /* search index; _not_ kdev_t */
        unsigned char           s_blocksize_bits;
        unsigned long           s_blocksize;
        loff_t                  s_maxbytes;  /* Max file size */
        struct file_system_type *s_type;
        const struct super_operations    *s_op;
        const struct dquot_operations    *dq_op;
        const struct quotactl_ops        *s_qcop;
        const struct export_operations *s_export_op;
        unsigned long           s_flags;
        unsigned long           s_iflags; /* internal SB_I_* flags */
        unsigned long           s_magic;
        struct dentry           *s_root;
        struct rw_semaphore     s_umount;
        int                     s_count;
```

```
        atomic_t                s_active;
#ifdef CONFIG_SECURITY
        void                    *s_security;
#endif
        const struct xattr_handler **s_xattr;
        const struct fscrypt_operations *s_cop;
        struct hlist_bl_head    s_anon;
        struct list_head        s_mounts;/*list of mounts;_not_for fs
use*/
        struct block_device     *s_bdev;
        struct backing_dev_info *s_bdi;
        struct mtd_info         *s_mtd;
        struct hlist_node       s_instances;
        unsigned int    s_quota_types; /*Bitmask of supported quota types
*/
        struct quota_info  s_dquot;   /* Diskquota specific options */
        struct sb_writers       s_writers;
        char s_id[32];                          /* Informational name */
        u8 s_uuid[16];                          /* UUID */
        void                    *s_fs_info;   /* Filesystem private info
*/
        unsigned int            s_max_links;
        fmode_t                 s_mode;

        /* Granularity of c/m/atime in ns.
           Cannot be worse than a second */
        u32                     s_time_gran;

        struct mutex s_vfs_rename_mutex;        /* Kludge */

        /*
         * Filesystem subtype.  If non-empty the filesystem type field
         * in /proc/mounts will be "type.subtype"
         */
        char *s_subtype;

        /*
         * Saved mount options for lazy filesystems using
         * generic_show_options()
         */
        char __rcu *s_options;
        const struct dentry_operations *s_d_op; /*default op for
dentries*/
        /*
         * Saved pool identifier for cleancache (-1 means none)
         */
        int cleancache_poolid;
```

```
          struct shrinker s_shrink;        /* per-sb shrinker handle */

          /* Number of inodes with nlink == 0 but still referenced */
          atomic_long_t s_remove_count;

          /* Being remounted read-only */
          int s_readonly_remount;

          /* AIO completions deferred from interrupt context */
          struct workqueue_struct *s_dio_done_wq;
          struct hlist_head s_pins;

          /*
           * Owning user namespace and default context in which to
           * interpret filesystem uids, gids, quotas, device nodes,
           * xattrs and security labels.
           */
          struct user_namespace *s_user_ns;

          struct list_lru          s_dentry_lru ____cacheline_aligned_in_smp;
          struct list_lru          s_inode_lru ____cacheline_aligned_in_smp;
          struct rcu_head          rcu;
          struct work_struct       destroy_work;

          struct mutex             s_sync_lock;  /* sync serialisation lock
  */

          /*
           * Indicates how deep in a filesystem stack this SB is
           */
          int s_stack_depth;

          /* s_inode_list_lock protects s_inodes */
          spinlock_t               s_inode_list_lock
____cacheline_aligned_in_smp;
          struct list_head         s_inodes;       /* all inodes */

          spinlock_t               s_inode_wblist_lock;
          struct list_head         s_inodes_wb;    /* writeback inodes */
  };
```

The superblock structure contains other structures which define and extend the information and functionalities of the superblock. Following are some of the elements of `super_block`:

- `s_list` is of type `struct list_head` and contains pointers to the list of mounted superblocks
- `s_dev` is the device identifier
- `s_maxbytes` contains the maximum file size
- `s_type` is a pointer of type `struct file_system_type`, which describes the filesystem type
- `s_op` is a pointer of type `struct super_operations`, containing operations on the superblock
- `s_export_op` is of type `struct export_operations` and helps the filesystem be exportable for remote systems to access, using network filesystems
- `s_root` is a pointer of type `struct dentry` and points to the dentry object of the filesystem's root directory

Each enumerated superblock instance contains a pointer to an abstract structure of function pointers that define the interface for superblock operations. Filesystems will need to implement their superblock operations and assign them to appropriate function pointers. This helps each filesystem implement superblock operations as per its layout of on-disk superblock and hide that logic under a common interface. `Struct super_operations` is defined in `<linux/fs.h>`:

```
struct super_operations {
        struct inode *(*alloc_inode)(struct super_block *sb);
        void (*destroy_inode)(struct inode *);

        void (*dirty_inode) (struct inode *, int flags);
        int (*write_inode) (struct inode *, struct writeback_control
*wbc);
        int (*drop_inode) (struct inode *);
        void (*evict_inode) (struct inode *);
        void (*put_super) (struct super_block *);
        int (*sync_fs)(struct super_block *sb, int wait);
        int (*freeze_super) (struct super_block *);
        int (*freeze_fs) (struct super_block *);
        int (*thaw_super) (struct super_block *);
        int (*unfreeze_fs) (struct super_block *);
        int (*statfs) (struct dentry *, struct kstatfs *);
        int (*remount_fs) (struct super_block *, int *, char *);
        void (*umount_begin) (struct super_block *);

        int (*show_options)(struct seq_file *, struct dentry *);
```

```
        int (*show_devname)(struct seq_file *, struct dentry *);
        int (*show_path)(struct seq_file *, struct dentry *);
        int (*show_stats)(struct seq_file *, struct dentry *);
#ifdef CONFIG_QUOTA
        ssize_t (*quota_read)(struct super_block *, int, char *, size_t,
loff_t);
        ssize_t (*quota_write)(struct super_block *, int, const char *,
size_t, loff_t);
        struct dquot **(*get_dquots)(struct inode *);
#endif
        int (*bdev_try_to_free_page)(struct super_block*, struct page*,
gfp_t);
        long (*nr_cached_objects)(struct super_block *,
                              struct shrink_control *);
        long (*free_cached_objects)(struct super_block *,
                              struct shrink_control *);
};
```

All elements in this structure point to functions that operate on the superblock object. All these operations are only called from a process context and without any locks being held, unless specified. Let's look at few important ones here:

- alloc_inode: This method is used to create and allocate space for the new inode object and initialize it under the superblock.
- destroy_inode: This destroys the given inode object and frees resources allocated for the inode. This is only used if alloc_inode was defined.
- dirty_inode: This is called by the VFS to mark a dirty inode (when inode is modified).
- write_inode: VFS invokes this method when it needs to write an inode on to the disk. The second argument points to struct writeback_control, a structure that tells the writeback code what to do.
- put_super: This is invoked when VFS needs to free the superblock.
- sync_fs: This is invoked to synchronize filesystem data with that of the underlying block device.
- statfs: Invoked to get filesystem statistics for the VFS.
- remount_fs: Invoked when the filesystem needs to be remounted.
- umount_begin: Invoked when the VFS is unmounting a filesystem.
- show_options: Invoked by VFS to show mount options.
- quota_read: Invoked by VFS to read from the filesystem quota file.

struct inode

Each instance of `struct inode` represents a file in `rootfs`. VFS defines this structure as an abstraction for filesystem-specific inodes. Irrespective of the type of inode structure and its representation on disk, each filesystem needs to enumerate its files as `struct inode` into `rootfs` for a common file view. This structure is defined in `<linux/fs.h>`:

```
struct inode {
      umode_t                    i_mode;
   unsigned short          i_opflags;
        kuid_t                    i_uid;
    kgid_t                  i_gid;
    unsigned int            i_flags;
#ifdef CONFIG_FS_POSIX_ACL
   struct posix_acl        *i_acl;
    struct posix_acl        *i_default_acl;
#endif
      const struct inode_operations   *i_op;
     struct super_block      *i_sb;
     struct address_space    *i_mapping;
#ifdef CONFIG_SECURITY
   void                    *i_security;
#endif
   /* Stat data, not accessed from path walking */
   unsigned long           i_ino;
    /*
        * Filesystems may only read i_nlink directly.  They shall use the
        * following functions for modification:
     *
        *     (set|clear|inc|drop)_nlink
     *    inode_(inc|dec)_link_count
    */
      union {
         const unsigned int i_nlink;
              unsigned int __i_nlink;
   };
      dev_t                    i_rdev;
   loff_t                  i_size;
    struct timespec          i_atime;
   struct timespec         i_mtime;
   struct timespec         i_ctime;
   spinlock_t              i_lock; /*i_blocks, i_bytes, maybe i_size*/
      unsigned short          i_bytes;
   unsigned int            i_blkbits;
      blkcnt_t                 i_blocks;
#ifdef __NEED_I_SIZE_ORDERED
      seqcount_t                i_size_seqcount;
```

```
#endif
     /* Misc */
        unsigned long          i_state;
  struct rw_semaphore      i_rwsem;

     unsigned long            dirtied_when;/*jiffies of first dirtying */
        unsigned long            dirtied_time_when;

    struct hlist_node       i_hash;
     struct list_head        i_io_list;/* backing dev IO list */
#ifdef CONFIG_CGROUP_WRITEBACK
    struct bdi_writeback    *i_wb;   /* the associated cgroup wb */

        /* foreign inode detection, see wbc_detach_inode() */
     int                     i_wb_frn_winner;
  u16                     i_wb_frn_avg_time;
        u16                     i_wb_frn_history;
#endif
     struct list_head        i_lru;  /* inode LRU list */
      struct list_head       i_sb_list;
        struct list_head         i_wb_list;/* backing dev writeback list */
        union {
           struct hlist_head       i_dentry;
          struct rcu_head         i_rcu;
    };
        u64                     i_version;
        atomic_t                i_count;
   atomic_t                i_dio_count;
      atomic_t                i_writecount;
#ifdef CONFIG_IMA
      atomic_t                i_readcount; /* struct files open RO */
#endif
/* former->i_op >default_file_ops */
        const struct file_operations  *i_fop;
        struct file_lock_context *i_flctx;
        struct address_space i_data;
        struct list_head i_devices;
        union {
           struct pipe_inode_info *i_pipe;
           struct block_device *i_bdev;
           struct cdev *i_cdev;
           char *i_link;
           unsigned i_dir_seq;
        };
        __u32 i_generation;
 #ifdef CONFIG_FSNOTIFY __u32 i_fsnotify_mask; /* all events this inode
cares about */
     struct hlist_head i_fsnotify_marks;
```

```
#endif
#if IS_ENABLED(CONFIG_FS_ENCRYPTION)
    struct fscrypt_info *i_crypt_info;
#endif
    void *i_private; /* fs or device private pointer */
};
```

Note that all fields are not mandatory and applicable to all filesystems; they are free to initialize appropriate fields that are relevant as per their definition of an inode. Each inode is bound to two important groups of operations defined by the underlying filesystem: first, a set of operations to manage inode data. These are represented through an instance of type `struct inode_operations` that is referred to by the `i_op` pointer of the inode. Second is a group of operations for accessing and manipulating underlying file data that the inode represents; these operations are encapsulated in an instance of type `struct file_operations` and bound to the `i_fop` pointer of inode instance.

In other words, each inode is bound to metadata operations represented by an instance of type struct `inode_operations`, and file data operations represented by an instance of type `struct file_operations`. However, user-mode applications access file data operations from a valid `file` object created to represent an open file for the caller process (we will discuss more on file object in next section):

```
struct inode_operations {
  struct dentry * (*lookup) (struct inode *,struct dentry *, unsigned int);
  const char * (*get_link) (struct dentry *, struct inode *, struct
delayed_call *);
  int (*permission) (struct inode *, int);
  struct posix_acl * (*get_acl)(struct inode *, int);
  int (*readlink) (struct dentry *, char __user *,int);
  int (*create) (struct inode *,struct dentry *, umode_t, bool);
  int (*link) (struct dentry *,struct inode *,struct dentry *);
  int (*unlink) (struct inode *,struct dentry *);
  int (*symlink) (struct inode *,struct dentry *,const char *);
  int (*mkdir) (struct inode *,struct dentry *,umode_t);
  int (*rmdir) (struct inode *,struct dentry *);
  int (*mknod) (struct inode *,struct dentry *,umode_t,dev_t);
  int (*rename) (struct inode *, struct dentry *,
  struct inode *, struct dentry *, unsigned int);
  int (*setattr) (struct dentry *, struct iattr *);
  int (*getattr) (struct vfsmount *mnt, struct dentry *, struct kstat *);
  ssize_t (*listxattr) (struct dentry *, char *, size_t);
  int (*fiemap)(struct inode *, struct fiemap_extent_info *, u64 start,
  u64 len);
  int (*update_time)(struct inode *, struct timespec *, int);
  int (*atomic_open)(struct inode *, struct dentry *,
  struct file *, unsigned open_flag,
```

```
    umode_t create_mode, int *opened);
    int (*tmpfile) (struct inode *, struct dentry *, umode_t);
    int (*set_acl)(struct inode *, struct posix_acl *, int);
} ____cacheline_aligned
```

Following is a brief description of few important operations:

- `lookup`: Used to locate inode instance of the file specified; this operation returns a dentry instance.
- `create`: This routine is invoked by VFS to construct an inode object for dentry specified as an argument.
- `link`: Used to support hard links. Called by the `link(2)` system call.
- `unlink`: Used to support deleting inodes. Called by the `unlink(2)` system call.
- `mkdir`: Used to support creation of subdirectories. Called by the `mkdir(2)` system call.
- `mknod`: Invoked by the `mknod(2)` system call to create a device, named pipe, inode, or socket.
- `listxattr`: Invoked by the VFS to list all extended attributes of a file.
- `update_time`: Invoked by the VFS to update a specific time or the `i_version` of the inode.

The following is VFS-defined `struct file_operations`, which encapsulates filesystem-defined operations on the underlying file data. Since this is declared to serve as a common interface for all filesystems, it contains function pointer interfaces suitable to support operations on various types of filesystems with distinct definitions of file data. Underlying filesystems are free to choose appropriate interfaces and leave the rest, depending on their notion of file and file data:

```
struct file_operations {
 struct module *owner;
 loff_t (*llseek) (struct file *, loff_t, int);
 ssize_t (*read) (struct file *, char __user *, size_t, loff_t *);
 ssize_t (*write) (struct file *, const char __user *, size_t, loff_t *);
 ssize_t (*read_iter) (struct kiocb *, struct iov_iter *);
 ssize_t (*write_iter) (struct kiocb *, struct iov_iter *);
 int (*iterate) (struct file *, struct dir_context *);
 int (*iterate_shared) (struct file *, struct dir_context *);
 unsigned int (*poll) (struct file *, struct poll_table_struct *);
 long (*unlocked_ioctl) (struct file *, unsigned int, unsigned long);
 long (*compat_ioctl) (struct file *, unsigned int, unsigned long);
 int (*mmap) (struct file *, struct vm_area_struct *);
 int (*open) (struct inode *, struct file *);
 int (*flush) (struct file *, fl_owner_t id);
```

```
 int (*release) (struct inode *, struct file *);
 int (*fsync) (struct file *, loff_t, loff_t, int datasync);
 int (*fasync) (int, struct file *, int);
 int (*lock) (struct file *, int, struct file_lock *);
 ssize_t (*sendpage) (struct file *, struct page *, int, size_t, loff_t *,
int);
 unsigned long (*get_unmapped_area)(struct file *, unsigned long, unsigned
long, unsigned long, unsigned long);
 int (*check_flags)(int);
 int (*flock) (struct file *, int, struct file_lock *);
 ssize_t (*splice_write)(struct pipe_inode_info *, struct file *, loff_t *,
size_t, unsigned int);
 ssize_t (*splice_read)(struct file *, loff_t *, struct pipe_inode_info *,
size_t, unsigned int);
 int (*setlease)(struct file *, long, struct file_lock **, void **);
 long (*fallocate)(struct file *file, int mode, loff_t offset,
 loff_t len);
 void (*show_fdinfo)(struct seq_file *m, struct file *f);
#ifndef CONFIG_MMU
 unsigned (*mmap_capabilities)(struct file *);
#endif
 ssize_t (*copy_file_range)(struct file *, loff_t, struct file *,
 loff_t, size_t, unsigned int);
 int (*clone_file_range)(struct file *, loff_t, struct file *, loff_t,
 u64);
 ssize_t (*dedupe_file_range)(struct file *, u64, u64, struct file *,
 u64);
};
```

Following is a brief description of a few important operations:

- llseek: Invoked when the VFS needs to move the file position index.
- read: Invoked by read(2) and other related system calls.
- write: Invoked by the write(2) and other related system calls.
- iterate: Invoked when VFS needs to read directory contents.
- poll: This is invoked by the VFS when a process needs to check for activity on the file. Called by select(2) and poll(2) system calls.
- unlocked_ioctl: The operation assigned to this pointer is invoked when the user-mode process calls the ioctl(2) system call on the file descriptor. This function is used to support special operations. Device drivers use this interface to support configuration operations on the target device.
- compat_ioctl: Similar to ioctl with an exception that it is used to convert arguments passed from a 32-bit process to be used with a 64-bit kernel.

- mmap: The routine assigned to this pointer is invoked when the user-mode process calls the mmap(2) system call. Functionality supported by this function is underlying filesystem dependent. For regular persistent files, this function is implemented to map the caller-specified data region of the file into the virtual address space of the caller process. For device files that support mmap, this routine maps underlying device address space into the caller's virtual address space.
- open: The function assigned to this interface is invoked by VFS when the user-mode process initiates the open(2) system call to create a file descriptor.
- flush: Invoked by the close(2) system call to flush a file.
- release: A function assigned to this interface is invoked by VFS when a user-mode process executes the close(2) system call to destroy a file descriptor.
- fasync: Invoked by the fcntl(2) system call when asynchronous mode is enabled for a file.
- splice_write: Invoked by the VFS to splice data from a pipe to a file.
- setlease: Invoked by the VFS to set or release a file lock lease.
- fallocate: Invoked by the VFS to pre-allocate a block.

Struct dentry

In our earlier discussion, we gained an understanding on how a typical disk filesystem represents each directory through an inode structure, and how a directory block on disk represents information of files under that directory. When user-mode applications initiate file access operations such as open() with a complete path such as /root/test/abc, the VFS will need to perform directory lookup operations to decode and validate each component specified in the path.

For efficient lookup and translation of components in a file path, VFS enumerates a special data structure, called dentry. A dentry object contains a string name of the file or directory, a pointer to its inode, and a pointer to the parent dentry. An instance of dentry is generated for each component in the file lookup path; for instance, in the case of /root/test/abc, a dentry is enumerated for root, another for test, and finally for file abc.

struct dentry is defined in kernel header </linux/dcache.h>:

```
struct dentry {
 /* RCU lookup touched fields */
   unsigned int d_flags;              /* protected by d_lock */
 seqcount_t d_seq;                /* per dentry seqlock */
   struct hlist_bl_node d_hash;     /* lookup hash list */
```

```
    struct dentry *d_parent;        /* parent directory */
    struct qstr d_name;
        struct inode *d_inode; /* Where the name -NULL is negative */
      unsigned char d_iname[DNAME_INLINE_LEN];        /* small names */

  /* Ref lookup also touches following */
    struct lockref d_lockref;        /* per-dentry lock and refcount */
        const struct dentry_operations *d_op;
      struct super_block *d_sb;        /* The root of the dentry tree */
unsigned long d_time;            /* used by d_revalidate */
        void *d_fsdata;                /* fs-specific data */

    union {
        struct list_head d_lru;        /* LRU list */
          wait_queue_head_t *d_wait;        /* in-lookup ones only */
  };
      struct list_head d_child;      /* child of parent list */
      struct list_head d_subdirs;      /* our children */
      /*
        * d_alias and d_rcu can share memory
    */
     union {
        struct hlist_node d_alias;        /* inode alias list */
          struct hlist_bl_node d_in_lookup_hash;
        struct rcu_head d_rcu;
    } d_u;
};
```

- d_parent is pointer to the parent dentry instance.
- d_name holds the name of the file.
- d_inode is a pointer to the inode instance of the file.
- d_flags contains several flags defined in <include/linux/dcache.h>.
- d_op points to the structure containing function pointers to various operations for the dentry object.

Let's now look at struct dentry_operations, which describes how a filesystem can overload the standard dentry operations:

```
struct dentry_operations {
  int (*d_revalidate)(struct dentry *, unsigned int);
      int (*d_weak_revalidate)(struct dentry *, unsigned int);
  int (*d_hash)(const struct dentry *, struct qstr *);
    int (*d_compare)(const struct dentry *,
              unsigned int, const char *, const struct qstr *);
  int (*d_delete)(const struct dentry *);
    int (*d_init)(struct dentry *);
```

```
    void (*d_release)(struct dentry *);
        void (*d_prune)(struct dentry *);
  void (*d_iput)(struct dentry *, struct inode *);
   char *(*d_dname)(struct dentry *, char *, int);
    struct vfsmount *(*d_automount)(struct path *);
    int (*d_manage)(const struct path *, bool);
        struct dentry *(*d_real)(struct dentry *, const struct inode *,
                          unsigned int);


} _____ca
```

Following is a brief description of a few important dentry operations:

- d_revalidate: Invoked when VFS needs to revalidate a dentry. Whenever a name lookup returns a dentry in the dcache, this is called.
- d_weak_revalidate: Invoked when VFS needs to revalidate a jumped dentry. This is invoked if a path-walk ends at a dentry that wasn't found on a lookup on the parent directory.
- d_hash: Invoked when VFS adds a dentry to the hash table.
- d_compare: Invoked to compare the filenames of two dentry instances. It compares a dentry name with a given name.
- d_delete: Invoked when the last reference to a dentry is removed.
- d_init: Invoked when a dentry is allocated.
- d_release: Invoked when a dentry is deallocated.
- d_iput: Invoked when an inode is released from the dentry.
- d_dname: Invoked when the pathname of the dentry must be generated. Handy for special filesystems to delay pathname generation (whenever the path is needed).

struct file

An instance of struct file represents an open file. This structure is created when a user process successfully opens a file, and contains the caller application's file access attributes such as offset into file data, access mode, and special flags, among others. This object is mapped to the caller's file descriptor table, and serves as the caller application's handle to the file. This structure is local to the process and is retained by a process until the relevant file is closed. A close operation on the file descriptor destroys the file instance.

```
struct file {
    union {
        struct llist_node       fu_llist;
```

```
        struct rcu_head           fu_rcuhead;
      } f_u;
    struct path                f_path;
    struct inode               *f_inode;        /* cached value */
        const struct file_operations    *f_op;


    /*
        * Protects f_ep_links, f_flags.
      * Must not be taken from IRQ context.
     */
        spinlock_t                f_lock;
    atomic_long_t             f_count;
  unsigned int              f_flags;
  fmode_t                   f_mode;
    struct mutex             f_pos_lock;
        loff_t                   f_pos;
      struct fown_struct       f_owner;
  const struct cred         *f_cred;
  struct file_ra_state      f_ra;


        u64                        f_version;
#ifdef CONFIG_SECURITY
    void                       *f_security;
#endif
   /* needed for tty driver, and maybe others */
     void                     *private_data;

#ifdef CONFIG_EPOLL
      /* Used by fs/eventpoll.c to link all the hooks to this file */
    struct list_head         f_ep_links;
       struct list_head        f_tfile_llink;
#endif /* #ifdef CONFIG_EPOLL */
      struct address_space    *f_mapping;
} __attribute__((aligned(4))); /* lest something weird decides that 2 is OK
*/
```

The f_inode pointer refers to the inode instance of the file. When a file object is constructed by VFS, the f_op pointer is initialized with the address of struct file_operations associated with the file's inode, as we discussed earlier.

Special filesystems

Unlike regular filesystems, which are designed to manage persistent file data backed on to a storage device, the kernel implements various special filesystems that manage a specific class of kernel in-core data structures. Since these filesystems do not deal with persistent data, they do not consume disk blocks, and the entire filesystem structure is maintained in-core. Presence of such filesystems enables simplified application development, debugging, and easier error detection. There are many filesystems in this category, each deliberately designed and implemented for a specific purpose. Following is brief description of a few important ones.

Procfs

Procfs is a special filesystem that enumerates kernel data structures as files. This filesystem serves as a debugging resource for kernel programmers, since it allows users to view the state of data structures through the virtual file interface. Procfs is mounted to the `/proc` directory (mount point) of rootfs.

Data in procfs files is not persistent, and is always constructed on the run; each file is an interface through which users can trigger associated operations. For instance, a read operation on a proc file invokes the associated read callback function bound to the file entry, and that function is implemented to populate the user buffer with appropriate data.

The number of files enumerated depends on the configuration and architecture for which the kernel was built. Following is a list of a few important files with useful data enumerated under `/proc`:

File name	Description
`/proc/cpuinfo`	Provides low-level cpu details such as vendor, model, clock speed, cache size, number of siblings, cores, CPU flags, and bogomips.
`/proc/meminfo`	Provides a summarized view of physical memory state.
`/proc/ioports`	Provides details on current usage of port I/O address space supported by the x86 class of machines. This file is not present on other architectures.
`/proc/iomem`	Shows a detailed layout describing current usage of memory address space.
`/proc/interrupts`	Shows a view of the IRQ descriptor table that contains details of IRQ lines and interrupt handlers bound to each.

`/proc/slabinfo`	Shows a detailed listing of slab caches and their current state.
`/proc/buddyinfo`	Shows the current state of buddy lists managed by the buddy system.
`/proc/vmstat`	Shows virtual memory management statistics.
`/proc/zoneinfo`	Shows per-node memory zone statistics.
`/proc/cmdline`	Shows boot arguments passed to the kernel.
`/proc/timer_list`	Shows a list of active pending timers, with details of clock source.
`/proc/timer_stats`	Provides detailed statistics on active timers, used for tracking timer usage and debugging.
`/proc/filesystems`	Presents a list of filesystem services currently active.
`/proc/mounts`	Shows currently mounted devices with their mountpoints.
`/proc/partitions`	Presents details of current storage partitions detected with associated /dev file enumerations.
`/proc/swaps`	Lists out active swap partitions with status details.
`/proc/modules`	Lists out names and status of kernel modules currently deployed.
`/proc/uptime`	Shows length of time kernel has been running since boot and spent in idle mode.
`/proc/kmsg`	Shows contents of kernel's message log buffer.
`/proc/kallsyms`	Presents kernel symbol table.
`/proc/devices`	Presents a list of registered block and character devices with their major numbers.
`/proc/misc`	Presents a list of devices registered through the misc interface with their misc identifiers.
`/proc/stat`	Presents system statistics.
`/proc/net`	Directory that contains various network stack-related pseudo files.
`/proc/sysvipc`	Subdirectory containing pseudo files that show the status of System V IPC objects, message queues, semaphores, and shared memory.

/proc also lists out a number of subdirectories that provide a detailed view of elements in process PCB or task structure. These folders are named by the PID of the process that they represent. Following is a list of important files that present process-related information:

File name	Description
/proc/pid/cmdline	Command-line name of the process.
/proc/pid/exe	A symbolic link to the executable file.
/proc/pid/environ	Lists out environmental variables accessible to the process.
/proc/pid/cwd	A symbolic link to the current working directory of the process.
/proc/pid/mem	A binary image that shows the virtual memory of the process.
/proc/pid/maps	Lists out virtual memory mappings for the process.
/proc/pid/fdinfo	A directory that lists out open file descriptors' current status and flags.
/proc/pid/fd	Directory that contains symlink to open file descriptors.
/proc/pid/status	Lists out current status of the process, including its memory usage.
/proc/pid/sched	Lists out scheduling statistics.
/proc/pid/cpuset	Lists out the cpu affinity mask for this process.
/proc/pid/cgroup	Shows cgroup details for the process.
/proc/pid/stack	Shows backtrace of the process-owned kernel stack.
/proc/pid/smaps	Shows memory consumed for each mapping into its address space.
/proc/pid/pagemap	Shows the physical mapping status for each virtual page of the process.
/proc/pid/syscall	Exposes the system call number and arguments for the system call currently being executed by the process.
/proc/pid/task	Directory containing child process/thread details.

 These listings were drawn up to familiarize you with proc files and their use. You are advised to visit the manual page of procfs for a detailed description of each of these files.

All of the files we listed so far are read-only; procfs also contains a branch /proc/sys that holds read-write files, which are referred to as kernel parameters. Files under /proc/sys are further classified as per the subsystems to which they apply. Listing out all those files is out of scope.

Sysfs

Sysfs is another pseudo filesystem that is introduced to export unified hardware and driver information to user mode. It enumerates information about devices and associated device drivers from the kernel's device model perspective to user space through virtual files. Sysfs is mounted to the **/sys** directory (mount point) of the rootfs. Similar to procfs, underlying drivers and kernel subsystems can be configured for power management and other functionalities through virtual file interfaces of sysfs. Sysfs also enables hotplug event management by Linux distros through appropriate daemons such as **udev**, which is configured to listen and respond to hotplug events.

Following is a brief description of important subdirectories of sysfs:

- **Devices**: One of the objectives behind the introduction of sysfs is to present a unified list of devices currently enumerated and managed by respective driver subsystems. The devices directory contains the global device hierarchy, which contains information for each physical and virtual device that has been discovered by the driver subsystems and registered with the kernel.
- **BUS**: This directory contains a listing of subdirectories, each representing the physical bus type that has support registered in the kernel. Each bus type directory contains two subdirectories: devices and drivers. The devices directory contains a listing of devices currently discovered or bound to that bus type. Each file in the listing is a symbolic link to the device file in device's directory in the global device tree. The drivers directory contains directories describing each device driver registered with the bus manager. Each of the driver directories lists out attributes that show the current configuration of driver parameters, which can be modified, and symbolic links that point to the physical device directory that the driver is bound to.
- **Class**: The class directory contains representations of device classes that are currently registered with the kernel. A device class describes a functional type of device. Each device class directory contains subdirectories representing devices currently allocated and registered under this class. For most of the class device objects, their directories contain symbolic links to the device and driver directories in the global device hierarchy and the bus hierarchy that are associated with that class object.

- **Firmware**: The `firmware` directory contains interfaces for viewing and manipulating platform-specific firmware that is run during power on/reset, such as BIOS or UEFI on x86 and OpenFirmware for PPC platforms.
- **Modules**: This directory contains subdirectories that represent each kernel module currently deployed. Each directory is enumerated with the name of the module it is representing. Each module directory contains information about a module such as refcount, modparams, and its core size.

Debugfs

Unlike procfs and sysfs, which are implemented to present specific information through the virtual file interface, *debugfs* is a generic memory filesystem that allows kernel developers to export any arbitrary information that is deemed useful for debugging. Debugfs provides function interfaces used to enumerate virtual files and is generally mounted to the `/sys/debug` directory. Debugfs is used by tracing mechanisms such as ftrace to present function and interrupt traces.

There are many other special filesystems such as pipefs, mqueue, and sockfs; we shall touch upon a few of them in later chapters.

Summary

Through this chapter, we have gained a generic understanding of a typical filesystem, its fabric and design, and what makes it an elemental part of an operating system. This chapter also emphasizes the importance and elegance of abstraction, using the common, layered architecture design which the kernel comprehensively imbibes. We have also stretched our understanding of the VFS and its common file interface that facilitates the common file API and its internal structures. In the next chapter, we will shall explore another facet of memory management called a virtual memory manager that deals with process virtual address spaces and page tables.

6
Interprocess Communication

A complex application-programming model might include a number of processes, each implemented to handle a specific job, which contribute to the end functionality of the application as a whole. Depending on the objective, design, and environment in which such applications are hosted, processes involved might be related (parent-child, siblings) or unrelated. Often, such processes need various resources to communicate, share data, and synchronize their execution to achieve desired results. These are provided by the operating system's kernel as services called **interprocess communication** (**IPC**). We have already discussed the usage of signals as an IPC mechanism; in this chapter, we shall begin to explore various other resources available for process communication and data sharing.

In this chapter we will cover the following topics:

- Pipes and FIFOs as messaging resources
- SysV IPC resources
- POSX IPC mechanisms

Pipes and FIFOs

Pipes form a basic unidirectional, self-synchronous means of communication between processes. As the name suggests, they have two ends: one where a process writes and the opposite end from where another process reads the data. Presumably what goes in first will be read out first in this kind of a setup. Pipes innately result in communication synchronization due to their limited capacity: if the writing process writes much faster than the reading process reads, the pipe's capacity will fail to hold excess data and invariably block the writing process until the reader reads and frees up data. Similarly, if the reader reads data faster than the writer, it will be left with no data to read, thus being blocked until data becomes available.

Pipes can be used as a messaging resource for both cases of communication: between related processes and between unrelated processes. When applied between related processes, pipes are referred to as **unnamed pipes**, since they are not enumerated as files under the `rootfs` tree. An unnamed pipe can be allocated through the `pipe()` API.

```
int pipe2(int pipefd[2], int flags);
```

API invokes a corresponding system call, which allocates appropriate data structures and sets up pipe buffers. It maps a pair of file descriptors, one for reading on the pipe buffer and another for writing on the pipe buffer. These descriptors are returned to the caller. The caller process normally forks the child process, which inherits the pipe file descriptors that can be used for messaging.

The following code excerpt shows the pipe system call implementation:

```
SYSCALL_DEFINE2(pipe2, int __user *, fildes, int, flags)
{
        struct file *files[2];
        int fd[2];
        int error;

        error = __do_pipe_flags(fd, files, flags);
        if (!error) {
                if (unlikely(copy_to_user(fildes, fd, sizeof(fd)))) {
                        fput(files[0]);
                        fput(files[1]);
                        put_unused_fd(fd[0]);
                        put_unused_fd(fd[1]);
                        error = -EFAULT;
                } else {
                        fd_install(fd[0], files[0]);
                        fd_install(fd[1], files[1]);
                }
        }
        return error;
}
```

Communication between unrelated processes requires the pipe file to be enumerated into **rootfs**. Such pipes are often called **named pipes**, and can be created either from the command line (`mkfifo`) or from a process using the `mkfifo` API.

```
int mkfifo(const char *pathname, mode_t mode);
```

A named pipe is created with the name specified and with appropriate permissions as specified by the mode argument. The `mknod` system call is invoked for creating a FIFO, which internally invokes VFS routines to set up the named pipe. Processes with access permissions can initiate operations on FIFOs through common VFS file APIs `open`, `read`, `write`, and `close`.

pipefs

Pipes and FIFOs are created and managed by a special filesystem called `pipefs`. It registers with VFS as a special filesystem. The following is a code excerpt from `fs/pipe.c`:

```
static struct file_system_type pipe_fs_type = {
        .name = "pipefs",
        .mount = pipefs_mount,
        .kill_sb = kill_anon_super,
};

static int __init init_pipe_fs(void)
{
        int err = register_filesystem(&pipe_fs_type);

        if (!err) {
                pipe_mnt = kern_mount(&pipe_fs_type);
                if (IS_ERR(pipe_mnt)) {
                        err = PTR_ERR(pipe_mnt);
                        unregister_filesystem(&pipe_fs_type);
                }
        }
        return err;
}

fs_initcall(init_pipe_fs);
```

It integrates pipe files into VFS by enumerating an `inode` instance representing each pipe; this allows applications to engage common file APIs `read` and `write`. The `inode` structure contains a union of pointers that are relevant for special files such as pipes and device files. For pipe file `inodes`, one of the pointers, `i_pipe`, is initialized to `pipefs`, defined as an instance of type `pipe_inode_info`:

```
struct inode {
        umode_t         i_mode;
        unsigned short i_opflags;
        kuid_t          i_uid;
        kgid_t          i_gid;
```

```
            unsigned int    i_flags;
            . . .
            . . .
            . . .
             union {
                      struct pipe_inode_info *i_pipe;
                      struct block_device *i_bdev;
                      struct cdev *i_cdev;
                      char *i_link;
                      unsigned i_dir_seq;
             };
             . . .
             . . .
             . . .
    };
```

`struct pipe_inode_info` contains all pipe-related metadata as defined by `pipefs`, which includes information of the pipe buffer and other important management data. This structure is defined in `<linux/pipe_fs_i.h>`:

```
struct pipe_inode_info {
        struct mutex mutex;
        wait_queue_head_t wait;
        unsigned int nrbufs, curbuf, buffers;
        unsigned int readers;
        unsigned int writers;
        unsigned int files;
        unsigned int waiting_writers;
        unsigned int r_counter;
        unsigned int w_counter;
        struct page *tmp_page;
        struct fasync_struct *fasync_readers;
        struct fasync_struct *fasync_writers;
        struct pipe_buffer *bufs;
        struct user_struct *user;
};
```

The `bufs` pointer refers to the pipe buffer; each pipe is by default assigned a total buffer of 65,535 bytes (64k) arranged as a circular array of 16 pages. User processes can alter the total size of the pipe buffer via a `fcntl()` operation on the pipe descriptor. The default maximum limit for the pipe buffer is 1,048,576 bytes, which can be changed by a privileged process via the `/proc/sys/fs/pipe-max-size` file interface. Following is a summarized table that describes the rest of the important elements:

Name	Description
`mutex`	Exclusion lock protecting the pipe
`wait`	Wait queue for readers and writers
`nrbufs`	Count of non-empty pipe buffers for this pipe
`curbuf`	Current pipe buffer
`buffers`	Total number of buffers
`readers`	Number of current readers
`writers`	Number of current writers
`files`	Number of struct file instances currently referring to this pipe
`waiting_writers`	Number of writers currently blocked on the pipe
`r_coutner`	Reader counter (relevant for FIFO)
`w_counter`	Writer counter (relevant for FIFO)
`*fasync_readers`	Reader side fasync
`*fasync_writers`	Writer side fasync
`*bufs`	Pointer to circular array of pipe buffers
`*user`	Pointer to the `user_struct` instance that represents the user who created this pipe

Reference to each page of the pipe buffer is wrapped into a circular array of instances of *type* `struct pipe_buffer`. This structure is defined in `<linux/pipe_fs_i.h>`:

```
struct pipe_buffer {
        struct page *page;
        unsigned int offset, len;
        const struct pipe_buf_operations *ops;
        unsigned int flags;
        unsigned long private;
};
```

`*page` is a pointer to the page descriptor of the page buffer, and the `offset` and `len` fields contain the offset to the data contained in the page buffer and its length. `*ops` is a pointer to a structure of type `pipe_buf_operations`, which encapsulates pipe buffer operations implemented by `pipefs`. It also implements file operations that are bound to pipe and FIFO inodes:

```
const struct file_operations pipefifo_fops = {
        .open = fifo_open,
        .llseek = no_llseek,
        .read_iter = pipe_read,
        .write_iter = pipe_write,
        .poll = pipe_poll,
        .unlocked_ioctl = pipe_ioctl,
        .release = pipe_release,
        .fasync = pipe_fasync,
};
```

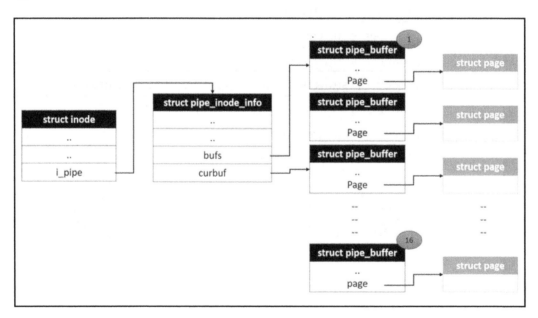

Message queues

Message queues are lists of message buffers through which an arbitrary number of processes can communicate. Unlike pipes, the writer does not have to wait for the reader to open the pipe and listen for data. Similar to a mailbox, writers can drop a fixed-length message wrapped in a buffer into the queue, which the reader can pick whenever it is ready. The message queue does not retain the message packet after it is picked by the reader, which means that each message packet is assured to be process persistent. Linux supports two distinct implementations of message queues: classic Unix SYSV message queues and contemporary POSIX message queues.

System V message queues

This is the classic AT&T message queue implementation suitable for messaging between an arbitrary number of unrelated processes. Sender processes wrap each message into a packet containing message data and a message number. The message queue implementation does not define the meaning of the message number, and it is left to the application designers to define appropriate meanings for message numbers and program readers and writers to interpret the same. This mechanism provides flexibility for programmers to use message numbers as message IDs or receiver IDs. It enables reader processes to selectively read messages that match specific IDs. However, messages with the same ID are always read in FIFO order (first in, first out).

Processes can create and open a SysV message queue with:

```
int msgget(key_t key, int msgflg);
```

The `key` parameter is a unique constant that serves as a magic number to identify the message queue. All programs that are required to access this message queue will need to use the same magic number; this number is usually hard-coded into relevant processes at compile time. However, applications need to ensure that the key value is unique for each message queue, and there are alternate library functions available through which unique keys can be dynamically generated.

The unique key and `msgflag` parameter values, if set to `IPC_CREATE`, will cause a new message queue to be set up. Valid processes that have access to the queue can read or write messages into the queue using `msgsnd` and `msgrcv` routines (we will not discuss them in detail here; refer to Linux system programming manuals):

```
int msgsnd(int msqid, const void *msgp, size_t msgsz, int msgflg);

ssize_t msgrcv(int msqid, void *msgp, size_t msgsz, long msgtyp,
               int msgflg);
```

Data structures

Each message queue is created by enumerating a set of data structures by the underlying SysV IPC subsystem. `struct msg_queue` is the core data structure, and an instance of this is enumerated for each message queue:

```
struct msg_queue {
        struct kern_ipc_perm q_perm;
        time_t q_stime; /* last msgsnd time */
        time_t q_rtime; /* last msgrcv time */
        time_t q_ctime; /* last change time */
        unsigned long q_cbytes; /* current number of bytes on queue */
        unsigned long q_qnum; /* number of messages in queue */
        unsigned long q_qbytes; /* max number of bytes on queue */
        pid_t q_lspid; /* pid of last msgsnd */
        pid_t q_lrpid; /* last receive pid */

        struct list_head q_messages; /* message list */
        struct list_head q_receivers;/* reader process list */
        struct list_head q_senders;  /*writer process list */
};
```

The `q_messages` field represents the head node of a double-linked circular list that contains all messages currently in the queue. Each message begins with a header followed by message data; each message can consume one of more pages depending on length of message data. The message header is always at the start of the first page and is represented by an instance of `struct msg_msg`:

```
/* one msg_msg structure for each message */
struct msg_msg {
        struct list_head m_list;
        long m_type;
        size_t m_ts; /* message text size */
        struct msg_msgseg *next;
        void *security;
```

```
                /* the actual message follows immediately */
};
```

The `m_list` field contains pointers to previous and next messages in the queue. The `*next` pointer refers to an instance of type `struct msg_msgseg`, which contains the address of the next page of message data. This pointer is relevant only when message data exceeds the first page. The second page frame starts with a descriptor `msg_msgseg`, which further contains a pointer to a subsequent page, and this order continues until the last page of the message data is reached:

```
struct msg_msgseg {
        struct msg_msgseg *next;
        /* the next part of the message follows immediately */
};
```

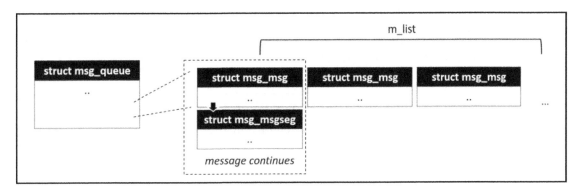

POSIX message queues

POSIX message queues implement priority-ordered messages. Each message written by a sender process is associated with an integer number which is interpreted as message priority; messages with a higher number are considered higher in priority. The message queue orders current messages as per priority and delivers them to the reader process in descending order (highest priority first). This implementation also supports a wider API interface with facilities of bounded wait send and receive operations and asynchronous message arrival notifications for receivers through signals or threads.

This implementation provides a distinct API interface to `create`, `open`, `read`, `write`, and `destroy` message queues. Following is a summarized description of APIs (we will not discuss usage semantics here, refer to system programming manuals for more details):

API interface	Description
`mq_open()`	Create or open a POSIX message queue
`mq_send()`	Write a message to the queue
`mq_timedsend()`	Similar to `mq_send`, but with a timeout parameter for bounded operations
`mq_receive()`	Fetch a message from the queue; this operation is possible on unbounded blocking calls
`mq_timedreceive()`	Similar to `mq_receive()` but with a timeout parameter that limits possible blocking for bounded time
`mq_close()`	Close a message queue
`mq_unlink()`	Destroy message queue
`mq_notify()`	Customize and set up message arrival notifications
`mq_getattr()`	Get attributes associated with a message queue
`mq_setattr()`	Set attributes specified on a message queue

POSIX message queues are managed by a special filesystem called `mqueue`. Each message queue is identified by a filename. Metadata for each queue is described by an instance of struct `mqueue_inode_info`, which symbolizes the inode object associated with the message queue file in the `mqueue` filesystem:

```
struct mqueue_inode_info {
        spinlock_t lock;
        struct inode vfs_inode;
        wait_queue_head_t wait_q;

        struct rb_root msg_tree;
        struct posix_msg_tree_node *node_cache;
        struct mq_attr attr;

        struct sigevent notify;
        struct pid *notify_owner;
        struct user_namespace *notify_user_ns;
        struct user_struct *user; /* user who created, for accounting */
        struct sock *notify_sock;
```

```
        struct sk_buff *notify_cookie;

        /* for tasks waiting for free space and messages, respectively */
        struct ext_wait_queue e_wait_q[2];

        unsigned long qsize; /* size of queue in memory (sum of all msgs)
*/
};
```

The `*node_cache` pointer refers to the `posix_msg_tree_node` descriptor that contains the header to a linked list of message nodes, in which each message is represented by a descriptor of type `msg_msg`:

```
struct posix_msg_tree_node {
        struct rb_node rb_node;
        struct list_head msg_list;
        int priority;
};
```

Shared memory

Unlike message queues, which offer a process-persistent messaging infrastructure, the shared memory service of IPC provides kernel-persistent memory that can be attached by an arbitrary number of processes that share common data. A shared memory infrastructure provides operation interfaces to allocate, attach, detach, and destroy shared memory regions. A process that needs access to shared data will *attach* or *map* a shared memory region into its address space; it can then access data in shared memory through the address returned by the mapping routine. This makes shared memory one of the fastest means of IPC since from a process's perspective it is akin to accessing local memory, which does not involve switch into kernel mode.

System V shared memory

Linux supports legacy SysV shared memory implementation under the IPC subsystem. Similar to SysV message queues, each shared memory region is identified by a unique IPC identifier.

Operation interfaces

The kernel provides distinct system call interfaces for initiating shared memory operations as follows:

Allocating shared memory

`shmget()` system call is invoked by a process to get an IPC identifier for a shared memory region; if the region does not exists, it creates one:

```
int shmget(key_t key, size_t size, int shmflg);
```

This function returns the identifier of the shared memory segment corresponding to the value contained in the *key* parameter. If other processes intend to use an existing segment, they can use the segment's *key* value when looking for its identifier. A new segment is however created if the *key* parameter is unique or has the value `IPC_PRIVATE`.
`size` indicates the number of bytes that needs to be allocated, as segments are allocated as memory pages. The number of pages to be allocated is obtained by rounding off the *size* value to the nearest multiple of a page size. \
The `shmflg` flag specifies how the segment needs to be created. It can contain two values:

- `IPC_CREATE`: This indicates creating a new segment. If this flag is unused, the segment associated with the key value is found, and if the user has the access permissions, the segment's identifier is returned.
- `IPC_EXCL`: This flag is always used with `IPC_CREAT`, to ensure that the call fails if the *key* value exists.

Attaching a shared memory

The shared memory region must be attached to its address space for a process to access it. `shmat()` is invoked to attach the shared memory to the address space of the calling process:

```
void *shmat(int shmid, const void *shmaddr, int shmflg);
```

The segment indicated by `shmid` is attached by this function. `shmaddr` specifies a pointer indicating the location in the process's address space where the segment is to be mapped. The third argument `shmflg` is a flag, which can be one of the following:

- `SHM_RND`: This is specified when `shmaddr` isn't a NULL value, indicating the function to attach the segment at the address, computed by rounding off the `shmaddr` value to the nearest multiple of page size; otherwise, the user must take care that `shmaddr` be page-aligned so that the segment gets attached correctly.
- `SHM_RDONLY`: This is to specify that the segment will only be read if the user has the necessary read permissions. Otherwise, both read and write access for the segment is given (the process must have the respective permissions).
- `SHM_REMAP`: This is a Linux-specific flag that indicates that any existing mapping at the address specified by `shmaddr` be replaced with the new mapping.

Detaching shared memory

Likewise, to detach the shared memory from the process address space, `shmdt()` is invoked. As IPC shared memory regions are persistent in the kernel, they continue to exist even after the processes detach:

```
int shmdt(const void *shmaddr);
```

The segment at the address specified by `shmaddr` is detached from the address space of the calling process.

Each of these interface operations invoke relevant system calls implemented in the `<ipc/shm.c>` source file.

Data structures

Each shared memory segment is represented by a `struct shmid_kernel` descriptor. This structure contains all metadata relevant to the management of SysV shared memory:

```
struct shmid_kernel /* private to the kernel */
{
        struct kern_ipc_perm shm_perm;
        struct file *shm_file; /* pointer to shared memory file */
        unsigned long shm_nattch; /* no of attached process */
        unsigned long shm_segsz; /* index into the segment */
        time_t shm_atim; /* last access time */
        time_t shm_dtim; /* last detach time */
        time_t shm_ctim; /* last change time */
```

```
        pid_t shm_cprid; /* pid of creating process */
        pid_t shm_lprid; /* pid of last access */
        struct user_struct *mlock_user;

        /* The task created the shm object. NULL if the task is dead. */
        struct task_struct *shm_creator;
        struct list_head shm_clist; /* list by creator */
};
```

For reliability and ease of management, the kernel's IPC subsystem manages shared memory segments through a special file system called shmfs. This filesystem is not mounted on to the rootfs tree; its operations are only accessible through SysV shared memory system calls. The *shm_file pointer refers to the struct file object of shmfs that represents a shared memory block. When a process initiates an attach operation, the underlying system call invokes do_mmap() to create relevant mapping into the caller's address space (through struct vm_area_struct) and steps into the *shmfs*-defined shm_mmap() operation to map corresponding shared memory:

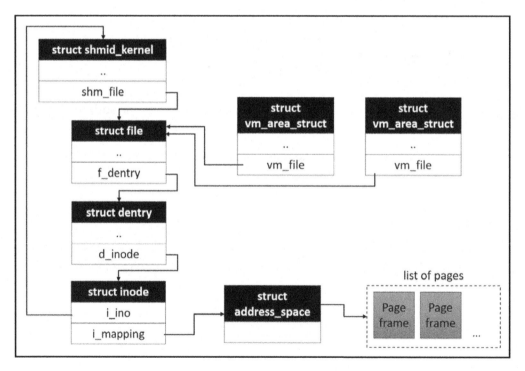

POSIX shared memory

The Linux kernel supports POSIX shared memory through a special filesystem called tmpfs, which is mounted on to /dev/shm of the rootfs. This implementation offers a distinct API which is consistent with the Unix file model, resulting in each shared memory allocation to be represented by a unique filename and inode. This interface is considered more flexible by application programmers since it allows standard POSIX file-mapping routines mmap() and unmap() for attaching and detaching memory segments into the caller process address space.

Following is a summarized description of interface routines:

API	Description
shm_open()	Create and open a shared memory segment identified by a filename
mmap()	POSIX standard file mapping interface for attaching shared memory to caller's address space
sh_unlink()	Destroy specified shared memory block
unmap()	Detach specified shared memory map from caller address space

The underlying implementation is similar to that of SysV shared memory with the difference that the mapping implementation is handled by the tmpfs filesystem.

Although shared memory is the easiest way of sharing common data or resources, it dumps the burden of implementing synchronization on the processes, as a shared memory infrastructure does not provide any synchronization or protection mechanism for the data or resources in the shared memory region. An application designer must consider synchronization of shared memory access between contending processes to ensure reliability and validity of shared data, for instance, preventing a possible write by two processes on the same region at a time, restricting a reading process to wait until a write is completed by another process, and so on. Often, to synchronize such race conditions another IPC resource called semaphores is used.

Semaphores

Semaphores are synchronization primitives provided by the IPC subsystem. They deliver a protective mechanism for shared data structures or resources against concurrent access by processes in a multithreaded environment. At its core, each semaphore is composed of an integer counter that can be atomically accessed by a caller process. Semaphore implementations provide two operations, one for waiting on a semaphore variable and another to signal the semaphore variable. In other words, waiting on the semaphore decreases the counter by 1 and signaling the semaphore increases the counter by 1. Typically, when a process wants to access a shared resource, it tries to decrease the semaphore counter. This attempt is however handled by the kernel as it blocks the attempting process until the counter yields a positive value. Similarly, when a process relinquishes the resource, it increases the semaphore counter, which wakes up any process that is waiting for the resource.

Semaphore versions

Traditionally all *nix systems implement the System V semaphore mechanism; however, POSIX has its own implementation of semaphores aiming at portability and leveling a few clumsy issues which the System V version carries. Let's begin by looking at System V semaphores.

System V semaphores

Semaphores in System V are not just a single counter as you might think, but rather a set of counters. This implies that a semaphore set can contain single or multiple counters (0 to n) with an identical semaphore ID. Each counter in the set can protect a shared resource, and a single semaphore set can protect multiple resources. The system call that helps create this kind of semaphore is as follows:

```
int semget(key_t key, int nsems, int semflg)
```

- key is used to identify the semaphore. If the key value is IPC_PRIVATE, a new set of semaphores is created.
- nsems indicates the semaphore set with the number of counters needed in the set
- semflg dictates how the semaphore should be created. It can contain two values:
  - IPC_CREATE: If the key does not exist, it creates a new semaphore
  - IPC_EXCL: If the key exists, it throws an error and fails

On success, the call returns the semaphore set identifier (a positive value).

A semaphore thus created contains uninitialized values and requires the initialization to be carried out using the `semctl()` function. After initialization, the semaphore set can be used by the processes:

```
int semop(int semid, struct sembuf *sops, unsigned nsops);
```

The `Semop()` function lets the process initiate operations on the semaphore set. This function offers a facility unique to the SysV semaphore implementation called **undoable operations** through a special flag called `SEM_UNDO`. When this flag is set, the kernel allows a semaphore to be restored to a consistent state if a process aborts before completing the relevant shared data access operation. For instance, consider a case where one of the processes locks the semaphore and begins its access operations on shared data; during this time if the process aborts before completion of shared data access, the semaphore will be left in an inconsistent state, making it unavailable for other contending processes. However, if the process had acquired a lock on the semaphore by setting the `SEM_UNDO` flag with `semop()`, its termination would allow the kernel to revert the semaphore to a consistent state (unlocked state) making it available for other contending processes in wait.

Data structures

Each SysV semaphore set is represented in the kernel by a descriptor of type `struct sem_array`:

```
/* One sem_array data structure for each set of semaphores in the system.
*/
struct sem_array {
        struct kern_ipc_perm ____cacheline_aligned_in_smp sem_perm;
        time_t sem_ctime;                /* last change time */
        struct sem *sem_base;            /*ptr to first semaphore in array
*/
        struct list_head pending_alter; /* pending operations */
                                         /* that alter the array */
        struct list_head pending_const; /* pending complex operations */
                                         /* that do not alter semvals */
        struct list_head list_id;        /* undo requests on this array */
        int sem_nsems;                   /* no. of semaphores in array */
        int complex_count;               /* pending complex operations */
        bool complex_mode;               /* no parallel simple ops */
    };
```

Each semaphore in the array is enumerated as an instance of struct sem defined in <ipc/sem.c>; the *sem_base pointer refers to the first semaphore object in the set. ;Each semaphore set contains a list of pending queue per process waiting; pending_alter is the head node for this pending queue of type struct sem_queue. Each semaphore set also contains per-semaphore undoable operations. list_id is a head node to a list of struct sem_undo instances; there is one instance in the list for each semaphore in the set. The following diagram sums up the semaphore set data structure and its lists:

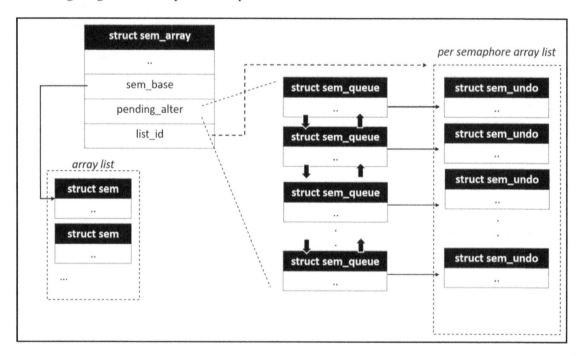

POSIX semaphores

POSIX semaphore semantics are rather simple when compared to System V. Each semaphore is a simple counter that can never be less than zero. The implementation provides function interfaces for initialization, increment, and decrement operations. They can be used for synchronizing threads by allocating the semaphore instance in memory accessible to all the threads. They can also be used for synchronizing processes by placing the semaphore in shared memory. Linux implementation of POSIX semaphores is optimized to deliver better performance for non-contending synchronization scenarios.

POSIX semaphores are available in two variants: named semaphores and unnamed semaphores. A named semaphore is identified by a filename and is suitable for use between unrelated processes. An unnamed semaphore is just a global instance of type `sem_t`; this form is generally preferred for use between threads. POSIX semaphore interface operations are part of the POSIX threads library implementation.

Function interfaces	Description
`sem_open()`	Opens an existing named semaphore file or creates a new named semaphore and returns its descriptor
`sem_init()`	Initializer routine for an unnamed semaphore
`sem_post()`	Operation to increment semaphore
`sem_wait()`	Operation to decrement semaphore, blocks if invoked when semaphore value is zero
`sem_timedwait()`	Extends `sem_wait()` with a timeout parameter for bounded wait
`sem_getvalue()`	Returns the current value of the semaphore counter
`sem_unlink()`	Removes a named semaphore identified with a file

Summary

In this chapter, we touched on various IPC mechanisms offered by the kernel. We explored the layout and relationship between various data structures for each mechanism, and also looked at both SysV and POSIX IPC mechanisms.

In the next chapter, we will take this discussion further into locking and kernel-synchronization mechanisms.

7
Virtual Memory Management

In the first chapter, we had brief discussion about an important abstraction called a *process*. We had discussed the process virtual address space and its isolation, and also have traversed thorough the memory management subsystem and gained a thorough understanding of various data structures and algorithms that go into physical memory management. In this chapter, let's extend our discussion on memory management with details of virtual memory management and page tables. We will look into the following aspects of the virtual memory subsystem:

- Process virtual address space and its segments
- Memory descriptor structure
- Memory mapping and VMA objects
- File-backed memory mappings
- Page cache
- Address translation with page tables

Process address space

The following diagram depicts the layout of a typical process address space in Linux systems, which is composed of a set of virtual memory segments:

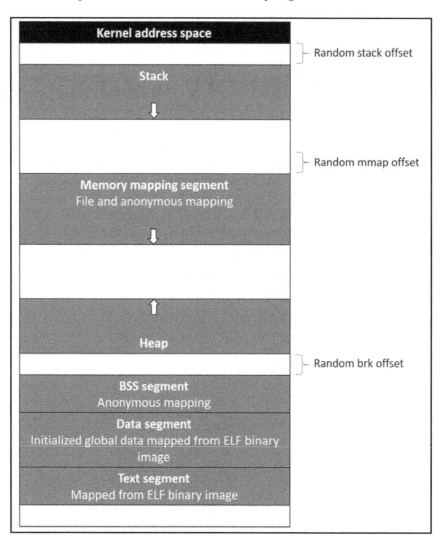

Each segment is physically mapped to one or more linear memory blocks (made out of one or more pages), and appropriate address translation records are placed in a process page table. Before we get into the complete details of how the kernel manages memory maps and constructs page tables, let's understand in brief each segment of the address space:

- **Stack** is the topmost segment, which expands downward. It contains **stack frames** that hold local variables and function parameters; a new frame is created on top of the stack upon entry into a called function, and is destroyed when the current function returns. Depending on the level of nesting of the function calls, there is always a need for the stack segment to dynamically expand to accommodate new frames. Such expansion is handled by the virtual memory manager through **page faults**: when the process attempts to touch an unmapped address at the top of the stack, the system triggers a page fault, which is handled by the kernel to check whether it is appropriate to grow the stack. If the current stack utilization is within `RLIMIT_STACK`, then it is considered appropriate and the stack is expanded. However, if the current utilization is maximum with no further scope to expand, then a segmentation fault signal is delivered to the process.

- **Mmap** is a segment below the stack; this segment is primarily used for mapping file data from page cache into process address space. This segment is also used for mapping shared objects or dynamic libraries. User-mode processes can initiate new mappings through the `mmap()` API. The Linux kernel also supports anonymous memory mapping through this segment, which serves as an alternative mechanism for dynamic memory allocations to store process data.

- **Heap** segment provides address space for dynamic memory allocation that allows a process to store runtime data. The kernel provides the `brk()` family of APIs, through which user-mode processes can expand or shrink the heap at runtime. However, most programming-language-specific standard libraries implement heap management algorithms for efficient utilization of heap memory. For instance, GNU glibc implements heap management that offers the `malloc()` family of functions for allocations.

The lower segments of the address space--**BSS**, **Data**, and **Text**--are related to the binary image of the process:

- The **BSS** stores **uninitialized** static variables, whose values are not initialized in the program code. The BSS is set up through anonymous memory mapping.
- The **data** segment contains global and static variables initialized in program source code. This segment is enumerated by mapping part of the program binary image that contains initialized data; this mapping is created of type **private memory mapping**, which ensures that changes to data variables' memory are not reflected on the disk file.
- The **text** segment is also enumerated by mapping the program binary file from memory; this mapping is of type RDONLY, resulting in a segmentation fault to be triggered on an attempt to write into this segment.

The kernel supports the address space randomization facility, which if enabled during build allows the VM subsystem to randomize start locations for **stack**, **mmap**, and **heap** segments for each new process. This provides processes with much-needed security from malicious programs that are capable of injecting faults. Hacker programs are generally hard-coded with fixed start addresses of memory segments of a valid process; with address space randomization, such malicious attacks would fail. However, text segments enumerated from the binary file of the application program are mapped to a fixed address as per the definition of the underlying architecture; this is configured into the linker script, which is applied while constructing the program binary file.

Process memory descriptor

The kernel maintains all information on process memory segments and the corresponding translation table in a memory descriptor structure, which is of type struct mm_struct. The process descriptor structure task_struct contains a pointer *mm to the memory descriptor for the process. We shall discuss a few important elements of the memory descriptor structure:

```
struct mm_struct {
            struct vm_area_struct *mmap; /* list of VMAs */
            struct rb_root mm_rb;
            u32 vmacache_seqnum; /* per-thread vmacache */
#ifdef CONFIG_MMU
            unsigned long (*get_unmapped_area) (struct file *filp,
unsigned long addr, unsigned long len,
unsigned long pgoff, unsigned long flags);
 #endif
            unsigned long mmap_base;                    /* base of mmap area */
```

```
            unsigned long mmap_legacy_base;   /* base of mmap area in
bottom-up allocations */
            unsigned long task_size;                    /* size of task vm
space */
            unsigned long highest_vm_end;      /* highest vma end address
*/
            pgd_t * pgd;
            atomic_t mm_users;              /* How many users with user space?
*/
            atomic_t mm_count;              /* How many references to "struct
mm_struct" (users count as 1) */
            atomic_long_t nr_ptes;      /* PTE page table pages */
 #if CONFIG_PGTABLE_LEVELS > 2
            atomic_long_t nr_pmds;      /* PMD page table pages */
 #endif
            int map_count;                          /* number of VMAs */
        spinlock_t page_table_lock;      /* Protects page tables and some
counters */
            struct rw_semaphore mmap_sem;

        struct list_head mmlist;      /* List of maybe swapped mm's. These
are globally strung
                                                      * together off
init_mm.mmlist, and are protected
                                                      * by mmlist_lock
                                                      */
        unsigned long hiwater_rss;      /* High-watermark of RSS usage */
         unsigned long hiwater_vm;       /* High-water virtual memory usage
*/
         unsigned long total_vm;          /* Total pages mapped */
         unsigned long locked_vm;         /* Pages that have PG_mlocked set
*/
         unsigned long pinned_vm;       /* Refcount permanently increased */
         unsigned long data_vm;           /* VM_WRITE & ~VM_SHARED &
~VM_STACK */
         unsigned long exec_vm;           /* VM_EXEC & ~VM_WRITE & ~VM_STACK
*/
         unsigned long stack_vm;          /* VM_STACK */
         unsigned long def_flags;
         unsigned long start_code, end_code, start_data, end_data;
         unsigned long start_brk, brk, start_stack;
         unsigned long arg_start, arg_end, env_start, env_end;
         unsigned long saved_auxv[AT_VECTOR_SIZE];              /* for
/proc/PID/auxv */
 /*
  * Special counters, in some configurations protected by the
  * page_table_lock, in other configurations by being atomic.
  */
```

```
        struct mm_rss_stat rss_stat;
        struct linux_binfmt *binfmt;
        cpumask_var_t cpu_vm_mask_var;
   /* Architecture-specific MM context */
        mm_context_t context;
        unsigned long flags;                    /* Must use atomic bitops to
   access the bits */
        struct core_state *core_state;   /* core dumping support */
        ...
        ...
        ...
   };
```

`mmap_base` refers to the start of the mmap segment in the virtual address space, and `task_size` contains the total size of the task in the virtual memory space. `mm_users` is an atomic counter that holds the count of LWPs that share this memory descriptor, `mm_count` holds the count of the number of processes currently using this descriptor, and the VM subsystem ensures that a memory descriptor structure is only released when `mm_count` is zero. The `start_code` and `end_code` fields contain the start and end virtual addresses for the code block mapped from the program's binary file. Similarly, `start_data` and `end_data` mark the beginning and end of the initialized data region mapped from the program's binary file.

The `start_brk` and `brk` fields represent the start and current end addresses of the heap segment; while `start_brk` remains constant throughout the process lifetime, `brk` is repositioned while allocating and releasing heap memory. Therefore, the total size of the active heap at a given moment in time is the size of the memory between the `start_brk` and `brk` fields. The elements `arg_start` and `arg_end` contain locations of the command-line argument list, and `env_start` and `env_end` contain the start and end locations for environment variables:

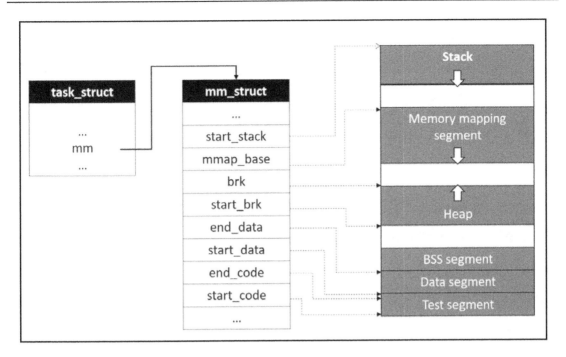

Each linear memory region mapped to a segment in virtual address space is represented through a descriptor of type `struct vm_area_struct`. Each VM area region is mapped with a virtual address interval that contains a start and end virtual addresses along with other attributes. The VM subsystem maintains a linked list of `vm_area_struct`(VMA) nodes representing current regions; this list is sorted in ascending order, with the first node representing the start virtual address interval and the node that follows containing the next address interval, and so on. The memory descriptor structure includes a pointer `*mmap`, which refers to this list of VM areas currently mapped.

The VM subsystem will need to scan the `vm_area` list while performing various operations on VM regions such as looking for a specific address within mapped address intervals, or appending a new VMA instance representing a new mapping. Such operations could be time consuming and inefficient especially for cases where a large number of regions are mapped into the list. As a workaround, the VM subsystem maintains a red-black tree for efficient access of `vm_area` objects. The memory descriptor structure includes the root node of the red-black tree `mm_rb`. With this arrangement, new VM regions can be quickly appended by searching the red-black tree for the region preceding the address interval for the new region; this eliminates the need to explicitly scan the linked list.

struct `vm_area_struct` **is defined in the kernel header** `<linux/mm_types.h>`:

```
/*
 * This struct defines a memory VMM memory area. There is one of these
 * per VM-area/task. A VM area is any part of the process virtual memory
 * space that has a special rule for the page-fault handlers (ie a shared
 * library, the executable area etc).
 */
 struct vm_area_struct {
            /* The first cache line has the info for VMA tree walking.
*/
            unsigned long vm_start; /* Our start address within vm_mm. */
            unsigned long vm_end; /* The first byte after our end
address within vm_mm. */
            /* linked list of VM areas per task, sorted by address */
            struct vm_area_struct *vm_next, *vm_prev;
            struct rb_node vm_rb;
            /*
             * Largest free memory gap in bytes to the left of this
VMA.
             * Either between this VMA and vma->vm_prev, or between one
of the
             * VMAs below us in the VMA rbtree and its ->vm_prev. This
helps
             * get_unmapped_area find a free area of the right size.
             */
            unsigned long rb_subtree_gap;
            /* Second cache line starts here. */
            struct mm_struct   *vm_mm; /* The address space we belong
to. */
            pgprot_t  vm_page_prot;       /* Access permissions of this
VMA. */
            unsigned long vm_flags;       /* Flags, see mm.h. */
            /*
             * For areas with an address space and backing store,
             * linkage into the address_space->i_mmap interval tree.
             */
            struct {
                    struct rb_node rb;
                    unsigned long rb_subtree_last;
            } shared;
        /*
             * A file's MAP_PRIVATE vma can be in both i_mmap tree and
anon_vma
             * list, after a COW of one of the file pages. A MAP_SHARED
vma
             * can only be in the i_mmap tree. An anonymous
MAP_PRIVATE, stack
```

```
                          * or brk vma (with NULL file) can only be in an anon_vma
   list.
               */
               struct list_head anon_vma_chain; /* Serialized by mmap_sem &
   page_table_lock */
               struct anon_vma *anon_vma;          /* Serialized by
   page_table_lock */
               /* Function pointers to deal with this struct. */
               const struct vm_operations_struct *vm_ops;
               /* Information about our backing store: */
               unsigned long vm_pgoff; /* Offset (within vm_file) in PAGE_SIZE
   units */
               struct file * vm_file; /* File we map to (can be NULL). */
               void * vm_private_data; /* was vm_pte (shared mem) */
   #ifndef CONFIG_MMU
               struct vm_region *vm_region; /* NOMMU mapping region */
    #endif
   #ifdef CONFIG_NUMA
               struct mempolicy *vm_policy; /* NUMA policy for the VMA */
    #endif
           struct vm_userfaultfd_ctx vm_userfaultfd_ctx;
    };
```

vm_start contains the start virtual address (lower address) of the region, which is the address of the first valid byte of the mapping, and vm_end contains the virtual address of the first byte beyond the mapped region (higher address). Thus, the length of the mapped memory region can be computed by subtracting vm_start from vm_end. The pointers *vm_next and *vm_prev refer to the next and previous VMA list, while the vm_rb element is for representing this VMA under the red-black tree. The *vm_mm pointer refers back to the process memory descriptor structure.

vm_page_prot contains access permissions for the pages in the region. vm_flags is a bit field that contains properties for memory in the mapped region. Flag bits are defined in the kernel header <linux/mm.h>.

Flag bits	Description
VM_NONE	Indicates inactive mapping.
VM_READ	If set, pages in the mapped area are readable.
VM_WRITE	If set, pages in the mapped area are writable.
VM_EXEC	This is set to mark a memory region as executable. Memory blocks containing executable instructions are set with this flag along with VM_READ.

VM_SHARED	If set, pages in the mapped region are shared.
VM_MAYREAD	Flag to indicate that VM_READ can be set on a currently mapped region. This flag is for use with the mprotect() system call.
VM_MAYWRITE	Flag to indicate that VM_WRITE can be set on a currently mapped region. This flag is for use with the mprotect() system call.
VM_MAYEXEC	Flag to indicate that VM_EXEC can be set on currently mapped region. This flag is for use with the mprotect() system call.
VM_GROWSDOWN	Mapping can grow downward; the stack segment is assigned this flag.
VM_UFFD_MISSING	This flag is set to indicate to VM subsystem that userfaultfd is enabled for this mapping, and is set to track page missing faults.
VM_PFNMAP	This flag is set to indicate that the memory region is mapped though PFN tracked pages, unlike regular page frames with page descriptors.
VM_DENYWRITE	Set to indicate that the current file mapping is not writable.
VM_UFFD_WP	This flag is set to indicate to the VM subsystem that userfaultfd is enabled for this mapping, and is set to track write-protect faults.
VM_LOCKED	Set when corresponding pages in the mapped memory region are locked.
VM_IO	Set when the device I/O area is mapped.
VM_SEQ_READ	Set when a process declares its intention to access the memory area within the mapped region sequentially.
VM_RAND_READ	Set when a process declares its intention to access the memory area within the mapped region at random.
VM_DONTCOPY	Set to indicate to the VM to disable copying this VMA on fork().
VM_DONTEXPAND	Set to indicate that the current mapping cannot expand on mremap().
VM_LOCKONFAULT	Lock pages in the memory map when they are faulted in. This flag is set when a process enables MLOCK_ONFAULT with the mlock2() system call.
VM_ACCOUNT	The VM subsystem performs additional checks to ensure there is memory available when performing operations on VMAs with this flag.
VM_NORESERVE	Whether the VM should suppress accounting.
VM_HUGETLB	Indicates that the current mapping contains huge TLB pages.
VM_DONTDUMP	If set, the current VMA is not included in the core dump.

VM_MIXEDMAP	Set when the VMA mapping contains both traditional page frames (managed through the page descriptor) and PFN-managed pages.
VM_HUGEPAGE	Set when the VMA is marked with MADV_HUGEPAGE to instruct the VM that pages under this mapping must be of type Transparent Huge Pages (THP). This flag works only with private anonymous mappings.
VM_NOHUGEPAGE	Set when the VMA is marked with MADV_NOHUGEPAGE.
VM_MERGEABLE	Set when the VMA is marked with MADV_MERGEABLE, which enables the kernel same-page merging (KSM) facility.
VM_ARCH_1	Architecture-specific extensions.
VM_ARCH_2	Architecture-specific extensions.

The following figure depicts the typical layout of a vm_area list as pointed to by the memory descriptor structure of the process:

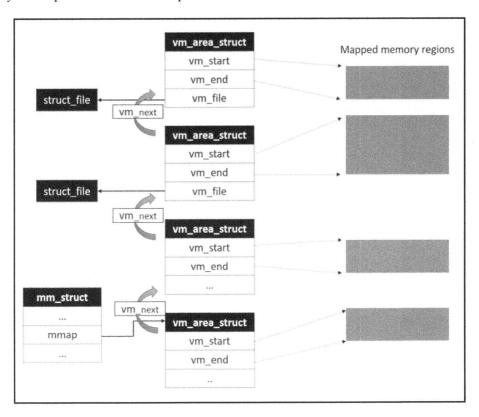

As depicted here, some memory regions mapped into the address space are file-backed (code regions form the application binary file, shared library, shared memory mappings, and so on). File buffers are managed by the kernel's page cache framework, which implements its own data structures to represent and manage file caches. The page cache tracks mappings to file regions by various user-mode process through an `address_space` data structure. The `shared` element of the `vm_area_struct` object enumerates this VMA into a red-black tree associated with the address space. We'll discuss more about the page cache and `address_space` objects in the next section.

Regions of the virtual address space such as heap, stack, and mmap are allocated through anonymous memory mappings. The VM subsystem groups all VMA instances of the process that represent anonymous memory regions into a list and represents them through a descriptor of type `struct anon_vma`. This structure enables quick access to all of the process VMAs that map anonymous pages; the `*anon_vma` pointer of each anonymous VMA structure refers to the `anon_vma` object.

However, when a process forks a child, all anonymous pages of the caller address space are shared with the child process under copy-on-write (COW). This causes new VMAs to be created (for the child) that represent the same anonymous memory regions of the parent. The memory manager would need to locate and track all VMAs that refer to the same regions for it to be able to support unmap and swap-out operations. As a solution, the VM subsystem uses another descriptor called `struct anon_vma_chain` that links all `anon_vma` structures of a process group. The `anon_vma_chain` element of the VMA structure is a list element of the anonymous VMA chain.

Each VMA instance is bound to a descriptor of type `vm_operations_struct`, which contains operations performed on the current VMA. The `*vm_ops` pointer of the VMA instance refers to the operations object:

```
/*
 * These are the virtual MM functions - opening of an area, closing and
 * unmapping it (needed to keep files on disk up-to-date etc), pointer
 * to the functions called when a no-page or a wp-page exception occurs.
 */
struct vm_operations_struct {
        void (*open)(struct vm_area_struct * area);
        void (*close)(struct vm_area_struct * area);
        int (*mremap)(struct vm_area_struct * area);
        int (*fault)(struct vm_area_struct *vma, struct vm_fault *vmf);
        int (*pmd_fault)(struct vm_area_struct *, unsigned long address,
                                              pmd_t *, unsigned int
flags);
        void (*map_pages)(struct fault_env *fe,
                    pgoff_t start_pgoff, pgoff_t end_pgoff);
```

```
            /* notification that a previously read-only page is about to
become
            * writable, if an error is returned it will cause a SIGBUS */
            int (*page_mkwrite)(struct vm_area_struct *vma, struct vm_fault
*vmf);
        /* same as page_mkwrite when using VM_PFNMAP|VM_MIXEDMAP */
            int (*pfn_mkwrite)(struct vm_area_struct *vma, struct vm_fault
*vmf);
    /* called by access_process_vm when get_user_pages() fails, typically
            * for use by special VMAs that can switch between memory and
hardware
            */
            int (*access)(struct vm_area_struct *vma, unsigned long addr,
                        void *buf, int len, int write);
    /* Called by the /proc/PID/maps code to ask the vma whether it
            * has a special name. Returning non-NULL will also cause this
            * vma to be dumped unconditionally. */
            const char * (*name)(struct vm_area_struct *vma);
    . . .
    . . .
```

The routine assigned to the *open() function pointer is invoked when the VMA is enumerated into the address space. Similarly, the routine assigned to the *close() function pointer is invoked when the VMA is detached from the virtual address space. The function assigned to the *mremap() interface is executed when the memory area mapped by the VMA is to be resized. When the physical region mapped by the VMA is inactive, the system triggers a page fault exception, and the function assigned to the *fault() pointer is invoked by the kernel's page-fault handler to read corresponding data of the VMA region into the physical page.

The kernel supports direct access operations (DAX) for files on storage devices that are similar to memory, such as nvrams, flash storage, and other persistent memory devices. Drivers for such storage devices are implemented to perform all read and write operations directly on storage, without any caching. When a user process attempts to map a file from a DAX storage device, the underlying disk driver directly maps the corresponding file pages to process the virtual address space. For optimal performance, user-mode processes can map large files from DAX storage by enabling VM_HUGETLB. Due to the large page sizes supported, page faults on DAX file maps cannot be handled through regular page fault handlers, and filesystems supporting DAX need to assign appropriate fault handlers to the *pmd_fault() pointer of the VMA.

Managing virtual memory areas

The kernel's VM subsystem implements various operations to manipulate the virtual memory regions of a process; these include functions to create, insert, modify, locate, merge, and delete VMA instances. We will discuss a few of the important routines.

Locating a VMA

The `find_vma()` routine locates the first region in the VMA list that satisfies the condition for a given address (`addr < vm_area_struct->vm_end`).

```c
/* Look up the first VMA which satisfies addr < vm_end, NULL if none. */
struct vm_area_struct *find_vma(struct mm_struct *mm, unsigned long addr)
{
        struct rb_node *rb_node;
        struct vm_area_struct *vma;

        /* Check the cache first. */
        vma = vmacache_find(mm, addr);
        if (likely(vma))
                return vma;
        rb_node = mm->mm_rb.rb_node;
        while (rb_node) {
                struct vm_area_struct *tmp;
                tmp = rb_entry(rb_node, struct vm_area_struct, vm_rb);
                if (tmp->vm_end > addr) {
                        vma = tmp;
                        if (tmp->vm_start <= addr)
                                break;
                        rb_node = rb_node->rb_left;
                } else
                        rb_node = rb_node->rb_right;
        }
        if (vma)
                vmacache_update(addr, vma);
        return vma;
}
```

The function first checks for the requested address in the recently accessed vma found in the per-thread vma cache. On a match, it returns the address of the VMA, else it steps into the red-black tree to locate the appropriate VMA. The root node of the tree is located in mm->mm_rb.rb_node. Through the helper function rb_entry(), each node is verified for the address within the virtual address interval of the VMA. If the target VMA with a lower start address and higher end address than the specified address is located, the function returns the address of the VMA instance. If the appropriate VMA is still not found, the search continues its lookup into the left or right child nodes of the rbtree. When a suitable VMA is found, a pointer to it is updated to the vma cache (anticipating the next call to find_vma() to locate the neighboring address in the same region), and it returns the address of the VMA instance.

When a new region is added immediately before or after an existing region (and therefore also between two existing regions), the kernel merges the data structures involved into a single structure —but, of course, only if the access permissions for all the regions involved are identical and contiguous data is mapped from the same backing store.

Merging VMA regions

When a new VMA is mapped immediately before or after an existing VMA with identical access attributes and data from a file-backed memory region, it is more optimal to merge them into a single VMA structure. vma_merge() is a helper function that is invoked to merge surrounding VMAs with identical attributes:

```
struct vm_area_struct *vma_merge(struct mm_struct *mm,
                        struct vm_area_struct *prev, unsigned long addr,
                        unsigned long end, unsigned long vm_flags,
                        struct anon_vma *anon_vma, struct file *file,
                        pgoff_t pgoff, struct mempolicy *policy,
                        struct vm_userfaultfd_ctx vm_userfaultfd_ctx)
{
        pgoff_t pglen = (end - addr) >> PAGE_SHIFT;
        struct vm_area_struct *area, *next;
        int err;
        . . .
        . . .
```

*mm refers to the memory descriptor of the process whose VMAs are to be merged; *prev refers to a VMA whose address interval precedes the new region; and the addr, end, and vm_flags contain the start, end, and flags of the new region. *file refers to the file instance whose memory region is mapped to the new region, and pgoff specifies the offset of the mapping within the file data.

This function first checks if the new region can be merged with the predecessor:

```
...
...
/*
 * Can it merge with the predecessor?
 */
if (prev && prev->vm_end == addr &&
            mpol_equal(vma_policy(prev), policy) &&
            can_vma_merge_after(prev, vm_flags,
                                anon_vma, file, pgoff,
                                vm_userfaultfd_ctx)) {
...
...
```

For this, it invokes a helper function `can_vma_merge_after()`, which checks if the end address of the predecessor corresponds to the start address of the new region, and if access flags are identical for both regions, it also checks offsets of file mappings to ensure that they are contiguous in file region, and that both regions do not contain any anonymous mappings:

```
                ...
                ...
                /*
                 * OK, it can. Can we now merge in the successor as well?
                 */
                if (next && end == next->vm_start &&
                            mpol_equal(policy, vma_policy(next)) &&
                            can_vma_merge_before(next, vm_flags,
                                                anon_vma, file,
                                                pgoff+pglen,
                                                vm_userfaultfd_ctx) &&
                            is_mergeable_anon_vma(prev->anon_vma,
                                                next->anon_vma,
    NULL)) {
                                            /* cases 1, 6 */
                            err = __vma_adjust(prev, prev->vm_start,
                                        next->vm_end, prev->vm_pgoff,
    NULL,
                                            prev);
                } else /* cases 2, 5, 7 */
                            err = __vma_adjust(prev, prev->vm_start,
                                        end, prev->vm_pgoff, NULL, prev);

                ...
                ...
    }
```

It then checks if merging is a possibility with the successor region; for this it invokes the helper function `can_vma_merge_before()`. This function carries out similar checks as before and if both the predecessor and the successor regions are found identical, then `is_mergeable_anon_vma()` is invoked to check if any anonymous mappings of the predecessor can be merged with those of the successor. Finally, another helper function `__vma_adjust()` is invoked to perform the final merging, which manipulates the VMA instances appropriately.

Similar types of helper functions exist for creating, inserting, and deleting memory regions, which are invoked as helper functions from `do_mmap()` and `do_munmap()`, called when user-mode applications attempt to `mmap()` and `unmap()` memory regions, respectively. We will not discuss details of these helper routines any further.

struct address_space

Memory caches are an integral part of modern memory management. In simple words, a **cache** is a collection of pages used for specific needs. Most operating systems implement a **buffer cache**, which is a framework that manages a list of memory blocks for caching persistent storage disk blocks. The buffer cache allows filesystems to minimize disk I/O operations by grouping and deferring disk sync until appropriate time.

The Linux kernel implements a **page cache** as a mechanism for caching; in simple words, the page cache is a collection of page frames that are dynamically managed for caching disk files and directories, and support virtual memory operations by providing pages for swapping and demand paging. It also handles pages allocated for special files, such as IPC shared memory and message queues. Application file I/O calls such as read and write cause the underlying filesystem to perform the relevant operation on pages in the page cache. Read operations on an unread file cause the requested file data to be fetched from disk into pages of the page cache, and write operations update the relevant file data in cached pages, which are then marked *dirty* and flushed to disk at specific intervals.

Groups of pages in cache that contain data of a specific disk file are represented through a descriptor of type `struct address_space`, so each `address_space` instance serves as an abstraction for a set of pages owned by either a file `inode` or block device file `inode`:

```
struct address_space {
        struct inode *host; /* owner: inode, block_device */
        struct radix_tree_root page_tree; /* radix tree of all pages */
        spinlock_t tree_lock; /* and lock protecting it */
        atomic_t i_mmap_writable;/* count VM_SHARED mappings */
        struct rb_root i_mmap; /* tree of private and shared mappings */
        struct rw_semaphore i_mmap_rwsem; /* protect tree, count, list */
```

```
              /* Protected by tree_lock together with the radix tree */
              unsigned long nrpages; /* number of total pages */
              /* number of shadow or DAX exceptional entries */
              unsigned long nrexceptional;
              pgoff_t writeback_index;/* writeback starts here */
              const struct address_space_operations *a_ops; /* methods */
              unsigned long flags; /* error bits */
              spinlock_t private_lock; /* for use by the address_space */
              gfp_t gfp_mask; /* implicit gfp mask for allocations */
              struct list_head private_list; /* ditto */
              void *private_data; /* ditto */
      } __attribute__((aligned(sizeof(long))));
```

The `*host` pointer refers to the owner `inode` whose data is contained in the pages represented by the current `address_space` object. For instance, if a page in the cache contains data of a file managed by the Ext4 filesystem, the corresponding VFS `inode` of the file stores the `address_space` object in its `i_data` field. The `inode` of the file and the corresponding `address_space` object is stored in the `i_data` field of the VFS `inode` object. The `nr_pages` field contains the count of pages under this `address_space`.

For efficient management of file pages in cache, the VM subsystem needs to track all virtual address mappings to regions of the same `address_space`; for instance, a number of user-mode processes might map pages of a shared library into their address space through `vm_area_struct` instances. The `i_mmap` field of the `address_space` object is the root element of a red-black tree that contains all `vm_area _struct` instances currently mapped to this `address_space`; since each `vm_area_struct` instance refers back to the memory descriptor of the respective process, it would always be possible to track process references.

All physical pages containing file data under the `address_space` object are organized through a radix tree for efficient access; the `page_tree` field is an instance of `struct radix_tree_root` that serves a root element for the radix tree of pages. This structure is defined in the kernel header `<linux/radix-tree.h>`:

```
    struct radix_tree_root {
            gfp_t gfp_mask;
            struct radix_tree_node __rcu *rnode;
    };
```

Each node of the radix tree is of type `struct radix_tree_node`; the `*rnode` pointer of the previous structure refers to the first node element of the tree:

```
struct radix_tree_node {
        unsigned char shift; /* Bits remaining in each slot */
        unsigned char offset; /* Slot offset in parent */
        unsigned int count;
        union {
                struct {
                        /* Used when ascending tree */
                        struct radix_tree_node *parent;
                        /* For tree user */
                        void *private_data;
                };
                /* Used when freeing node */
                struct rcu_head rcu_head;
        };
        /* For tree user */
        struct list_head private_list;
        void __rcu *slots[RADIX_TREE_MAP_SIZE];
        unsigned long tags[RADIX_TREE_MAX_TAGS][RADIX_TREE_TAG_LONGS];
};
```

The `offset` field specifies the node slot offset in the parent, `count` holds the total count of child nodes, and `*parent` is a pointer to the parent node. Each node can refer to 64 tree nodes (specified by the macro `RADIX_TREE_MAP_SIZE`) through the slots array, where unused slot entries are initialized with NULL.

For efficient management of pages under an address space, it is important for the memory manager to set a clear distinction between clean and dirty pages; this is made possible through **tags** assigned for pages of each node of the `radix` tree. The tagging information is stored in the `tags` field of the node structure, which is a two-dimensional array . The first dimension of the array distinguishes between the possible tags, and the second contains a sufficient number of elements of unsigned longs so that there is a bit for each page that can be organized in the node. Following is the list of tags supported:

```
/*
 * Radix-tree tags, for tagging dirty and writeback pages within
 * pagecache radix trees
 */
#define PAGECACHE_TAG_DIRTY 0
#define PAGECACHE_TAG_WRITEBACK 1
#define PAGECACHE_TAG_TOWRITE 2
```

The Linux `radix` tree API provides various operation interfaces to set, `clear`, and `get` tags:

```
void *radix_tree_tag_set(struct radix_tree_root *root,
                             unsigned long index, unsigned int
tag);
void *radix_tree_tag_clear(struct radix_tree_root *root,
                             unsigned long index, unsigned int
tag);
int radix_tree_tag_get(struct radix_tree_root *root,
                             unsigned long index, unsigned int
tag);
```

The following diagram depicts the layout of pages under the `address_space` object:

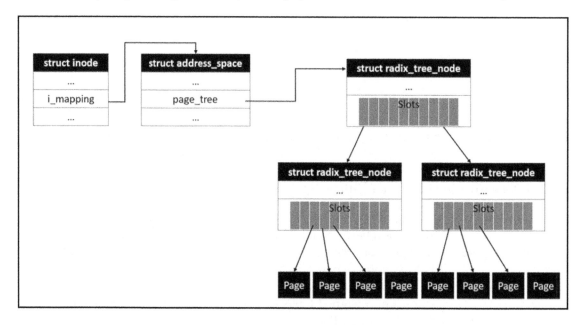

Each address space object is bound to a set of functions that implement various low-level operations between address space pages and the back-store block device. The a_ops pointer of the `address_space` structure refers to the descriptor containing address space operations. These operations are invoked by VFS to initiate data transfers between pages in cache associated with an address map and back-store block device:

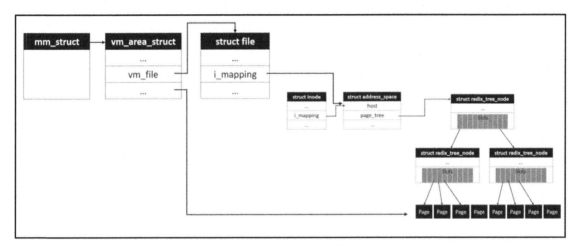

Page tables

All access operations on process virtual address regions are put through address translation before reaching the appropriate physical memory regions. The VM subsystem maintains page tables to translate linear page addresses into physical addresses. Even though the page table layout is architecture specific, for most architectures, the kernel uses a four-level paging structure, and we will consider the x86-64 kernel page table layout for this discussion.

The following diagram depicts the layout of the page table for x86-64:

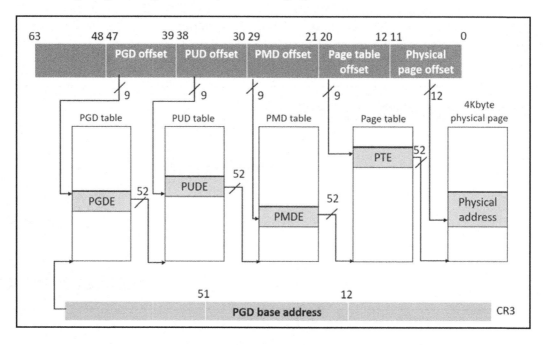

The address of the page global directory, which is the top-level page table, is initialized into control register cr3. This is a 64-bit register following bit break-up:

Bits	Description
2:0	Ignored
4:3	Page level write-through and page-level cache disable
11:5	Reserved
51:12	Address of page global directory
63:52	Reserved

Out of 64 bit-wide linear addresses supported by x86-64, Linux currently uses 48 bits that enable 256 TB of linear address space, which is considered large enough for current use. This 48-bit linear address is split into five parts, with the first 12 bits containing the offset of the memory location in the physical frame and rest of the parts containing offsets into appropriate page table structures:

Linear address bits	Description
11:0 (12 bits)	Index of physical page
20:12 (9 bits)	Index of page table
29:21 (9 bits)	Index of page middle directory
38:30 (9 bits)	Index of page upper directory
47:39 (9 bits)	Index of page global directory

Each of the page table structures can support 512 records, of which each record provides the base address of the next-level page structure. During translation of a given linear address, MMU extracts the top 9 bits containing the index into the page global directory (PGD), which is then added to the base address of PGD (found in cr3); this lookup results in the discovery of the base address for page upper directory (PUD). Next, MMU retrieves the PUD offset (9 bits) found in the linear address, and adds it to the base address of PUD structure to reach the PUD entry (PUDE) that yields the base address of page middle directory (PMD). The PMD offset found in the linear address is then added to the base address of PMD to reach the relevant PMD entry (PMDE), which yields the base address of the page table. The page table offset (9 bits) found in the linear address is then added to the base address discovered from the PMD entry to reach the page table entry (PTE), which in turn yields the start address of the physical frame of the requested data. Finally, the page offset (12 bits) found in the linear address is added to the PTE discovered base address to reach the memory location to be accessed.

Summary

In this chapter, we focused on specifics of virtual memory management with respect to process virtual address space and memory maps. We discussed critical data structures of the VM subsystem, memory descriptor structure (`struct mm_struct`), and VMA descriptor (`struct vm_area_struct`). We looked at the page cache and its data structures (`struct address_space`) used in reverse mapping of file buffers into various process address spaces. Finally, we explored the page table layout of Linux, which is widely used in many architectures. Having gained a thorough understanding of filesystems and virtual memory management, in the next chapter, we will extend this discussion into the IPC subsystem and its resources.

8
Kernel Synchronization and Locking

Kernel address space is shared by all user-mode processes, which enables concurrent access to kernel services and data structures. For reliable functioning of the system, it is imperative that kernel services be implemented to be re-entrant. Kernel code paths accessing global data structures need to be synchronized to ensure consistency and validity of shared data. In this chapter, we will get into details of various resources at the disposal of kernel programmers for synchronization of kernel code paths and protection of shared data from concurrent access.

This chapter will cover the following topics:

- Atomic operations
- Spinlocks
- Standard mutexes
- Wait/wound mutex
- Semaphores
- Sequence locks
- Completions

Atomic operations

A computation operation is considered to be **atomic** if it appears to the rest of the system to occur instantaneously. Atomicity guarantees indivisible and uninterruptible execution of the operation initiated. Most CPU instruction set architectures define instruction opcodes that can perform atomic read-modify-write operations on a memory location. These operations have a succeed-or-fail definition, that is, they either successfully change the state of the memory location or fail with no apparent effect. These operations are handy for manipulation of shared data atomically in a multi-threaded scenario. They also serve as foundational building blocks for implementation of exclusion locks, which are engaged to protect shared memory locations from concurrent access by parallel code paths.

Linux kernel code uses atomic operations for various use cases, such as reference counters in shared data structures (which are used to track concurrent access to various kernel data structures), wait-notify flags, and for enabling exclusive ownership of data structures to a specific code path. To ensure portability of kernel services that directly deal with atomic operations, the kernel provides a rich library of architecture-neutral interface macros and inline functions that serve as abstractions to processor-dependent atomic instructions. Relevant CPU-specific atomic instructions under these neutral interfaces are implemented by the architecture branch of the kernel code.

Atomic integer operations

Generic atomic operation interfaces include support for integer and bitwise operations. Integer operations are implemented to operate on special kernel-defined types called `atomic_t` (32-bit integer) and `atomic64_t` (64-bit integer). Definitions for these types can be found in the generic kernel header `<linux/types.h>`:

```
typedef struct {
        int counter;
} atomic_t;

#ifdef CONFIG_64BIT
typedef struct {
        long counter;
} atomic64_t;
#endif
```

The implementation provides two groups of integer operations; one set applicable on 32 bit and the other group for 64 bit atomic variables. These interface operations are implemented as a set of macros and inline functions. Following is a summarized list of operations applicable on `atomic_t` type variables:

Interface macro/Inline function	Description
`ATOMIC_INIT(i)`	Macro to initialize an atomic counter
`atomic_read(v)`	Read value of the atomic counter v
`atomic_set(v, i)`	Atomically set counter v to value specified in i
`atomic_add(int i, atomic_t *v)`	Atomically add i to counter v
`atomic_sub(int i, atomic_t *v)`	Atomically subtract i from counter v
`atomic_inc(atomic_t *v)`	Atomically increment counter v
`atomic_dec(atomic_t *v)`	Atomically decrement counter v

Following is a list of functions that perform relevant **read-modify-write** (**RMW**) operations and return the result (that is, they return the value that was written to the memory address after the modification):

Operation	Description
`bool atomic_sub_and_test(int i, atomic_t *v)`	Atomically subtracts i from v and returns `true` if the result is zero, or `false` otherwise
`bool atomic_dec_and_test(atomic_t *v)`	Atomically decrements v by 1 and returns `true` if the result is 0, or `false` for all other cases
`bool atomic_inc_and_test(atomic_t *v)`	Atomically adds i to v and returns `true` if the result is 0, or `false` for all other cases
`bool atomic_add_negative(int i, atomic_t *v)`	Atomically adds i to v and returns `true` if the result is negative, or `false` when result is greater than or equal to zero
`int atomic_add_return(int i, atomic_t *v)`	Atomically adds i to v and returns the result

`int atomic_sub_return(int i, atomic_t *v)`	Atomically subtracts i from v and returns the result
`int atomic_fetch_add(int i, atomic_t *v)`	Atomically adds i to v and return pre-addition value at v
`int atomic_fetch_sub(int i, atomic_t *v)`	Atomically subtracts i from v, and return pre-subtract value at v
`int atomic_cmpxchg(atomic_t *v, int old, int new)`	Reads the value at location v, and checks if it is equal to old; if `true`, swaps value at v with *new*, and always returns value read at v
`int atomic_xchg(atomic_t *v, int new)`	Swaps the old value stored at location v with new, and returns old value v

For all of these operations, 64-bit variants exist for use with `atomic64_t`; these functions have the naming convention `atomic64_*()`.

Atomic bitwise operations

Kernel-provided generic atomic operation interfaces also include bitwise operations. Unlike integer operations, which are implemented to operate on the `atomic(64)_t` type, these bit operations can be applied on any memory location. The arguments to these operations are the position of the bit or bit number, and a pointer with a valid address. The bit range is 0-31 for 32-bit machines and 0-63 for 64-bit machines. Following is a summarized list of bitwise operations available:

Operation interface	Description
`set_bit(int nr, volatile unsigned long *addr)`	Atomically set the bit nr in location starting from addr
`clear_bit(int nr, volatile unsigned long *addr)`	Atomically clear the bit nr in location starting from addr
`change_bit(int nr, volatile unsigned long *addr)`	Atomically flip the bit nr in the location starting from addr

`int test_and_set_bit(int nr, volatile unsigned long *addr)`	Atomically set the bit nr in the location starting from `addr`, and return old value at the nr^{th} bit
`int test_and_clear_bit(int nr, volatile unsigned long *addr)`	Atomically clear the bit nr in the location starting from `addr`, and return old value at the nr^{th} bit
`int test_and_change_bit(int nr, volatile unsigned long *addr)`	Atomically flip the bit nr in the location starting from `addr`, and return old value at the nr^{th} bit

For all the operations with a return type, the value returned is the old state of the bit that was read out of the memory address before the specified modification happened. Non-atomic versions of these operations also exist; they are efficient and useful for cases that might need bit manipulations, initiated from code statements in a mutually exclusive critical block. These are declared in the kernel header `<linux/bitops/non-atomic.h>`.

Introducing exclusion locks

Hardware-specific atomic instructions can operate only on CPU word- and doubleword-size data; they cannot be directly applied on shared data structures of custom size. For most multi-threaded scenarios, often it can be observed that shared data is of custom sizes, for example, a structure with *n* elements of various types. Concurrent code paths accessing such data usually comprise a bunch of instructions that are programmed to access and manipulate shared data; such access operations must be executed *atomically* to prevent races. To ensure atomicity of such code blocks, mutual exclusion locks are used. All multi-threading environments provide implementation of exclusion locks that are based on exclusion protocols. These locking implementations are built on top of hardware-specific atomic instructions.

The Linux kernel implements operation interfaces for standard exclusion mechanisms such as mutual and reader-writer exclusions. It also contains support for various other contemporary lightweight and lock-free synchronization mechanisms. Most kernel data structures and other shared data elements such as shared buffers and device registers are protected from concurrent access through appropriate exclusion-locking interfaces offered by the kernel. In this section we will explore available exclusions and their implementation details.

Spinlocks

Spinlocks are one of the simplest and lightweight mutual exclusion mechanisms widely implemented by most concurrent programming environments. A spinlock implementation defines a lock structure and operations that manipulate the lock structure. The lock structure primarily hosts an atomic lock counter among other elements, and operations interfaces include:

- An **initializer routine**, that initializes a spinlock instance to the default (unlock) state
- A **lock routine**, that attempts to acquire spinlock by altering the state of the lock counter atomically
- An **unlock routine**, that releases the spinlock by altering counter into unlock state

When a caller context attempts to acquire spinlock while it is locked (or held by another context), the lock function iteratively polls or spins for the lock until available, causing the caller context to hog the CPU until lock is acquired. It is due to this fact that this exclusion mechanism is aptly named spinlock. It is therefore advised to ensure that code within critical sections is atomic or non-blocking, so that lock can be held for a short, deterministic duration, as it is apparent that holding a spinlock for a long duration could prove disastrous.

As discussed, spinlocks are built around processor-specific atomic operations; the architecture branch of the kernel implements core spinlock operations (assembly programmed). The kernel wraps the architecture-specific implementation through a generic platform-neutral interface that is directly usable by kernel service; this enables portability of the service code which engages spinlocks for protection of shared resources.

Generic spinlock interfaces can be found in the kernel header <linux/spinlock.h> while architecture-specific definitions are part of <asm/spinlock.h>. The generic interface provides a bunch of lock() and unlock() operations, each implemented for a specific use case. We will discuss each of these interfaces in the sections to follow; for now, let's begin our discussion with the standard and most basic variants of lock() and unlock() operations offered by the interface. The following code sample shows the usage of a basic spinlock interface:

```
DEFINE_SPINLOCK(s_lock);
spin_lock(&s_lock);
/* critical region ... */
spin_unlock(&s_lock);
```

Let's examine the implementation of these functions under the hood:

```
static __always_inline void spin_lock(spinlock_t *lock)
{
        raw_spin_lock(&lock->rlock);
}

...
...

static __always_inline void spin_unlock(spinlock_t *lock)
{
        raw_spin_unlock(&lock->rlock);
}
```

Kernel code implements two variants of spinlock operations; one suitable for SMP platforms and the other for uniprocessor platforms. Spinlock data structure and operations related to the architecture and type of build (SMP and UP) are defined in various headers of the kernel source tree. Let's familiarize ourselves with the role and importance of these headers:

`<include/linux/spinlock.h>` contains generic spinlock/rwlock declarations.

The following headers are related to SMP platform builds:

- `<asm/spinlock_types.h>` contains `arch_spinlock_t/arch_rwlock_t` and initializers
- `<linux/spinlock_types.h>` defines the generic type and initializers
- `<asm/spinlock.h>` contains the `arch_spin_*()` and similar low-level operation implementations
- `<linux/spinlock_api_smp.h>` contains the prototypes for the `_spin_*()` APIs
- `<linux/spinlock.h>` builds the final `spin_*()` APIs

The following headers are related to uniprocessor (UP) platform builds:

- `<linux/spinlock_type_up.h>` contains the generic, simplified UP spinlock type
- `<linux/spinlock_types.h>` defines the generic type and initializers
- `<linux/spinlock_up.h>` contains the `arch_spin_*()` and similar version of UP builds (which are NOPs on non-debug, non-preempt builds)
- `<linux/spinlock_api_up.h>` builds the `_spin_*()` APIs
- `<linux/spinlock.h>` builds the final `spin_*()` APIs

The generic kernel header `<linux/spinlock.h>` contains a conditional directive to decide on the appropriate (SMP or UP) API to pull.

```
/*
 * Pull the _spin_*()/_read_*()/_write_*() functions/declarations:
 */
#if defined(CONFIG_SMP) || defined(CONFIG_DEBUG_SPINLOCK)
# include <linux/spinlock_api_smp.h>
#else
# include <linux/spinlock_api_up.h>
#endif
```

The `raw_spin_lock()` and `raw_spin_unlock()` macros dynamically expand to the appropriate version of spinlock operations based on the type of platform (SMP or UP) chosen in the build configuration. For SMP platforms, `raw_spin_lock()` expands to the `__raw_spin_lock()` operation implemented in the kernel source file `kernel/locking/spinlock.c`. Following is the locking operation code defined with a macro:

```
/*
 * We build the __lock_function inlines here. They are too large for
 * inlining all over the place, but here is only one user per function
 * which embeds them into the calling _lock_function below.
 *
 * This could be a long-held lock. We both prepare to spin for a long
 * time (making _this_ CPU preemptable if possible), and we also signal
 * towards that other CPU that it should break the lock ASAP.
 */

#define BUILD_LOCK_OPS(op, locktype)                                    \
void __lockfunc __raw_##op##_lock(locktype##_t *lock)                   \
{                                                                       \
        for (;;) {                                                      \
                preempt_disable();                                      \
                if (likely(do_raw_##op##_trylock(lock)))               \
                        break;                                          \
                preempt_enable();                                       \
                                                                        \
                if (!(lock)->break_lock)                                \
                        (lock)->break_lock = 1;                         \
                while (!raw_##op##_can_lock(lock) && (lock)->break_lock)\
                        arch_##op##_relax(&lock->raw_lock);             \
        }                                                               \
        (lock)->break_lock = 0;                                         \
}
```

This routine is composed of nested loop constructs, an outer `for` loop construct, and an inner `while` loop that spins until the specified condition is satisfied. The first block of code in the outer loop attempts to acquire lock atomically by invoking the architecture-specific `##_trylock()` routine. Notice that this function is invoked with kernel preemption disabled on the local processor. If lock is acquired successfully, it breaks out of the loop construct and the call returns with preemption turned off. This ensures that the caller context holding the lock is not preemptable during execution of a critical section. This approach also ensures that no other context can contend for the same lock on the local CPU until the current owner releases it.

However, if it fails to acquire lock, preemption is enabled through the `preempt_enable()` call, and the caller context enters the inner loop. This loop is implemented through a conditional `while` that spins until lock is found to be available. Each iteration of the loop checks for lock, and when it detects that the lock is not available yet, it invokes an architecture-specific relax routine (which executes a CPU-specific nop instruction) before spinning again to check for lock. Recall that during this time preemption is enabled; this ensures that the caller context is preemptable and does not hog CPU for long duration, which can happen especially when lock is highly contended. It also allows the possibility of two or more threads scheduled on the same CPU to contend for the same lock, possibly by preempting each other.

When a spinning context detects that lock is available through `raw_spin_can_lock()`, it breaks out of the `while` loop, causing the caller to iterate back to the beginning of the outer loop (`for` loop) where it again attempts to grab lock through `##_trylock()` by disabling preemption:

```
/*
 * In the UP-nondebug case there's no real locking going on, so the
 * only thing we have to do is to keep the preempt counts and irq
 * flags straight, to suppress compiler warnings of unused lock
 * variables, and to add the proper checker annotations:
 */
#define ___LOCK(lock) \
  do { __acquire(lock); (void)(lock); } while (0)

#define __LOCK(lock) \
  do { preempt_disable(); ___LOCK(lock); } while (0)

#define _raw_spin_lock(lock) __LOCK(lock)
```

Unlike the SMP variant, spinlock implementation for UP platforms is quite simple; in fact, the lock routine just disables kernel preemption and puts the caller into a critical section. This works since there is no possibility of another context to contend for the lock with preemption suspended.

Alternate spinlock APIs

Standard spinlock operations that we discussed so far are suitable for the protection of shared resources that are accessed only from the process context kernel path. However, there might be scenarios where a specific shared resource or data might be accessed from both the process and interrupt context code of a kernel service. For instance, think of a device driver service that might contain both process context and interrupt context routines, both programmed to access the shared driver buffer for execution of appropriate I/O operations.

Let's presume that a spinlock was engaged to protect the driver's shared resource from concurrent access, and all routines of the driver service (both process and interrupt context) seeking access to the shared resource are programmed with appropriate critical sections using standard spin_lock() and spin_unlock() operations. This strategy would ensure protection of the shared resource by enforcing exclusion, but can cause a *hard lock condition* on the CPU at random times, due to *lock* contention by the interrupt path code on the same CPU where the *lock* was held by a process context path. To further understand this, let's assume the following events occur in the same order:

1. Process context routine of the driver acquires *lock* (using the standard spin_lock() call).
2. While the critical section is in execution, an interrupt occurs and is driven to the local CPU, causing the process context routine to preempt and give away the CPU for interrupt handlers.
3. Interrupt context path of the driver (ISR) starts and tries to acquire *lock* (using the standard spin_lock() call), which then starts to spin for *lock* to be available.

For the duration of the ISR, the process context is preempted and can never resume execution, resulting in a *lock* that can never be released, and the CPU is hard locked with a spinning interrupt handler that never yields.

To prevent such occurrences, the process context code needs to disable interrupts on the current processor while it takes the *lock*. This will ensure that an interrupt can never preempt the current context until the completion of the critical section and lock release. Note that interrupts can still occur but are routed to other available CPUs, on which the interrupt handler can spin until *lock* becomes available. The spinlock interface provides an alternate locking routine `spin_lock_irqsave()`, which disables interrupts on the current processor along with kernel preemption. The following snippet shows the routine's underlying code:

```
unsigned long __lockfunc __raw_##op##_lock_irqsave(locktype##_t *lock)  \
{                                                                        \
        unsigned long flags;                                             \
                                                                         \
        for (;;) {                                                       \
                preempt_disable();                                       \
                local_irq_save(flags);                                   \
                if (likely(do_raw_##op##_trylock(lock)))                 \
                        break;                                           \
                local_irq_restore(flags);                                \
                preempt_enable();                                        \
                                                                         \
                if (!(lock)->break_lock)                                 \
                        (lock)->break_lock = 1;                          \
                while (!raw_##op##_can_lock(lock) && (lock)->break_lock)\
                        arch_##op##_relax(&lock->raw_lock);              \
        }                                                                \
        (lock)->break_lock = 0;                                          \
        return flags;                                                    \
}
```

`local_irq_save()` is invoked to disable hard interrupts for the current processor; notice how on failure to acquire the lock, interrupts are enabled by calling `local_irq_restore()`. Note that a `lock` taken by the caller using `spin_lock_irqsave()` needs to be unlocked using `spin_lock_irqrestore()`, which enables both kernel preemption and interrupts for the current processor before releasing lock.

Similar to hard interrupt handlers, it is also possible for soft interrupt context routines such as *softirqs*, *tasklets*, and other such *bottom halves* to contend for a *lock* held by the process context code on the same processor. This can be prevented by disabling the execution of *bottom halves* while acquiring *lock* in the process context. `spin_lock_bh()` is another variant of the locking routine that takes care of suspending the execution of interrupt context bottom halves on the local CPU.

```
void __lockfunc __raw_##op##_lock_bh(locktype##_t *lock)                 \
```

```
{                                                                    \
        unsigned long flags;                                         \
                                                                     \
        /* */                                                        \
        /* Careful: we must exclude softirqs too, hence the */       \
        /* irq-disabling. We use the generic preemption-aware */     \
        /* function: */                                              \
        /**/                                                         \
        flags = _raw_##op##_lock_irqsave(lock);                      \
        local_bh_disable();                                          \
        local_irq_restore(flags);                                    \
}
```

local_bh_disable() suspends bottom half execution for the local CPU. To release a *lock* acquired by spin_lock_bh(), the caller context will need to invoke spin_unlock_bh(), which releases spinlock and BH lock for the local CPU.

Following is a summarized list of the kernel spinlock API interface:

Function	Description
spin_lock_init()	Initialize spinlock
spin_lock()	Acquire lock, spins on contention
spin_trylock()	Attempt to acquire lock, returns error on contention
spin_lock_bh()	Acquire lock by suspending BH routines on the local processor, spins on contention
spin_lock_irqsave()	Acquire lock by suspending interrupts on the local processor by saving current interrupt state, spins on contention
spin_lock_irq()	Acquire lock by suspending interrupts on the local processor, spins on contention
spin_unlock()	Release the lock
spin_unlock_bh()	Release lock and enable bottom half for the local processor
spin_unlock_irqrestore()	Release lock and restore local interrupts to previous state
spin_unlock_irq()	Release lock and restore interrupts for the local processor
spin_is_locked()	Return state of the lock, nonzero if lock is held or zero if lock is available

Reader-writer spinlocks

Spinlock implementation discussed until now protects shared data by enforcing standard mutual exclusion between concurrent code paths racing for shared data access. This form of exclusion is not suitable for the protection of shared data which is often read by concurrent code paths, with infrequent writers or updates. Reader-writer locks enforce exclusion between reader and writer paths; this allows concurrent readers to share lock and a reader task will need to wait for the lock while a writer owns the lock. Rw-locks enforce standard exclusion between concurrent writers, which is desired.

Rw-locks are represented by struct rwlock_t declared in kernel header <linux/rwlock_types.h>:

```
typedef struct {
        arch_rwlock_t raw_lock;
#ifdef CONFIG_GENERIC_LOCKBREAK
        unsigned int break_lock;
#endif
#ifdef CONFIG_DEBUG_SPINLOCK
        unsigned int magic, owner_cpu;
        void *owner;
#endif
#ifdef CONFIG_DEBUG_LOCK_ALLOC
        struct lockdep_map dep_map;
#endif
} rwlock_t;
```

rwlocks can be initialized statically through the macro DEFINE_RWLOCK(v_rwlock) or dynamically at runtime through rwlock_init(v_rwlock).

Reader code paths will need to invoke the read_lock routine.

```
read_lock(&v_rwlock);
/* critical section with read only access to shared data */
read_unlock(&v_rwlock);
```

Writer code paths use the following:

```
write_lock(&v_rwlock);
/* critical section for both read and write */
write_unlock(&v_lock);
```

Both read and write lock routines spin when lock is contended. The interface also offers non-spinning versions of lock functions called read_trylock() and write_trylock(). It also offers interrupt-disabling versions of the locking calls, which are handy when either the read or write path happens to execute in interrupt or bottom-half context.

Following is a summarized list of interface operations:

Function	Description
read_lock()	Standard read lock interface, spins on contention
read_trylock()	Attempts to acquire lock, returns error if lock is unavailable
read_lock_bh()	Attempts to acquire lock by suspending BH execution for the local CPU, spins on contention
read_lock_irqsave()	Attempts to acquire lock by suspending interrupts for the current CPU by saving current state of local interrupts, spins on contention
read_unlock()	Releases read lock
read_unlock_irqrestore()	Releases lock held and restores local interrupts to the previous state
read_unlock_bh()	Releases read lock and enables BH on the local processor
write_lock()	Standard write lock interface, spins on contention
write_trylock()	Attempts to acquire lock, returns error on contention
write_lock_bh()	Attempts to acquire write lock by suspending bottom halves for the local CPU, spins on contention
wrtie_lock_irqsave()	Attempts to acquire write lock by suspending interrupts for the local CPU by saving current state of local interrupts,. spins on contention
write_unlock()	Releases write lock
write_unlock_irqrestore()	Releases lock and restores local interrupts to the previous state
write_unlock_bh()	Releases write lock and enables BH on the local processor

Underlying calls for all of these operations are similar to that of spinlock implementations and can be found in headers specified in the aforementioned spinlock section.

Mutex locks

Spinlocks by design are better suited for scenarios where *lock* is held for short, fixed intervals of time, since *busy-waiting* for an indefinite duration would have a dire impact on performance of the system. However, there are ample situations where a *lock* is held for longer, non-deterministic durations; **sleeping locks** are precisely designed to be engaged for such situations. Kernel mutexes are an implementation of sleeping locks: when a caller task attempts to acquire a mutex that is unavailable (already owned by another context), it is put into sleep and moved out into a wait queue, forcing a context switch allowing the CPU to run other productive tasks. When the mutex becomes available, the task in the wait queue is woken up and moved by the unlock path of the mutex, which can then attempt to *lock* the mutex.

Mutexes are represented by `struct mutex`, defined in `include/linux/mutex.h` and corresponding operations implemented in the source file `kernel/locking/mutex.c`:

```
struct mutex {
        atomic_long_t owner;
        spinlock_t wait_lock;
#ifdef CONFIG_MUTEX_SPIN_ON_OWNER
        struct optimistic_spin_queue osq; /* Spinner MCS lock */
#endif
        struct list_head wait_list;
#ifdef CONFIG_DEBUG_MUTEXES
        void *magic;
#endif
#ifdef CONFIG_DEBUG_LOCK_ALLOC
        struct lockdep_map dep_map;
#endif
};
```

In its basic form, each mutex contains a 64-bit `atomic_long_t` counter (`owner`), which is used both for holding lock state, and to store a reference to the task structure of the current task owning the lock. Each mutex contains a wait-queue (`wait_list`), and a spin lock(`wait_lock`) that serializes access to `wait_list`.

The mutex API interface provides a set of macros and functions for initialization, lock, unlock, and to access the status of the mutex. These operation interfaces are defined in `<include/linux/mutex.h>`.

A mutex can be declared and initialized with the macro `DEFINE_MUTEX(name)`.

There is also an option of initializing a valid mutex dynamically through
`mutex_init(mutex)`.

As discussed earlier, on contention, lock operations put the caller thread into sleep, which requires the caller thread to be put into TASK_INTERRUPTIBLE, TASK_UNINTERRUPTIBLE, or TASK_KILLABLE states, before moving it into the mutex wait list. To support this, the mutex implementation offers two variants of lock operations, one for **uninterruptible** and other for **interruptible** sleep. Following is a list of standard mutex operations with a short description for each:

```
/**
 * mutex_lock - acquire the mutex
 * @lock: the mutex to be acquired
 *
 * Lock the mutex exclusively for this task. If the mutex is not
 * available right now, Put caller into Uninterruptible sleep until mutex
 * is available.
 */
    void mutex_lock(struct mutex *lock);

/**
 * mutex_lock_interruptible - acquire the mutex, interruptible
 * @lock: the mutex to be acquired
 *
 * Lock the mutex like mutex_lock(), and return 0 if the mutex has
 * been acquired else put caller into interruptible sleep until the mutex
 * until mutex is available. Return -EINTR if a signal arrives while
sleeping
 * for the lock.
 */
    int __must_check mutex_lock_interruptible(struct mutex *lock);

/**
 * mutex_lock_Killable - acquire the mutex, interruptible
 * @lock: the mutex to be acquired
 *
 * Similar to mutex_lock_interruptible(),with a difference that the call
 * returns -EINTR only when fatal KILL signal arrives while sleeping for
the
 * lock.
 */
    int __must_check mutex_lock_killable(struct mutex *lock);

/**
 * mutex_trylock - try to acquire the mutex, without waiting
 * @lock: the mutex to be acquired
 *
```

```
 * Try to acquire the mutex atomically. Returns 1 if the mutex
 * has been acquired successfully, and 0 on contention.
 *
 */
    int mutex_trylock(struct mutex *lock);

/**
 * atomic_dec_and_mutex_lock - return holding mutex if we dec to 0,
 * @cnt: the atomic which are to dec
 * @lock: the mutex to return holding if we dec to 0
 *
 * return true and hold lock if we dec to 0, return false otherwise. Please
 * note that this function is interruptible.
 */
    int atomic_dec_and_mutex_lock(atomic_t *cnt, struct mutex *lock);

/**
 * mutex_is_locked - is the mutex locked
 * @lock: the mutex to be queried
 *
 * Returns 1 if the mutex is locked, 0 if unlocked.
 */
    static inline int mutex_is_locked(struct mutex *lock);

/**
 * mutex_unlock - release the mutex
 * @lock: the mutex to be released
 *
 * Unlock the mutex owned by caller task.
 *
 */
    void mutex_unlock(struct mutex *lock);
```

Despite being possible blocking calls, mutex locking functions have been greatly optimized for performance. They are programmed to engage fast and slow path approaches while attempting lock acquisition. Let's explore the code under the hood of the locking calls to better understand fast path and slow path. The following code excerpt is of the `mutex_lock()` routine from `<kernel/locking/mutex.c>`:

```
void __sched mutex_lock(struct mutex *lock)
{
  might_sleep();

  if (!__mutex_trylock_fast(lock))
    __mutex_lock_slowpath(lock);
}
```

Lock acquisition is first attempted by invoking a non-blocking fast path call
`__mutex_trylock_fast()`. If it fails to acquire lock through due to contention, it enters
slow path by invoking `__mutex_lock_slowpath()`:

```
static __always_inline bool __mutex_trylock_fast(struct mutex *lock)
{
  unsigned long curr = (unsigned long)current;

  if (!atomic_long_cmpxchg_acquire(&lock->owner, 0UL, curr))
    return true;

  return false;
}
```

This function is programmed to acquire lock atomically if available. It invokes the
`atomic_long_cmpxchg_acquire()` macro, which attempts to assign the current thread as
the owner of the mutex; this operation will succeed if the mutex is available, in which case
the function returns `true`. Should some other thread own the mutex, this function will fail
and return `false`. On failure, the caller thread will enter the slow path routine.

Conventionally, the concept of slow path has always been to put the caller task into sleep
while waiting for the lock to become available. However, with the advent of many-core
CPUs, there is a growing need for scalability and improved performance, so with an
objective to achieve scalability, the mutex slow path implementation has been reworked
with an optimization called **optimistic spinning**, a.k.a. **midpath**, which can improve
performance considerably.

The core idea of optimistic spinning is to push contending tasks into poll or spin instead of
sleep when the mutex owner is found to be running. Once the mutex becomes available
(which is expected to be sooner, since the owner is found to be running) it is assumed that a
spinning task could always acquire it quicker as compared to a suspended or sleeping task
in the mutex wait list. However, such spinning is only a possibility when there are no other
higher-priority tasks in ready state. With this feature, spinning tasks are more likely to be
cache-hot, resulting in deterministic execution that yields noticeable performance
improvement:

```
static int __sched
__mutex_lock(struct mutex *lock, long state, unsigned int subclass,
        struct lockdep_map *nest_lock, unsigned long ip)
{
  return __mutex_lock_common(lock, state, subclass, nest_lock, ip, NULL,
false);
}

. . .
```

```
      . . .
      . . .

static noinline void __sched __mutex_lock_slowpath(struct mutex *lock)
{
        __mutex_lock(lock, TASK_UNINTERRUPTIBLE, 0, NULL, _RET_IP_);
}

static noinline int __sched
__mutex_lock_killable_slowpath(struct mutex *lock)
{
   return __mutex_lock(lock, TASK_KILLABLE, 0, NULL, _RET_IP_);
}

static noinline int __sched
__mutex_lock_interruptible_slowpath(struct mutex *lock)
{
   return __mutex_lock(lock, TASK_INTERRUPTIBLE, 0, NULL, _RET_IP_);
}
```

The __mutex_lock_common() function contains a slow path implementation with optimistic spinning; this routine is invoked by all sleep variants of mutex locking functions with appropriate flags as argument. This function first attempts to acquire mutex through optimistic spinning implemented through cancellable mcs spinlocks (osq field in mutex structure) associated with the mutex. When the caller task fails to acquire mutex with optimistic spinning, as a last resort this function switches to conventional slow path, resulting in the caller task to be put into sleep and queued into the mutex wait_list until woken up by the unlock path.

Debug checks and validations

Incorrect use of mutex operations can cause deadlocks, failure of exclusion, and so on. To detect and prevent such possible occurrences, the mutex subsystem is equipped with appropriate checks or validations instrumented into mutex operations. These checks are by default disabled, and can be enabled by choosing the configuration option CONFIG_DEBUG_MUTEXES=y during kernel build.

Following is a list of checks enforced by instrumented debug code:

- Mutex can be owned by one task at a given point in time
- Mutex can be released (unlocked) only by the valid owner, and an attempt to release mutex by a context that does not own the lock will fail
- Recursive locking or unlocking attempts will fail
- A mutex can only be initialized via the initializer call, and any attempt to *memset* mutex will never succeed
- A caller task may not exit with a mutex lock held
- Dynamic memory areas where held locks reside must not be freed
- A mutex can be initialized once, and any attempt to re-initialize an already initialized mutex will fail
- Mutexes may not be used in hard/soft interrupt context routines

Deadlocks can trigger due to many reasons, such as the execution pattern of the kernel code and careless usage of locking calls. For instance, let's consider a situation where concurrent code paths need to take ownership of L_1 and L_2 locks by nesting the locking functions. It must be ensured that all the kernel functions that require these locks are programmed to acquire them in the same order. When such ordering is not strictly imposed, there is always a possibility of two different functions trying to lock $L1$ and $L2$ in opposite order, which could trigger lock inversion deadlock, when these functions execute concurrently.

The kernel lock validator infrastructure has been implemented to check and prove that none of the locking patterns observed during kernel runtime could ever cause deadlock. This infrastructure prints data pertaining to locking pattern such as:

- Point-of-acquire tracking, symbolic lookup of function names, and list of all locks held in the system
- Owner tracking
- Detection of self-recursing locks and printing out all relevant info
- Detection of lock inversion deadlocks and printing out all affected locks and tasks

The lock validator can be enabled by choosing `CONFIG_PROVE_LOCKING=y` during kernel build.

Wait/wound mutexes

As discussed in the earlier section, unordered nested locking in the kernel functions could pose a risk of lock-inversion deadlocks, and kernel developers avoid this by defining rules for nested lock ordering and perform runtime checks through the lock validator infrastructure. Yet, there are situations where lock ordering is dynamic, and nested locking calls cannot be hardcoded or imposed as per preconceived rules.

One such use case is to do with GPU buffers; these buffers are to be owned and accessed by various system entities such as GPU hardware, GPU driver, user-mode applications, and other video-related drivers. User mode contexts can submit the dma buffers for processing in an arbitrary order, and the GPU hardware may process them at arbitrary times. If locking is used to control the ownership of the buffers, and if multiple buffers must be manipulated at the same time, deadlocks cannot be avoided. Wait/wound mutexes are designed to facilitate dynamic ordering of nested locks, without causing lock-inversion deadlocks. This is achieved by forcing the context in contention to *wound*, meaning forcing it to release the holding lock.

For instance, let's presume two buffers, each protected with a lock, and further consider two threads, say T_1 and T_2, seek ownership of the buffers by attempting locks in opposite order:

```
Thread T1       Thread T2
===========     ==========
lock(bufA);     lock(bufB);
lock(bufB);     lock(bufA);
 ....            ....
 ....            ....
unlock(bufB);   unlock(bufA);
unlock(bufA);   unlock(bufB);
```

Execution of T_1 and T_2 concurrently might result in each thread waiting for the lock held by the other, causing deadlock. Wait/wound mutex prevents this by letting the *thread that grabbed the lock first* to remain in sleep, waiting for nested lock to be available. The other thread is *wound*, causing it to release its holding lock and start over again. Suppose T_1 got to lock on bufA before T_2 could acquire lock on bufB. T_1 would be considered as the thread that *got there first* and is put to sleep for lock on bufB, and T_2 would be wound, causing it to release lock on bufB and start all over. This avoids deadlock and T_2 would start all over when T_1 releases locks held.

Operation interfaces:

Wait/wound mutexes are represented through `struct ww_mutex` defined in the header `<linux/ww_mutex.h>`:

```
struct ww_mutex {
        struct mutex base;
        struct ww_acquire_ctx *ctx;
# ifdef CONFIG_DEBUG_MUTEXES
        struct ww_class *ww_class;
#endif
};
```

The first step to use wait/wound mutex is to define a *class*, which is a mechanism to represent a group of locks. When concurrent tasks contend for the same locks, they must do so by specifying this class.

A class can be defined using a macro:

```
static DEFINE_WW_CLASS(bufclass);
```

Each class declared is an instance of type `struct ww_class` and contains an atomic counter `stamp`, which is used to hold a sequence number that records which one of the contending tasks *got there first*. Other fields are used by the kernel's lock validator to verify correct usage of the wait/wound mechanism.

```
struct ww_class {
        atomic_long_t stamp;
        struct lock_class_key acquire_key;
        struct lock_class_key mutex_key;
        const char *acquire_name;
        const char *mutex_name;
};
```

Each contending thread must invoke `ww_acquire_init()` before attempting nested locking calls. This sets up the context by assigning a sequence number to track locks.

```
/**
 * ww_acquire_init - initialize a w/w acquire context
 * @ctx: w/w acquire context to initialize
 * @ww_class: w/w class of the context
 *
 * Initializes a context to acquire multiple mutexes of the given w/w
class.
 *
 * Context-based w/w mutex acquiring can be done in any order whatsoever
 * within a given lock class. Deadlocks will be detected and handled with
```

```
the
 * wait/wound logic.
 *
 * Mixing of context-based w/w mutex acquiring and single w/w mutex locking
 * can result in undetected deadlocks and is so forbidden. Mixing different
 * contexts for the same w/w class when acquiring mutexes can also result
in
 * undetected deadlocks, and is hence also forbidden. Both types of abuse
will
 * will be caught by enabling CONFIG_PROVE_LOCKING.
 *
 */
    void ww_acquire_init(struct ww_acquire_ctx *ctx, struct ww_clas
*ww_class);
```

Once the context is set up and initialized, tasks can begin acquiring locks with either
`ww_mutex_lock()` or `ww_mutex_lock_interruptible()` calls:

```
/**
 * ww_mutex_lock - acquire the w/w mutex
 * @lock: the mutex to be acquired
 * @ctx: w/w acquire context, or NULL to acquire only a single lock.
 *
 * Lock the w/w mutex exclusively for this task.
 *
 * Deadlocks within a given w/w class of locks are detected and handled
with
 * wait/wound algorithm. If the lock isn't immediately available this
function
 * will either sleep until it is(wait case) or it selects the current
context
 * for backing off by returning -EDEADLK (wound case).Trying to acquire the
 * same lock with the same context twice is also detected and signalled by
 * returning -EALREADY. Returns 0 if the mutex was successfully acquired.
 *
 * In the wound case the caller must release all currently held w/w mutexes
 * for the given context and then wait for this contending lock to be
 * available by calling ww_mutex_lock_slow.
 *
 * The mutex must later on be released by the same task that
 * acquired it. The task may not exit without first unlocking the
mutex.Also,
 * kernel memory where the mutex resides must not be freed with the mutex
 * still locked. The mutex must first be initialized (or statically
defined) b
 * before it can be locked. memset()-ing the mutex to 0 is not allowed. The
 * mutex must be of the same w/w lock class as was used to initialize the
 * acquired context.
```

```
 * A mutex acquired with this function must be released with
ww_mutex_unlock.
 */
    int ww_mutex_lock(struct ww_mutex *lock, struct ww_acquire_ctx *ctx);

/**
 * ww_mutex_lock_interruptible - acquire the w/w mutex, interruptible
 * @lock: the mutex to be acquired
 * @ctx: w/w acquire context
 *
 */
    int  ww_mutex_lock_interruptible(struct ww_mutex *lock,
                                        struct  ww_acquire_ctx *ctx);
```

When a task grabs all nested locks (using any of these locking routines) associated with a class, it needs to notify acquisition of ownership using the function `ww_acquire_done()`. This call marks the end of the acquisition phase, and the task can proceed to process shared data:

```
/**
 * ww_acquire_done - marks the end of the acquire phase
 * @ctx: the acquire context
 *
 * Marks the end of the acquire phase, any further w/w mutex lock calls
using
 * this context are forbidden.
 *
 * Calling this function is optional, it is just useful to document w/w
mutex
 * code and clearly designated the acquire phase from actually using the
 * locked data structures.
 */
    void ww_acquire_done(struct ww_acquire_ctx *ctx);
```

When a task completes its processing of shared data, it can begin releasing all of the locks held, with calls to the `ww_mutex_unlock()` routine. Once all of the locks are released, the *context* must be released with a call to `ww_acquire_fini()`:

```
/**
 * ww_acquire_fini - releases a w/w acquire context
 * @ctx: the acquire context to free
 *
 * Releases a w/w acquire context. This must be called _after_ all acquired
 * w/w mutexes have been released with ww_mutex_unlock.
 */
    void ww_acquire_fini(struct ww_acquire_ctx *ctx);
```

Semaphores

Until early versions of 2.6 kernel releases, semaphores were the primary form of sleep locks. A typical semaphore implementation comprises a counter, wait queue, and set of operations that can increment/decrement the counter atomically.

When a semaphore is used to protect a shared resource, its counter is initialized to a number greater than zero, which is considered to be unlocked state. A task seeking access to a shared resource begins by invoking the decrement operation on the semaphore. This call checks the semaphore counter; if it is found to be greater than zero, the counter is decremented and the function returns success. However, if the counter is found to be zero, the decrement operation puts the caller task to sleep until the counter is found to have increased to a number greater than zero.

This simple design offers great flexibility, which allows adaptability and application of semaphores for different situations. For instance, for cases where a resource needs to be accessible to a specific number of tasks at any point in time, the semaphore count can be initialized to the number of tasks that require access, say 10, which allows a maximum of 10 tasks access to shared resource at any time. For yet other cases, such as a number of tasks that require mutually exclusive access to a shared resource, the semaphore count can be initialized to 1, resulting in a maximum of one task to access the resource at any given point in time.

Semaphore structure and its interface operations are declared in the kernel header `<include/linux/semaphore.h>`:

```
struct semaphore {
        raw_spinlock_t     lock;
        unsigned int       count;
        struct list_head   wait_list;
};
```

Spinlock (the `lock` field) serves as a protection for `count`, that is, semaphore operations (inc/dec) are programmed to acquire `lock` before manipulating `count`. `wait_list` is used to queue tasks to sleep while they wait for the semaphore count to increase beyond zero.

Semaphores can be declared and initialized to 1 through a macro: `DEFINE_SEMAPHORE(s)`.

A semaphore can also be initialized dynamically to any positive number through the following:

```
void sema_init(struct semaphore *sem, int val)
```

Following is a list of operation interfaces with a brief description of each. Routines with naming convention `down_xxx()` attempt to decrement the semaphore, and are possible blocking calls (except `down_trylock()`), while routine `up()` increments the semaphore and always succeeds:

```
/**
 * down_interruptible - acquire the semaphore unless interrupted
 * @sem: the semaphore to be acquired
 *
 * Attempts to acquire the semaphore.  If no more tasks are allowed to
 * acquire the semaphore, calling this function will put the task to sleep.
 * If the sleep is interrupted by a signal, this function will return -
EINTR.
 * If the semaphore is successfully acquired, this function returns 0.
 */
    int down_interruptible(struct semaphore *sem);

/**
 * down_killable - acquire the semaphore unless killed
 * @sem: the semaphore to be acquired
 *
 * Attempts to acquire the semaphore.  If no more tasks are allowed to
 * acquire the semaphore, calling this function will put the task to sleep.
 * If the sleep is interrupted by a fatal signal, this function will return
 * -EINTR.  If the semaphore is successfully acquired, this function
returns
 * 0.
 */
    int down_killable(struct semaphore *sem);

/**
 * down_trylock - try to acquire the semaphore, without waiting
 * @sem: the semaphore to be acquired
 *
 * Try to acquire the semaphore atomically.  Returns 0 if the semaphore has
 * been acquired successfully or 1 if it it cannot be acquired.
 *
 */
    int down_trylock(struct semaphore *sem);

/**
 * down_timeout - acquire the semaphore within a specified time
 * @sem: the semaphore to be acquired
 * @timeout: how long to wait before failing
 *
 * Attempts to acquire the semaphore.  If no more tasks are allowed to
 * acquire the semaphore, calling this function will put the task to sleep.
```

```
 * If the semaphore is not released within the specified number of jiffies,
 * this function returns -ETIME.  It returns 0 if the semaphore was
acquired.
 */
    int down_timeout(struct semaphore *sem, long timeout);

/**
 * up - release the semaphore
 * @sem: the semaphore to release
 *
 * Release the semaphore.  Unlike mutexes, up() may be called from any
 * context and even by tasks which have never called down().
 */
    void up(struct semaphore *sem);
```

Unlike mutex implementation, semaphore operations do not support debug checks or validations; this constraint is due to their inherent generic design which allows them to be used as exclusion locks, event notification counters, and so on. Ever since mutexes made their way into the kernel (2.6.16), semaphores are no longer the preferred choice for exclusion, and the use of semaphores as locks has considerably reduced, and for other purposes, the kernel has alternate interfaces. Most of the kernel code using semaphores has be converted into mutexes with a few minor exceptions. Yet semaphores still exist and are likely to remain at least until all of the kernel code using them is converted to mutex or other suitable interfaces.

Reader-writer semaphores

This interface is an implementation of sleeping reader-writer exclusion, which serves as an alternative for spinning ones. Reader-writer semaphores are represented by `struct rw_semaphore`, declared in the kernel header `<linux/rwsem.h>`:

```
struct rw_semaphore {
        atomic_long_t count;
        struct list_head wait_list;
        raw_spinlock_t wait_lock;
#ifdef CONFIG_RWSEM_SPIN_ON_OWNER
        struct optimistic_spin_queue osq; /* spinner MCS lock */
        /*
         * Write owner. Used as a speculative check to see
         * if the owner is running on the cpu.
         */
        struct task_struct *owner;
#endif
#ifdef CONFIG_DEBUG_LOCK_ALLOC
      struct lockdep_map dep_map;
```

```
#endif
};
```

This structure is identical to that of a mutex, and is designed to support optimistic spinning with osq; it also includes debug support through the kernel's *lockdep*. Count serves as an exclusion counter, which is set to 1, allowing a maximum of one writer to own the lock at a point in time. This works since mutual exclusion is only enforced between contending writers, and any number of readers can concurrently share the read lock. wait_lock is a spinlock which protects the semaphore wait_list.

An rw_semaphore can be instantiated and initialized statically through DECLARE_RWSEM(name), and alternatively, it can be dynamically initialized through init_rwsem(sem).

As with the case of rw-spinlocks, this interface too offers distinct routines for lock acquisition in reader and writer paths. Following is a list of interface operations:

```
/* reader interfaces */
    void down_read(struct rw_semaphore *sem);
    void up_read(struct rw_semaphore *sem);
/* trylock for reading -- returns 1 if successful, 0 if contention */
    int down_read_trylock(struct rw_semaphore *sem);
    void up_read(struct rw_semaphore *sem);

/* writer Interfaces */
    void down_write(struct rw_semaphore *sem);
    int __must_check down_write_killable(struct rw_semaphore *sem);

/* trylock for writing -- returns 1 if successful, 0 if contention */
    int down_write_trylock(struct rw_semaphore *sem);
    void up_write(struct rw_semaphore *sem);
/* downgrade write lock to read lock */
    void downgrade_write(struct rw_semaphore *sem);

/* check if rw-sem is currently locked */
    int rwsem_is_locked(struct rw_semaphore *sem);
```

These operations are implemented in the source file <kernel/locking/rwsem.c>; the code is quite self explanatory and we will not discuss it any further.

Sequence locks

Conventional reader-writer locks are designed with reader priority, and they might cause a writer task to wait for a non-deterministic duration, which might not be suitable on shared data with time-sensitive updates. This is where sequential lock comes in handy, as it aims at providing a quick and lock-free access to shared resources. Sequential locks are best when the resource that needs to be protected is small and simple, with write access being quick and non-frequent, as internally sequential locks fall back on the spinlock primitive.

Sequential locks introduce a special counter that is incremented every time a writer acquires a sequential lock along with a spinlock. After the writer completes, it releases the spinlock and increments the counter again and opens the access for other writers. For read, there are two types of readers: sequence readers and locking readers. The **sequence reader** checks for the counter before it enters the critical section and then checks again at the end of it without blocking any writer. If the counter remains the same, it implies that no writer had accessed the section during read, but if there is an increment of the counter at the end of the section, it is an indication that a writer had accessed, which calls for the reader to re-read the critical section for updated data. A **locking reader**, as the name implies, will get a lock and block other readers and writers when it is in progress; it will also wait when another locking reader or writer is in progress.

A sequence lock is represented by the following type:

```
typedef struct {
        struct seqcount seqcount;
        spinlock_t lock;
} seqlock_t;
```

We can initialize a sequence lock statically using the following macro:

```
#define DEFINE_SEQLOCK(x) \
            seqlock_t x = __SEQLOCK_UNLOCKED(x)
```

Actual initialization is done using the __SEQLOCK_UNLOCKED(x), which is defined here:

```
#define __SEQLOCK_UNLOCKED(lockname)                  \
    {                                                 \
            .seqcount = SEQCNT_ZERO(lockname),        \
            .lock = __SPIN_LOCK_UNLOCKED(lockname)    \
    }
```

To dynamically initialize sequence lock, we need to use the `seqlock_init` macro, which is defined as follows:

```
#define seqlock_init(x)                                  \
    do {                                                 \
            seqcount_init(&(x)->seqcount);               \
            spin_lock_init(&(x)->lock);                  \
    } while (0)
```

API

Linux provides many APIs for using sequence locks, which are defined in `</linux/seqlock.h>`. Some of the important ones are listed here:

```
static inline void write_seqlock(seqlock_t *sl)
{
        spin_lock(&sl->lock);
        write_seqcount_begin(&sl->seqcount);
}

static inline void write_sequnlock(seqlock_t *sl)
{
        write_seqcount_end(&sl->seqcount);
        spin_unlock(&sl->lock);
}

static inline void write_seqlock_bh(seqlock_t *sl)
{
        spin_lock_bh(&sl->lock);
        write_seqcount_begin(&sl->seqcount);
}

static inline void write_sequnlock_bh(seqlock_t *sl)
{
        write_seqcount_end(&sl->seqcount);
        spin_unlock_bh(&sl->lock);
}

static inline void write_seqlock_irq(seqlock_t *sl)
{
        spin_lock_irq(&sl->lock);
        write_seqcount_begin(&sl->seqcount);
}

static inline void write_sequnlock_irq(seqlock_t *sl)
{
```

```
            write_seqcount_end(&sl->seqcount);
            spin_unlock_irq(&sl->lock);
    }

    static inline unsigned long __write_seqlock_irqsave(seqlock_t *sl)
    {
            unsigned long flags;

            spin_lock_irqsave(&sl->lock, flags);
            write_seqcount_begin(&sl->seqcount);
            return flags;
    }
```

The following two functions are used for reading by starting and finalizing a read section:

```
    static inline unsigned read_seqbegin(const seqlock_t *sl)
    {
            return read_seqcount_begin(&sl->seqcount);
    }

    static inline unsigned read_seqretry(const seqlock_t *sl, unsigned start)
    {
            return read_seqcount_retry(&sl->seqcount, start);
    }
```

Completion locks

Completion locks are an efficient way to achieve code synchronization if you need one or multiple threads of execution to wait for completion of some event, such as waiting for another process to reach a point or state. Completion locks may be preferred over a semaphore for a couple of reasons: multiple threads of execution can wait for a completion, and using complete_all(), they can all be released at once. This is way better than a semaphore waking up to multiple threads. Secondly, semaphores can lead to race conditions if a waiting thread deallocates the synchronization object; this problem doesn't exist when using completion.

Completion can be used by including <linux/completion.h> and by creating a variable of type struct completion, which is an opaque structure for maintaining the state of completion. It uses a FIFO to queue the threads waiting for the completion event:

```
    struct completion {
            unsigned int done;
            wait_queue_head_t wait;
    };
```

Completion basically consists of initializing the completion structure, waiting through any of the variants of `wait_for_completion()` call, and finally signalling the completion through `complete()` or the `complete_all()` call. There are also functions to check the state of completions during its lifetime.

Initialization

The following macro can be used for static declaration and initialization of a completion structure:

```
#define DECLARE_COMPLETION(work) \
        struct completion work = COMPLETION_INITIALIZER(work)
```

The following inline function will initialize a dynamically created completion structure:

```
static inline void init_completion(struct completion *x)
{
        x->done = 0;
        init_waitqueue_head(&x->wait);
}
```

The following inline function will be used to reinitialize a completion structure if you need to reuse it. This can be used after `complete_all()`:

```
static inline void reinit_completion(struct completion *x)
{
        x->done = 0;
}
```

Waiting for completion

If any thread needs to wait for a task to complete, it will call `wait_for_completion()` on the initialized completion structure. If the `wait_for_completion` operation happens after the call to `complete()` or `complete_all()`, the thread simply continues, as the reason it wanted to wait for has been satisfied; else, it waits till `complete()` is signalled. There are variants available for the `wait_for_completion()` calls:

```
extern void wait_for_completion_io(struct completion *);
extern int wait_for_completion_interruptible(struct completion *x);
extern int wait_for_completion_killable(struct completion *x);
extern unsigned long wait_for_completion_timeout(struct completion *x,
                                            unsigned long timeout);
extern unsigned long wait_for_completion_io_timeout(struct completion *x,
                                            unsigned long timeout);
```

```
extern long wait_for_completion_interruptible_timeout(
        struct completion *x, unsigned long timeout);
extern long wait_for_completion_killable_timeout(
        struct completion *x, unsigned long timeout);
extern bool try_wait_for_completion(struct completion *x);
extern bool completion_done(struct completion *x);

extern void complete(struct completion *);
extern void complete_all(struct completion *);
```

Signalling completion

The execution thread that wants to signal the completion of the intended task calls `complete()` to a waiting thread so that it can continue. Threads will be awakened in the same order in which they were queued. In the case of multiple waiters, it calls `complete_all()`:

```
void complete(struct completion *x)
{
        unsigned long flags;

        spin_lock_irqsave(&x->wait.lock, flags);
        if (x->done != UINT_MAX)
                x->done++;
        __wake_up_locked(&x->wait, TASK_NORMAL, 1);
        spin_unlock_irqrestore(&x->wait.lock, flags);
}
EXPORT_SYMBOL(complete);
void complete_all(struct completion *x)
{
        unsigned long flags;

        spin_lock_irqsave(&x->wait.lock, flags);
        x->done = UINT_MAX;
        __wake_up_locked(&x->wait, TASK_NORMAL, 0);
        spin_unlock_irqrestore(&x->wait.lock, flags);
}
EXPORT_SYMBOL(complete_all);
```

Summary

Throughout this chapter, we not only understood the various protection and synchronization mechanisms provided by the kernel, but also made an underlying attempt at appreciating the effectiveness of these options, with their varied functionalities and shortcomings. Our takeaway from this chapter has to be the tenacity with which the kernel addresses these varying complexities for providing protection and synchronization of data. Another notable fact remains in the way the kernel maintains ease of coding along with design panache when tackling these issues.

In our next chapter, we will look at another crucial aspect of how interrupts are handled by the kernel.

9
Interrupts and Deferred Work

An **interrupt** is an electrical signal delivered to the processor indicating occurrence of a significant event that needs immediate attention. These signals can originate either from external hardware (connected to the system) or from circuits within the processor. In this chapter we will look into the kernel's interrupt management subsystem and explore the following:

- Programmable interrupt controllers
- Interrupt vector table
- IRQs
- IRQ chip and IRQ descriptors
- Registering and unregistering interrupt handlers
- IRQ line-control operations
- IRQ stacks
- Need for deferred routines
- Softirqs
- Tasklets
- Workqueues

Interrupt signals and vectors

When an interrupt originates from an external device, it is referred to as a **hardware interrupt**. These signals are generated by external hardware to seek the attention of the processor on occurrence of a significant external event, for instance a key hit on the keyboard, a click on a mouse button, or moving the mouse trigger hardware interrupts through which the processor is notified about the availability of data to be read. Hardware interrupts occur asynchronously with respect to the processor clock (meaning they can occur at random times), and hence are also termed as **asynchronous interrupts**.

Interrupts triggered from within the CPU due to events generated by program instructions currently in execution are referred to as **software interrupts**. A software interrupt is caused either by an **exception** triggered by program instructions currently in execution or on execution of a privileged instruction that raises an interrupt. For instance, when a program instruction attempts to divide a number by zero, the arithmetic logic unit of the processor raises an interrupt called a divide-by-zero exception. Similarly, when a program in execution intends to invoke a kernel service call, it executes a special instruction (sysenter) that raises an interrupt to shift the processor into privileged mode, which paves the path for the execution of the desired service call. These events occur synchronously with respect to the processor's clock and hence are also called **synchronous interrupts**.

In response to the occurrence of an interrupt event, CPUs are designed to preempt the current instruction sequence or thread of execution, and execute a special function called **interrupt service routine (ISR)**. To locate the appropriate *ISR* that corresponds to an interrupt event, **interrupt vector tables** are used. An **interrupt vector** is an address in memory that contains a reference to a software-defined **interrupt service** to be executed in response to an interrupt. Processor architectures define the total count of **interrupt vectors** supported, and describe the layout of each interrupt vector in memory. In general, for most processor architectures, all supported vectors are set up in memory as a list called an **interrupt vector table**, whose address is programmed into a processor register by the platform software.

Let's consider specifics of the *x86* architecture as an example for better understanding. The x86 family of processors supports a total of 256 interrupt vectors, of which the first 32 are reserved for processor exceptions and the rest used for software and hardware interrupts. Implementation of a vector table by x86 is referred to as an **interrupt descriptor table (IDT)**, which is an array of descriptors of either 8 byte (for 32-bit machines) or 16 byte (for 64-bit *x86* machines) sizes. During early boot, the architecture-specific branch of the kernel code sets up the **IDT** in memory and programs the **IDTR** register (special x86 register) of the processor with the physical start address and length of the **IDT**. When an interrupt occurs, the processor locates relevant vector descriptors by multiplying the reported vector number by the size of the vector descriptor (*vector number x 8* on x86_32 machines, and *vector no x 16* on x86_64 machines) and adding the result to the base address of the **IDT.** Once a valid *vector descriptor* is reached, the processor continues with the execution of actions specified within the descriptor.

On x86 platforms, each *vector descriptor* implements a *gate* (interrupt, task, or trap), which is used to transfer control of execution across segments. Vector descriptors representing hardware interrupts implement an *interrupt gate*, which refers to the base address and offset of the segment containing interrupt handler code. An *interrupt gate* disables all maskable interrupts before passing control to a specified interrupt handler. Vector descriptors representing *exceptions* and software interrupts implement a *trap gate*, which also refers to the location of code designated as a handler for the event. Unlike an *interrupt gate*, a *trap gate* does not disable maskable interrupts, which makes it suitable for execution of soft interrupt handlers.

Programmable interrupt controller

Now let's focus on external interrupts and explore how processors identify the occurrence of an external hardware interrupt, and how they discover the vector number associated with the interrupt. CPUs are designed with a dedicated input pin (intr pin) used to signal external interrupts. Each external hardware device capable of issuing interrupt requests usually consists of one or more output pins called **Interrupt Request lines (IRQ)**, used to signal an interrupt request on the CPU. All computing platforms use a hardware circuit called a **programmable interrupt controller (PIC)** to multiplex the CPU's interrupt pin across various interrupt request lines. All of the existing IRQ lines originating from on-board device controllers are routed to input pins of the interrupt controller, which monitors each IRQ line for an interrupt signal, and upon arrival of an interrupt, converts the request into a cpu-understandable vector number and relays the interrupt signal on to the CPU's interrupt pin. In simple words, a programmable interrupt controller multiplexes multiple device interrupt request lines into a single interrupt line of the processor:

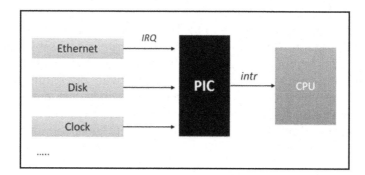

Design and implementation of interrupt controllers is platform specific. Intel *x86* multiprocessor platforms use **Advanced Programmable Interrupt Controller (APIC)**. The APIC design splits interrupt controller functionality into two distinct chipsets: the first component is an **I/O APIC** that resides on the system bus. All shared peripheral hardware IRQ lines are routed to the I/O APIC; this chip translates an interrupt request into vector code. The second is a per-CPU controller called **Local APIC** (usually integrated into the processor core) which delivers hardware interrupts to specific CPU cores. **I/O APIC** routes the interrupt events to a **Local APIC** of the chosen CPU core. It is programmed with a redirection table, which is used for making interrupt routing decisions. CPU **Local APICs** manage all external interrupts for a specific CPU core; additionally, they deliver events from CPU local hardware such as timers and can also receive and generate **inter-processor interrupts (IPIs)** that can occur on an SMP platform.

Interrupts and Deferred Work

The following diagram depicts the split architecture of **APIC**. The flow of events now begins with individual devices raising IRQ on the **I/O APIC**, which routes the request to a specific **Local APIC**, which in turn delivers the interrupt to a specific CPU core:

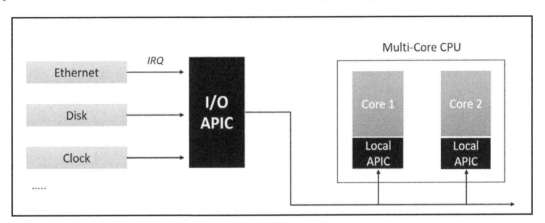

Similar to the **APIC** architecture, multicore ARM platforms split the **generic interrupt controller (GIC)** implementation into two. The first component is called a **distributor,** which is global to the system and has several peripheral hardware interrupt sources physically routed to it. The second component is replicated per-CPU and is called the **cpu interface**. The *distributor* component is programmed with distribution logic of **shared peripheral interrupts**(*SPI)* to known CPU interfaces.

Interrupt controller operations

The architecture-specific branch of the kernel code implements interrupt controller specific operations for management of IRQ lines such as masking/unmasking individual interrupts, setting priorities, and SMP affinity. These operations are required to be invoked from architecture-independent code paths of the kernel for manipulation of individual IRQ lines, and to facilitate such calls, the kernel defines an architecture-independent abstraction layer through a structure called `struct irq_chip`. This structure can be found in the kernel header `<include/linux/irq.h>`:

```
struct irq_chip {
    struct device *parent_device;
    const char    *name;
    unsigned int (*irq_startup)(struct irq_data *data);
    void (*irq_shutdown)(struct irq_data *data);
    void (*irq_enable)(struct irq_data *data);
    void (*irq_disable)(struct irq_data *data);
```

```
        void (*irq_ack)(struct irq_data *data);
        void (*irq_mask)(struct irq_data *data);
        void (*irq_mask_ack)(struct irq_data *data);
        void (*irq_unmask)(struct irq_data *data);
        void (*irq_eoi)(struct irq_data *data);

        int (*irq_set_affinity)(struct irq_data *data, const struct cpumask
                                *dest, bool force);
        int (*irq_retrigger)(struct irq_data *data);
        int (*irq_set_type)(struct irq_data *data, unsigned int flow_type);
        int (*irq_set_wake)(struct irq_data *data, unsigned int on);
        void (*irq_bus_lock)(struct irq_data *data);
        void (*irq_bus_sync_unlock)(struct irq_data *data);
        void (*irq_cpu_online)(struct irq_data *data);
        void (*irq_cpu_offline)(struct irq_data *data);
        void (*irq_suspend)(struct irq_data *data);
        void (*irq_resume)(struct irq_data *data);
        void (*irq_pm_shutdown)(struct irq_data *data);
        void (*irq_calc_mask)(struct irq_data *data);
        void (*irq_print_chip)(struct irq_data *data, struct seq_file *p);
        int (*irq_request_resources)(struct irq_data *data);
        void (*irq_release_resources)(struct irq_data *data);
        void (*irq_compose_msi_msg)(struct irq_data *data, struct msi_msg
*msg);
        void (*irq_write_msi_msg)(struct irq_data *data, struct msi_msg *msg);
        int (*irq_get_irqchip_state)(struct irq_data *data, enum
irqchip_irq_state which, bool *state);
        int (*irq_set_irqchip_state)(struct irq_data *data, enum
irqchip_irq_state which, bool state);

        int (*irq_set_vcpu_affinity)(struct irq_data *data, void *vcpu_info);
        void (*ipi_send_single)(struct irq_data *data, unsigned int cpu);
        void (*ipi_send_mask)(struct irq_data *data, const struct cpumask
*dest);        unsigned long flags;
};
```

The structure declares a set of function pointers to account for all peculiarities of IRQ chips found across various hardware platforms. Thus, a particular instance of the structure defined by board-specific code usually supports only a subset of possible operations. Following are x86 multicore platform versions of `irq_chip` instances defining operations of I/O APIC and LAPIC.

```
static struct irq_chip ioapic_chip __read_mostly = {
                .name          = "IO-APIC",
                .irq_startup   = startup_ioapic_irq,
                .irq_mask      = mask_ioapic_irq,
                .irq_unmask    = unmask_ioapic_irq,
```

```
        .irq_ack           = irq_chip_ack_parent,
        .irq_eoi           = ioapic_ack_level,
        .irq_set_affinity = ioapic_set_affinity,
        .irq_retrigger     = irq_chip_retrigger_hierarchy,
        .flags             = IRQCHIP_SKIP_SET_WAKE,
};


static struct irq_chip lapic_chip __read_mostly = {
        .name              = "local-APIC",
        .irq_mask          = mask_lapic_irq,
        .irq_unmask        = unmask_lapic_irq,
        .irq_ack           = ack_lapic_irq,
};
```

IRQ descriptor table

Another important abstraction is with respect to IRQ numbers associated with hardware interrupts. Interrupt controllers identify each IRQ source with a unique hardware IRQ number. The kernel's generic interrupt-management layer maps each hardware IRQ to a unique identifier called Linux IRQ; these numbers abstract hardware IRQs, thereby ensuring portability of kernel code. All of the peripheral device drivers are programmed to use the Linux IRQ number to bind or register their interrupt handlers.

Linux IRQs are represented by IRQ descriptor structure, which is defined by struct irq_desc; for each IRQ source, an instance of this structure is enumerated during early kernel boot. A list of IRQ descriptors is maintained in an array indexed by the IRQ number, called the IRQ descriptor table:

```
  struct irq_desc {
      struct irq_common_data    irq_common_data;
      struct irq_data           irq_data;
      unsigned int __percpu    *kstat_irqs;
      irq_flow_handler_t        handle_irq;
#ifdef CONFIG_IRQ_PREFLOW_FASTEOI
      irq_preflow_handler_t     preflow_handler;
#endif
      struct irqaction          *action;    /* IRQ action list */
      unsigned int              status_use_accessors;
      unsigned int              core_internal_state__do_not_mess_with_it;
      unsigned int              depth;    /* nested irq disables */
      unsigned int              wake_depth;/* nested wake enables */
      unsigned int              irq_count;/* For detecting broken IRQs */
      unsigned long             last_unhandled;
      unsigned int              irqs_unhandled;
```

```
        atomic_t                threads_handled;
        int                     threads_handled_last;
        raw_spinlock_t          lock;
        struct cpumask          *percpu_enabled;
        const struct cpumask    *percpu_affinity;
#ifdef CONFIG_SMP
        const struct cpumask        *affinity_hint;
        struct irq_affinity_notify  *affinity_notify;


        . . .
        . . .
        . . .
};
```

`irq_data` is an instance of `struct irq_data`, and this contains low-level information that is relevant for interrupt management, such as Linux IRQ number, hardware IRQ number, and a pointer to interrupt controller operations (`irq_chip`) among other important fields:

```
/**
 * struct irq_data - per irq chip data passed down to chip functions
 * @mask:          precomputed bitmask for accessing the chip registers
 * @irq:           interrupt number
 * @hwirq:         hardware interrupt number, local to the interrupt domain
 * @common:        point to data shared by all irqchips
 * @chip:          low level interrupt hardware access
 * @domain:        Interrupt translation domain; responsible for mapping
 *                 between hwirq number and linux irq number.
 * @parent_data:   pointer to parent struct irq_data to support hierarchy
 *                 irq_domain
 * @chip_data:     platform-specific per-chip private data for the chip
 *                 methods, to allow shared chip implementations
 */

struct irq_data {
        u32 mask;
        unsigned int irq;
        unsigned long hwirq;
        struct irq_common_data *common;
        struct irq_chip *chip;
        struct irq_domain *domain;
#ifdef CONFIG_IRQ_DOMAIN_HIERARCHY
        struct irq_data *parent_data;
#endif
        void *chip_data;
};
```

The `handle_irq` element of the `irq_desc` structure is a function pointer of type `irq_flow_handler_t`, which refers to a high-level function that deals with flow management on the line. The generic irq layer provides as set of predefined irq flow functions; an appropriate routine is assigned to each interrupt line based on its type.

- `handle_level_irq()`: Generic implementation for level-triggered interrupts
- `handle_edge_irq()`: Generic implementation for edge-triggered interrupts
- `handle_fasteoi_irq()`: Generic implementation for interrupts that only need an EOI at the end of the handler
- `handle_simple_irq()`: Generic implementation for simple interrupts
- `handle_percpu_irq()`: Generic implementation for per-CPU interrupts
- `handle_bad_irq()`: Used for spurious interrupts

The `*action` element of the `irq_desc` structure is a pointer to one or a chain of action descriptors, which contain driver-specific interrupt handlers among other important elements. Each action descriptor is an instance of `struct irqaction` defined in the kernel header `<linux/interrupt.h>`:

```
/**
 * struct irqaction - per interrupt action descriptor
 * @handler: interrupt handler function
 * @name: name of the device
 * @dev_id: cookie to identify the device
 * @percpu_dev_id: cookie to identify the device
 * @next: pointer to the next irqaction for shared interrupts
 * @irq: interrupt number
 * @flags: flags
 * @thread_fn: interrupt handler function for threaded interrupts
 * @thread: thread pointer for threaded interrupts
 * @secondary: pointer to secondary irqaction (force threading)
 * @thread_flags: flags related to @thread
 * @thread_mask: bitmask for keeping track of @thread activity
 * @dir: pointer to the proc/irq/NN/name entry
 */
struct irqaction {
        irq_handler_t handler;
        void * dev_id;
        void __percpu * percpu_dev_id;
        struct irqaction * next;
        irq_handler_t thread_fn;
        struct task_struct * thread;
        struct irqaction * secondary;
        unsigned int irq;
        unsigned int flags;
```

```
        unsigned long thread_flags;
        unsigned long thread_mask;
        const char * name;
        struct proc_dir_entry * dir;
};
```

High-level interrupt-management interfaces

The generic IRQ layer provides a set of function interfaces for device drivers to grab IRQ descriptors and bind interrupt handlers, release IRQs, enable or disable interrupt lines, and so on. We will explore all of the generic interfaces in this section.

Registering an interrupt handler

```
typedef irqreturn_t (*irq_handler_t)(int, void *);

/**
 * request_irq - allocate an interrupt line
 * @irq: Interrupt line to allocate
 * @handler: Function to be called when the IRQ occurs.
 * @irqflags: Interrupt type flags
 * @devname: An ascii name for the claiming device
 * @dev_id: A cookie passed back to the handler function
 */
int request_irq(unsigned int irq, irq_handler_t handler, unsigned long flags,
                const char *name, void *dev);
```

request_irq() instantiates an irqaction object with values passed as parameters and binds it to the irq_desc specified as the first (irq) parameter. This call allocates interrupt resources and enables the interrupt line and IRQ handling. handler is a function pointer of type irq_handler_t, which takes the address of a driver-specific interrupt handler routine. flags is a bitmask of options related to interrupt management. Flag bits are defined in the kernel header <linux/interrupt.h>:

- IRQF_SHARED: Used while binding an interrupt handler to a shared IRQ line.
- IRQF_PROBE_SHARED: Set by callers when they expect sharing mismatches to occur.
- IRQF_TIMER: Flag to mark this interrupt as a timer interrupt.
- IRQF_PERCPU: Interrupt is per CPU.
- IRQF_NOBALANCING: Flag to exclude this interrupt from IRQ balancing.

- `IRQF_IRQPOLL`: Interrupt is used for polling (only the interrupt that is registered first in a shared interrupt is considered for performance reasons).
- `IRQF_NO_SUSPEND`: Do not disable this IRQ during suspend. Does not guarantee that this interrupt will wake the system from a suspended state.
- `IRQF_FORCE_RESUME`: Force-enable it on resume even if `IRQF_NO_SUSPEND` is set.
- `IRQF_EARLY_RESUME`: Resume IRQ early during syscore instead of at device resume time.
- `IRQF_COND_SUSPEND`: If the IRQ is shared with a `NO_SUSPEND` user, execute this interrupt handler after suspending interrupts. For system wakeup devices, users need to implement wakeup detection in their interrupt handlers.

Since each flag value is a bit, a logical OR (that is, |) of a subset of these can be passed, and if none apply, then a value 0 for the `flags` parameter is valid. The address assigned to `dev` is considered as a unique cookie and serves as an identifier for the action instance in a shared IRQ case. The value of this parameter can be NULL while registering interrupt handlers without the `IRQF_SHARED` flag.

On success, `request_irq()` returns zero; a nonzero return value indicates failure to register the specified interrupt handler. The return error code `-EBUSY` denotes failure to register or bind the handler to a specified IRQ that is already in use.

Interrupt handler routines have the following prototype:

```
irqreturn_t handler(int irq, void *dev_id);
```

`irq` specifies the IRQ number, and `dev_id` is the unique cookie used while registering the handler. `irqreturn_t` is a typedef to an enumerated integer constant:

```
enum irqreturn {
        IRQ_NONE        = (0 << 0),
        IRQ_HANDLED             = (1 << 0),
        IRQ_WAKE_THREAD         = (1 << 1),
};

typedef enum irqreturn irqreturn_t;
```

The interrupt handler should return `IRQ_NONE` to indicate that the interrupt was not handled. It is also used to indicate that the source of the interrupt was not from its device in a shared IRQ case. When interrupt handling has completed normally, it must return `IRQ_HANDLED` to indicate success. `IRQ_WAKE_THREAD` is a special flag, returned to wake up the threaded handler; we elaborate on it in the next section.

Deregistering an interrupt handler

A driver's interrupt handlers can be deregistered through a call to the `free_irq()` routine:

```
/**
 * free_irq - free an interrupt allocated with request_irq
 * @irq: Interrupt line to free
 * @dev_id: Device identity to free
 *
 * Remove an interrupt handler. The handler is removed and if the
 * interrupt line is no longer in use by any driver it is disabled.
 * On a shared IRQ the caller must ensure the interrupt is disabled
 * on the card it drives before calling this function. The function
 * does not return until any executing interrupts for this IRQ
 * have completed.
 * Returns the devname argument passed to request_irq.
 */
const void *free_irq(unsigned int irq, void *dev_id);
```

`dev_id` is the unique cookie (assigned while registering the handler) to identify the handler to be deregistered in a shared IRQ case; this argument can be NULL for other cases. This function is a potential blocking call, and must not be invoked from an interrupt context: it blocks calling context until completion of any interrupt handler currently in execution, for the specified IRQ line.

Threaded interrupt handlers

Handlers registered through `request_irq()` are executed by the interrupt-handling path of the kernel. This code path is asynchronous, and runs by suspending scheduler preemption and hardware interrupts on the local processor, and so is referred to as a hard IRQ context. Thus, it is imperative to program the driver's interrupt handler routines to be short (do as little work as possible) and atomic (non blocking), to ensure responsiveness of the system. However, not all hardware interrupt handlers can be short and atomic: there are a magnitude of convoluted devices generating interrupt events, whose responses involve complex variable-time operations.

Conventionally, drivers are programmed to handle such complications with a split-handler design for the interrupt handler, called **top half** and **bottom half**. Top half routines are invoked in hard interrupt context, and these functions are programmed to execute *interrupt critical* operations, such as physical I/O on the hardware registers, and schedule the bottom half for deferred execution. Bottom half routines are usually programmed to deal with the rest of the *interrupt non-critical* and *deferrable work*, such as processing of data generated by the top half, interacting with process context, and accessing user address space. The kernel offers multiple mechanisms for scheduling and execution of bottom half routines, each with a distinct interface API and policy of execution. We'll elaborate on the design and usage details of formal bottom half mechanisms in the next section.

As an alternative to using formal bottom-half mechanisms, the kernel supports setting up interrupt handlers that can execute in a thread context, called **threaded interrupt handlers**. Drivers can set up threaded interrupt handlers through an alternate interface routine called `request_threaded_irq()`:

```
/**
 * request_threaded_irq - allocate an interrupt line
 * @irq: Interrupt line to allocate
 * @handler: Function to be called when the IRQ occurs.
 * Primary handler for threaded interrupts
 * If NULL and thread_fn != NULL the default
 * primary handler is installed
 * @thread_fn: Function called from the irq handler thread
 * If NULL, no irq thread is created
 * @irqflags: Interrupt type flags
 * @devname: An ascii name for the claiming device
 * @dev_id: A cookie passed back to the handler function
 */
    int request_threaded_irq(unsigned int irq, irq_handler_t handler,
                            irq_handler_t thread_fn, unsigned long
irqflags,
                            const char *devname, void *dev_id);
```

The function assigned to `handler` serves as the primary interrupt handler that executes in a hard IRQ context. The routine assigned to `thread_fn` is executed in a thread context, and is scheduled to run when the primary handler returns `IRQ_WAKE_THREAD`. With this split handler setup, there are two possible use cases: the primary handler can be programmed to execute interrupt-critical work and defer non-critical work to the thread handler for later execution, similar to that of the bottom half. The alternative is a design that defers the entire interrupt-handling code into the thread handler and restricts the primary handler only for verification of the interrupt source and waking up thread routine. This use case might require the corresponding interrupt line to be masked until completion of the thread handler, to avoid the nesting of interrupts. This can be accomplished either by programming the primary handler to turn off the interrupt at source before waking up the thread handler or through a flag bit `IRQF_ONESHOT` assigned while registering the threaded interrupt handler.

The following are `irqflags` related to threaded interrupt handlers:

- `IRQF_ONESHOT`: The interrupt is not re-enabled after the hard IRQ handler is finished. This is used by threaded interrupts that need to keep the IRQ line disabled until the threaded handler has been run.
- `IRQF_NO_THREAD`: The interrupt cannot be threaded. This is used in shared IRQs to restrict the use of threaded interrupt handlers.

A call to this routine with NULL assigned to `handler` will cause the kernel to use the default primary handler, which simply returns `IRQ_WAKE_THREAD`. And a call to this function with NULL assigned to `thread_fn` is synonymous with `request_irq()`:

```
static inline int __must_check
request_irq(unsigned int irq, irq_handler_t handler, unsigned long flags,
            const char *name, void *dev)
{
        return request_threaded_irq(irq, handler, NULL, flags, name, dev);
}
```

Another alternate interface for setting up an interrupt handler is `request_any_context_irq()`. This routine has a similar signature to that of `requeust_irq()` but slightly varies in its functionality:

```
/**
 * request_any_context_irq - allocate an interrupt line
 * @irq: Interrupt line to allocate
 * @handler: Function to be called when the IRQ occurs.
 * Threaded handler for threaded interrupts.
 * @flags: Interrupt type flags
 * @name: An ascii name for the claiming device
```

```
 * @dev_id: A cookie passed back to the handler function
 *
 * This call allocates interrupt resources and enables the
 * interrupt line and IRQ handling. It selects either a
 * hardirq or threaded handling method depending on the
 * context.
 * On failure, it returns a negative value. On success,
 * it returns either IRQC_IS_HARDIRQ or IRQC_IS_NESTED..
 */
int request_any_context_irq(unsigned int irq,irq_handler_t handler,
                            unsigned long flags,const char *name,void
*dev_id)
```

This function differs from `request_irq()` in that it looks into the IRQ descriptor for properties of the interrupt line as set up by the architecture-specific code, and decides whether to establish the function assigned as a traditional hard IRQ handler or as a threaded interrupt handler. On success, `IRQC_IS_HARDIRQ` is returned if the handler was established to run in hard IRQ context, or `IRQC_IS_NESTED` otherwise.

Control interfaces

The generic IRQ layer provides routines to carry out control operations on IRQ lines. Following is the list of functions for masking and unmasking specific IRQ lines:

```
void disable_irq(unsigned int irq);
```

This disables the specified IRQ line by manipulating the counter in the IRQ descriptor structure. This routine is a possible blocking call, as it waits until any running handlers for this interrupt complete. Alternatively, the function `disable_irq_nosync()` can also be used to *disable* the given IRQ line; this call does not check and wait for any running handlers for the given interrupt line to complete:

```
void disable_irq_nosync(unsigned int irq);
```

Disabled IRQ lines can be enabled with a call to:

```
void enable_irq(unsigned int irq);
```

Note that IRQ enable and disable operations nest, that is, multiple calls to *disable* an IRQ line require the same number of *enable* calls for that IRQ line to be reenabled. This means that `enable_irq()` will enable the given IRQ only when a call to it matches the last *disable* operation.

By choice, interrupts can also be disabled/enabled for the local CPU; the following pairs of macros can be used for the same:

- `local_irq_disable()`: To disable interrupts on the local processor.
- `local_irq_enable()`: Enables interrupts for the local processor.
- `local_irq_save(unsigned long flags)`: Disables interrupts on the local CPU by saving current interrupt state in *flags*.
- `local_irq_restore(unsigned long flags)`: Enables interrupts on the local CPU by restoring interrupts to a previous state.

IRQ stacks

Historically, for most architectures, interrupt handlers shared the kernel stack of the running process that was interrupted. As discussed in the first chapter, the process kernel stack is typically 8 KB for 32-bit architectures and 16 KB for 64-bit architectures. A fixed kernel stack might not always be enough for kernel work and IRQ processing routines, resulting in judicious allocation of data both by kernel code and interrupt handlers. To address this, the kernel build (for a few architectures) is configured by default to set up an additional per-CPU hard IRQ stack for use by interrupt handlers, and a per-CPU soft IRQ stack for use by software interrupt code. Following are the x86-64 bit architecture-specific stack declarations in kernel header `<arch/x86/include/asm/processor.h>`:

```
/*
 * per-CPU IRQ handling stacks
 */
struct irq_stack {
        u32                          stack[THREAD_SIZE/sizeof(u32)];
} __aligned(THREAD_SIZE);

DECLARE_PER_CPU(struct irq_stack *, hardirq_stack);
DECLARE_PER_CPU(struct irq_stack *, softirq_stack);
```

Apart from these, x86-64-bit builds also include special stacks; more details can be found in the kernel source documentation `<x86/kernel-stacks>`:

- Double fault stack
- Debug stack
- NMI stack
- Mce stack

Deferred work

As introduced in an earlier section, **bottom halves** are kernel mechanisms for executing deferred work, and can be engaged by any kernel code to defer execution of non-critical work until some time in the future. To support implementation and for management of deferred routines, the kernel implements special frameworks, called **softirqs**, **tasklets**, and **work queues**. Each of these frameworks constitute a set of data structures, and function interfaces, used for registering, scheduling, and queuing of the bottom half routines. Each mechanism is designed with a distinct *policy* for management and execution of bottom halfs. Drivers and other kernel services that require deferred execution will need to bind and schedule their BH routines through the appropriate framework.

Softirqs

The term **softirq** loosely translates to **soft interrupt**, and as the name suggests, deferred routines managed by this framework are executed at a high priority but with hard interrupt lines enabled. Thus, softirq bottom halves (or softirqs) can preempt all other tasks except hard interrupt handlers. However, usage of softirqs is restricted to static kernel code and this mechanism is not available for dynamic kernel modules.

Each softirq is represented through an instance of type `struct softirq_action` declared in the kernel header `<linux/interrupt.h>`. This structure contains a function pointer that can hold the address of the bottom half routine:

```
struct softirq_action
{
        void (*action)(struct softirq_action *);
};
```

Current versions of the kernel have 10 softirqs, each indexed through an enum in the kernel header `<linux/interrupt.h>`. These indexes serve as an identity and are treated as the relative priority of the softirq, and entries with lower indexes are considered higher in priority, with index 0 being the highest priority softirq:

```
enum
{
        HI_SOFTIRQ=0,
        TIMER_SOFTIRQ,
        NET_TX_SOFTIRQ,
        NET_RX_SOFTIRQ,
        BLOCK_SOFTIRQ,
        IRQ_POLL_SOFTIRQ,
        TASKLET_SOFTIRQ,
```

```
            SCHED_SOFTIRQ,
            HRTIMER_SOFTIRQ, /* Unused, but kept as tools rely on the
                                 numbering. Sigh! */
            RCU_SOFTIRQ, /* Preferable RCU should always be the last softirq */

            NR_SOFTIRQS
    };
```

The kernel source file `<kernel/softirq.c>` declares an array called `softirq_vec` of size `NR_SOFTIRQS`, with each offset containing a `softirq_action` instance of the corresponding softirq indexed in the enum:

```
    static struct softirq_action softirq_vec[NR_SOFTIRQS]
    __cacheline_aligned_in_smp;

    /* string constants for naming each softirq */
    const char * const softirq_to_name[NR_SOFTIRQS] = {
            "HI", "TIMER", "NET_TX", "NET_RX", "BLOCK", "IRQ_POLL",
            "TASKLET", "SCHED", "HRTIMER", "RCU"
    };
```

Framework provides a function `open_softriq()` used for initializing the softirq instance with the corresponding bottom-half routine:

```
    void open_softirq(int nr, void (*action)(struct softirq_action *))
    {
            softirq_vec[nr].action = action;
    }
```

`nr` is the index of the softirq to be initialized and `*action` is a function pointer to be initialized with the address of the bottom-half routine. The following code excerpt is taken from the timer service, and shows the invocation of `open_softirq` to register a softirq:

```
    /*kernel/time/timer.c*/
    open_softirq(TIMER_SOFTIRQ, run_timer_softirq);
```

Kernel services can signal the execution of softirq handlers using a function `raise_softirq()`. This function takes the index of the softirq as an argument:

```
    void raise_softirq(unsigned int nr)
    {
            unsigned long flags;

            local_irq_save(flags);
            raise_softirq_irqoff(nr);
            local_irq_restore(flags);
    }
```

The following code excerpt is from `<kernel/time/timer.c>`:

```
void run_local_timers(void)
{
        struct timer_base *base = this_cpu_ptr(&timer_bases[BASE_STD]);

        hrtimer_run_queues();
        /* Raise the softirq only if required. */
        if (time_before(jiffies, base->clk)) {
                if (!IS_ENABLED(CONFIG_NO_HZ_COMMON) || !base->nohz_active)
                        return;
                /* CPU is awake, so check the deferrable base. */
                base++;
                if (time_before(jiffies, base->clk))
                        return;
        }
        raise_softirq(TIMER_SOFTIRQ);
}
```

The kernel maintains a per-CPU bitmask for keeping track of softirqs raised for execution, and the function `raise_softirq()` sets the corresponding bit (index mentioned as argument) in the local CPUs softirq bitmask to mark the specified softirq as pending.

Pending softirq handlers are checked and executed at various points in the kernel code. Principally, they are executed in the interrupt context, immediately after the completion of hard interrupt handlers with IRQ lines enabled. This guarantees swift processing of softirqs raised from hard interrupt handlers, resulting in optimal cache usage. However, the kernel allows an arbitrary task to suspend execution of softirq processing on a local processor either through `local_bh_disable()` or `spin_lock_bh()` calls. Pending softirq handlers are executed in the context of an arbitrary task that re-enables softirq processing by invoking either `local_bh_enable()` or `spin_unlock_bh()` calls. And lastly, softirq handlers can also be executed by a per-CPU kernel thread `ksoftirqd`, which is woken up when a softirq is raised by any process-context kernel routine. This thread is also woken up from the interrupt context when too many softirqs accumulate due to high load.

Softirqs are most suitable for completion of priority work deferred from hard interrupt handlers since they run immediately on completion of hard interrupt handlers. However, softirqs handlers are reentrant, and must be programmed to engage appropriate protection mechanisms while accessing data structures, if any. The reentrant nature of softirqs may cause unbounded latencies, impacting the efficiency of the system as a whole, which is why their usage is restricted, and new ones are almost never added, unless it is absolute necessity for the execution of high-frequency threaded deferred work. For all other types of deferred work, tasklets and work queues are suggested.

Tasklets

The **tasklet** mechanism is a sort of wrapper around the softirq framework; in fact, tasklet handlers are executed by softirqs. Unlike softirqs, tasklets are not reentrant, which guarantees that the same tasklet handler can never run concurrently. This helps minimize overall latencies, provided programmers examine and impose relevant checks to ensure that work done in a tasklet is non-blocking and atomic. Another difference is with respect to their usage: unlike softirqs (which are restricted), any kernel code can use tasklets, and this includes dynamically linked services.

Each tasklet is represented through an instance of type `struct tasklet_struct` declared in kernel header `<linux/interrupt.h>`:

```
struct tasklet_struct
{
        struct tasklet_struct *next;
        unsigned long state;
        atomic_t count;
        void (*func)(unsigned long);
        unsigned long data;
};
```

Upon initialization, `*func` holds the address of the handler routine and `data` is used to pass a data blob as a parameter to the handler routine during invocation. Each tasklet carries a `state`, which can be either `TASKLET_STATE_SCHED`, which indicates that it is scheduled for execution, or `TASKLET_STATE_RUN`, which indicates it is in execution. An atomic counter is used to *enable* or *disable* a tasklet; when `count` equals a *non-zero* value, it indicates that the tasklet is *disabled,* and *zero* indicates that it is *enabled*. A disabled tasklet cannot be executed even if scheduled, until it is enabled at some future time.

Kernel services can instantiate a new tasklet statically through any of the following macros:

```
#define DECLARE_TASKLET(name, func, data) \
struct tasklet_struct name = { NULL, 0, ATOMIC_INIT(0), func, data }

#define DECLARE_TASKLET_DISABLED(name, func, data) \
struct tasklet_struct name = { NULL, 0, ATOMIC_INIT(1), func, data }
```

New tasklets can be instantiated dynamically at runtime through the following:

```
void tasklet_init(struct tasklet_struct *t,
                  void (*func)(unsigned long), unsigned long data)
{
        t->next = NULL;
        t->state = 0;
        atomic_set(&t->count, 0);
```

```
        t->func = func;
        t->data = data;
}
```

The kernel maintains two per-CPU tasklet lists for queuing scheduled tasklets, and the definitions of these lists can be found in the source file `<kernel/softirq.c>`:

```
/*
 * Tasklets
 */
struct tasklet_head {
        struct tasklet_struct *head;
        struct tasklet_struct **tail;
};

static DEFINE_PER_CPU(struct tasklet_head, tasklet_vec);
static DEFINE_PER_CPU(struct tasklet_head, tasklet_hi_vec);
```

`tasklet_vec` is considered normal list, and all queued tasklets present in this list are run by `TASKLET_SOFTIRQ` (one of the 10 softirqs). `tasklet_hi_vec` is a high-priority tasklet list, and all queued tasklets present in this list are executed by `HI_SOFTIRQ`, which happens to be the highest priority softirq. A tasklet can be queued for execution into the appropriate list by invoking `tasklet_schedule()` or `tasklet_hi_scheudule()`.

The following code shows the implementation of `tasklet_schedule()`; this function is invoked with the address of the tasklet instance to be queued as a parameter:

```
extern void __tasklet_schedule(struct tasklet_struct *t);

static inline void tasklet_schedule(struct tasklet_struct *t)
{
        if (!test_and_set_bit(TASKLET_STATE_SCHED, &t->state))
                __tasklet_schedule(t);
}
```

The conditional construct checks if the specified tasklet is already scheduled; if not, it atomically sets the state to `TASKLET_STATE_SCHED` and invokes `__tasklet_shedule()` to enqueue the tasklet instance into the pending list. If the specified tasklet is already found to be in the `TASKLET_STATE_SCHED` state, it is not rescheduled:

```
void __tasklet_schedule(struct tasklet_struct *t)
{
        unsigned long flags;

        local_irq_save(flags);
        t->next = NULL;
        *__this_cpu_read(tasklet_vec.tail) = t;
```

```
        __this_cpu_write(tasklet_vec.tail, &(t->next));
        raise_softirq_irqoff(TASKLET_SOFTIRQ);
        local_irq_restore(flags);
}
```

This function silently enqueues the specified tasklet to the tail of the `tasklet_vec` and raises the `TASKLET_SOFTIRQ` on the local processor.

Following is the code for the `tasklet_hi_scheudle()` routine:

```
extern void __tasklet_hi_schedule(struct tasklet_struct *t);

static inline void tasklet_hi_schedule(struct tasklet_struct *t)
{
        if (!test_and_set_bit(TASKLET_STATE_SCHED, &t->state))
                __tasklet_hi_schedule(t);
}
```

Actions executed in this routine are similar to that of `tasklet_schedule()`, with an exception that it invokes `__tasklet_hi_scheudle()` to enqueue the specified tasklet into the tail of `tasklet_hi_vec`:

```
void __tasklet_hi_schedule(struct tasklet_struct *t)
{
        unsigned long flags;

        local_irq_save(flags);
        t->next = NULL;
        *__this_cpu_read(tasklet_hi_vec.tail) = t;
        __this_cpu_write(tasklet_hi_vec.tail, &(t->next));
        raise_softirq_irqoff(HI_SOFTIRQ);
        local_irq_restore(flags);
}
```

This call raises `HI_SOFTIRQ` on the local processor, which turns all tasklets queued in `tasklet_hi_vec` into the highest-priority bottom halves (higher in priority over the rest of the softirqs).

Another variant is `tasklet_hi_schedule_first()`, which inserts the specified tasklet to the head of `tasklet_hi_vec` and raises `HI_SOFTIRQ`:

```
extern void __tasklet_hi_schedule_first(struct tasklet_struct *t);


 */
static inline void tasklet_hi_schedule_first(struct tasklet_struct *t)
{
```

```
            if (!test_and_set_bit(TASKLET_STATE_SCHED, &t->state))
                    __tasklet_hi_schedule_first(t);
}

/*kernel/softirq.c */
void __tasklet_hi_schedule_first(struct tasklet_struct *t)
{
        BUG_ON(!irqs_disabled());
        t->next = __this_cpu_read(tasklet_hi_vec.head);
        __this_cpu_write(tasklet_hi_vec.head, t);
        __raise_softirq_irqoff(HI_SOFTIRQ);
}
```

Other interface routines exist that are used to enable, disable, and kill scheduled tasklets.

```
void tasklet_disable(struct tasklet_struct *t);
```

This function disables the specified tasklet by incrementing its *disable count*. The tasklet may still be scheduled, but it is not executed until it has been enabled again. If the tasklet is currently running when this call is invoked, this function busy-waits until the tasklet completes.

```
void tasklet_enable(struct tasklet_struct *t);
```

This attempts to enable a tasklet that had been previously disabled by decrementing its *disable count*. If the tasklet has already been scheduled, it will run soon:

```
void tasklet_kill(struct tasklet_struct *t);
```

This function is called to kill the given tasklet, to ensure that the it cannot be scheduled to run again. If the tasklet specified is already scheduled by the time this call is invoked, then this function waits until its execution completes:

```
void tasklet_kill_immediate(struct tasklet_struct *t, unsigned int cpu);
```

This function is called to kill an already scheduled tasklet. It immediately removes the specified tasklet from the list even if the tasklet is in the TASKLET_STATE_SCHED state.

Workqueues

Workqueues (wqs) are mechanisms for the execution of asynchronous process context routines. As the name aptly suggests, a workqueue (wq) is a list of *work* items, each containing a function pointer that takes the address of a routine to be executed asynchronously. Whenever some kernel code (that belongs to a subsystem or a service) intends to defer some work for asynchronous process context execution, it must initialize the *work* item with the address of the handler function, and enqueue it onto a workqueue. The kernel uses a dedicated pool of kernel threads, called *kworker* threads, to execute functions bound to each *work* item in the queue, sequentially.

Interface API

The workqueue API offers two types of functions interfaces: first, a set of interface routines to instantiate and queue *work* items onto a global workqueue, which is shared by all kernel subsystems and services, and second, a set of interface routines to set up a new workqueue, and queue work items onto it. We will begin to explore workqueue interfaces with macros and functions related to the global shared workqueue.

Each *work* item in the queue is represented by an instance of type `struct work_struct`, which is declared in the kernel header `<linux/workqueue.h>`:

```
struct work_struct {
        atomic_long_t data;
        struct list_head entry;
        work_func_t func;
#ifdef CONFIG_LOCKDEP
        struct lockdep_map lockdep_map;
#endif
};
```

`func` is a pointer that takes the address of the deferred routine; a new struct work object can be created and initialized through macro `DECLARE_WORK`:

```
#define DECLARE_WORK(n, f) \
  struct work_struct n = __WORK_INITIALIZER(n, f)
```

`n` is the name of the instance to be created and `f` is the address of the function to be assigned. A work instance can be scheduled into the workqueue through `schedule_work()`:

```
bool schedule_work(struct work_struct *work);
```

This function enqueues the given *work* item on the local CPU workqueue, but does not guarantee its execution on it. It returns *true* if the given *work* is successfully enqueued, or *false* if the given *work* is already found in the workqueue. Once queued, the function associated with the *work* item is executed on any of the available CPUs by the relevant `kworker` thread. Alternatively, a *work* item can be marked for execution on a specific CPU, while scheduling it into the queue (which might yield better cache utilization); this can be done with a call to `scheudule_work_on()`:

```
bool schedule_work_on(int cpu, struct work_struct *work);
```

`cpu` is the identifier to which the *work* task is to be bound. For instance, to schedule a *work* task onto a local CPU, the caller can invoke:

```
schedule_work_on(smp_processor_id(), &t_work);
```

`smp_processor_id()` is a kernel macro (defined in `<linux/smp.h>`) that returns the local CPU identifier.

The interface API also offers a variant of scheduling calls, which allow the caller to queue *work* tasks whose execution is guaranteed to be delayed at least until a specified timeout. This is achieved by binding a *work* task with a timer, which can be initialized with an expiry timeout, until which time the *work* task is not scheduled into the queue:

```
struct delayed_work {
        struct work_struct work;
        struct timer_list timer;

        /* target workqueue and CPU ->timer uses to queue ->work */
        struct workqueue_struct *wq;
        int cpu;
};
```

`timer` is an instance of a dynamic timer descriptor, which is initialized with the expiry interval and armed while scheduling a *work* task. We'll discuss kernel timers and other time-related concepts more in the next chapter.

Callers can instantiate `delayed_work` and initialize it statically through a macro:

```
#define DECLARE_DELAYED_WORK(n, f) \
        struct delayed_work n = __DELAYED_WORK_INITIALIZER(n, f, 0)
```

Similar to normal *work* tasks, delayed *work* tasks can be scheduled to run on any of the available CPUs or be scheduled to execute on a specified core. To schedule delayed *work* that can run on any of the available processors, callers can invoke `schedule_delayed_work()`, and to schedule delayed *work* onto specific CPUs, use the function `schedule_delayed_work_on()`:

```
bool schedule_delayed_work(struct delayed_work *dwork,unsigned long delay);
bool schedule_delayed_work_on(int cpu, struct delayed_work *dwork,
                                                    unsigned long
delay);
```

Note that if the delay is zero, then the specified *work* item is scheduled for immediate execution.

Creating dedicated workqueues

Timing of the execution of *work* items scheduled onto the global workqueue is not predictable: one long-running *work* item can always cause indefinite delays for the rest. Alternatively, the workqueue framework allows the allocation of dedicated workqueues, which can be owned by a kernel subsystem or a service. Interface APIs used to create and schedule work into these queues provide control flags, through which owners can set special attributes such as CPU locality, concurrency limits, and priority, which have an influence on the execution of work items queued.

A new workqueue can be set up through a call to `alloc_workqueue()`; the following excerpt taken from `<fs/nfs/inode.c>` shows sample usage:

```
struct workqueue_struct *wq;
...
wq = alloc_workqueue("nfsiod", WQ_MEM_RECLAIM, 0);
```

This call takes three arguments: the first is a string constant to `name` the workqueue. The second argument is the bitfield of `flags`, and the third an integer called `max_active`. The last two are used to specify control attributes of the queue. On success, this function returns the address of the workqueue descriptor.

The following is a list of flag options:

- `WQ_UNBOUND`: Workqueues created with this flag are managed by kworker-pools that are not bound to any specific CPU. This causes all *work* items scheduled to this queue to run on any available processor. *Work* items in this queue are executed as soon as possible by kworker pools.
- `WQ_FREEZABLE`: A workqueue of this type is freezable, which means that it is affected by system suspend operations. During suspend, all current *work* items are drained and no new *work* item can run until the system is unfreezed or resumed.
- `WQ_MEM_RECLAIM`: This flag is used to mark a workqueue that contains *work* items involved in memory reclaim paths. This causes the framework to ensure that there is always a *worker* thread available to run *work* items on this queue.
- `WQ_HIGHPRI`: This flag is used to mark a workqueue as high priority. Work items in high-priority workqueues have a higher precedence over normal ones, in that these are executed by a high-priority pool of *kworker* threads. The kernel maintains a dedicated pool of high-priority kworker threads for each CPU, which are distinct from normal kworker pools.
- `WQ_CPU_INTENSIVE`: This flag marks work items on this workqueue to be CPU intensive. This helps the system scheduler to regulate the execution of *work* items that are expected to hog the CPU for long intervals. This means runnable CPU-intensive *work* items will not prevent other work items in the same kworker-pool from starting. A runnable non-CPU-intensive *work* item can always delay the execution of *work* items marked as CPU intensive. This flag is meaningless for an unbound wq.
- `WQ_POWER_EFFICIENT`: Workqueues marked with this flag are per-CPU by default, but become unbound if the system was booted with the `workqueue.power_efficient` kernel param set. Per-CPU workqueues that are identified to contribute significantly to power consumption are identified and marked with this flag, and enabling the power_efficient mode leads to noticeable power savings at the cost of a slight performance penalty.

The final argument `max_active` is an integer, which must specify the count of *work* items that can be executed simultaneously from this workqueue on any given CPU.

Once a dedicated workqueue is set up, *work* items can be scheduled through any of the following calls:

```
bool queue_work(struct workqueue_struct *wq, struct work_struct *work);
```

wq is a pointer to a queue; it enqueues the specified *work* item on the local CPU, but does not guarantee execution on local processor. This call returns *true* if the given work item is successfully queued, and *false* if the given work item is already scheduled.

Alternatively, callers can enqueue a work item bound to a specific CPU with a call to:

```
bool queue_work_on(int cpu,struct workqueue_struct *wq,struct work_struct
                                                             *work);
```

Once a work item is enqueued into a workqueue of the specified cpu, it returns *true* if the given work item is successfully queued and *false* if the given work item is already found in the queue.

Similar to shared workqueue APIs, delayed scheduling options also are available for dedicated workqueues. The following calls are to be used for delayed scheduling of *work* items:

```
bool queue_delayed_work_on(int cpu, struct workqueue_struct *wq, struct
delayed_work *dwork,unsigned long delay);
```

```
bool queue_delayed_work(struct workqueue_struct *wq, struct delayed_work
*dwork, unsigned long delay
```

Both calls delay scheduling of the given work until the timeout specified by the delay has elapsed, with the exception that queue_delayed_work_on() enqueues the given *work* item on the specified CPU and guarantees its execution on it. Note that if the delay specified is zero and the workqueue is idle, then the given *work* item is scheduled for immediate execution.

Summary

Through this chapter, we have touched base with interrupts, the various components that fabricate the whole infrastructure, and how the kernel manages it efficiently. We understood how the kernel engages abstraction to smoothly handle varied interrupt signals routed from various controllers. The kernel's effort in simplifying complex programming approaches is again brought to the fore through the high-level interrupt-management interfaces. We also stretched our understanding on all the key routines and important data structures of the interrupt subsystem. We also explored kernel mechanisms for handling deferred work.

In the next chapter, we will explore the kernel's timekeeping subsystem to understand key concepts such as time measurement, interval timers, and timeout and delay routines.

10
Clock and Time Management

The Linux time management subsystem manages various time-related activities and keeps track of timing data such as current time and date, time elapsed since system boot up (system uptime) and timeouts, for example, how long to wait for a particular event to be initiated or terminated, locking the system after a timeout period has elapsed, or raising a signal to kill an unresponsive process.

There are two types of timing activities handled by the Linux time management subsystem:

- Keeping the current time and date
- Maintaining timers

Time representation

Depending on the use cases, time is represented in three different ways in Linux:

1. **Wall time (or real time):** This is the actual time and date in the real world, such as 07:00 AM, 10 Aug 2017, and is used for timestamps on files and packets sent through the network.
2. **Process time:** This is the time consumed by a process in its life span. It includes the time consumed by the process in user mode and the time consumed by the kernel code when executing on behalf of the process. This is useful for statistical purposes, auditing, and profiling.
3. **Monotonic time:** This is the time elapsed since system bootup. It's ever incrementing and monotonic in nature (system uptime).

These three times are measured in either of the following ways:

1. **Relative time:** This is the time relative to some specific event, such as 7 minutes since system bootup, or 2 minutes since last input from user.
2. **Absolute time:** This is a unique point in time without any reference to a previous event, such as 10:00 AM, 12 Aug 2017. In Linux, absolute time is represented as the number of elapsed seconds since 00:00:00 midnight of 1 January 1970 (UTC)

Wall time is ever incrementing (unless it has been modified by the user), even between reboots and shutdowns, but process time and system uptime start from some predefined point in time (*usually zero*) every time a new process is created or when the system starts.

Timing hardware

Linux relies on appropriate hardware devices to maintain time. These hardware devices can be categorized broadly into two types: system clock and timers.

Real-time clock (RTC)

Keeping track of the current time and date is very crucial, not just to let the user know about it but to use it as a timestamp for various resources in the system, specifically, files present in secondary storage. Every file has metadata information such as the date of creation and last modification date, and every time a file is created or modified, these two fields are updated with the current time in the system. These fields are used by several apps to manage files such as to sort, group, or even delete them (if the file hasn't been accessed a for long time). The *make* tool uses this timestamp to determine whether a source file has been edited since the last time it accessed it; only then is it compiled, otherwise left untouched.

The system clock RTC keeps track of the current time and date; backed by an additional battery, it continues to tick even when the system is turned off.

RTC can raise interrupts on IRQ8 periodically. This feature can be used as an alarm facility, by programming the RTC to raise interrupt on IRQ8 when it reaches a specific time. In IBM-compatible PCs, the RTC is mapped to the 0x70 and 0x71 I/O ports. It can be accessed through the /dev/rtc device file.

Timestamp counter (TSC)

This is a counter implemented in every x86 microprocessor by means of a 64-bit register called TSC the register. It counts the number of clock signals arriving on the CLK pin of the processor. The current counter value can be read by accessing the TSC register. The number of ticks counted per second can be calculated as 1/(clock frequency); for a 1 GHz clock it translates to once every nanosecond.

Knowing the duration between two consecutive ticks is very crucial. The fact that one processor clock's frequency might not be the same as others makes it vary across processors. CPU clock frequency is calculated during system boot by the `calibrate_tsc()` callback routine of the x86_platform_ops structure defined in the `arch/x86/include/asm/x86_init.h` header file:

```
struct x86_platform_ops {
        unsigned long (*calibrate_cpu)(void);
        unsigned long (*calibrate_tsc)(void);
        void (*get_wallclock)(struct timespec *ts);
        int (*set_wallclock)(const struct timespec *ts);
        void (*iommu_shutdown)(void);
        bool (*is_untracked_pat_range)(u64 start, u64 end);
        void (*nmi_init)(void);
        unsigned char (*get_nmi_reason)(void);
        void (*save_sched_clock_state)(void);
        void (*restore_sched_clock_state)(void);
        void (*apic_post_init)(void);
        struct x86_legacy_features legacy;
        void (*set_legacy_features)(void);
};
```

This data structure manages other timing operations too, such as getting time from the RTC through `get_wallclock()` or setting time on the RTC through the `set_wallclock()` callback.

Programmable interrupt timer (PIT)

There are certain tasks that need to be carried out by the kernel at regular intervals, such as:

- Updating the current time and date (at midnight)
- Updating the system running time (uptime)
- Keeping track of the time consumed by each process so that they don't exceed the time allotted to run on the CPU
- Keeping track of various timer activities

In order to carry out these tasks, interrupts must be periodically raised. Every time this periodic interrupt is raised, the kernel knows it's time to update the aforementioned timing data. The PIT is the piece of hardware responsible for issuing this periodic interrupt, called timer interrupt. The PIT keeps on issuing timer interrupts on IRQ0 periodically at approximately 1000 Hz frequency, once every millisecond. This periodic interrupt is called the **tick** and the frequency at which it's issued is called the **tick rate**. The tick rate frequency is defined by the kernel macro **HZ** and is measured in hertz.

System responsiveness depends on the tick rate: the shorter the ticks, the more responsive a system would be, and vice versa. With shorter ticks, `poll()` and `select()` system calls will have a faster response time. However, the considerable drawback of a shorter tick rate is that the CPU will be working in kernel mode (executing the interrupt handler for the timer interrupt) most of the time, leaving less time for user-mode code (programs) to execute on it. In a high-performance CPU, it wouldn't be much of an overhead, but in slower CPUs, the overall system performance would be affected considerably.

To reach a balance between response time and system performance, a tick rate of 100 Hz is used in most machines. Except for *Alpha* and *m68knommu*, which use a 1000 Hz tick rate, the rest of the common architectures, including *x86* (arm, powerpc, sparc, mips, and so on) use a 100 Hz tick rate. Common PIT hardware found in *x86* machines is Intel 8253. It's I/O mapped and accessed through addresses 0x40 – 0x43. The PIT is initialized by `setup_pit_timer()`, defined in the `arch/x86/kernel/i8253.c` file:

```
void __init setup_pit_timer(void)
{
        clockevent_i8253_init(true);
        global_clock_event = &i8253_clockevent;
}
```

This calls `clockevent_i8253_init()` internally, defined in `<drivers/clocksource/i8253.c>`:

```
void __init clockevent_i8253_init(bool oneshot)
```

```
{
        if (oneshot)
                i8253_clockevent.features |= CLOCK_EVT_FEAT_ONESHOT;
        /*
        * Start pit with the boot cpu mask. x86 might make it global
        * when it is used as broadcast device later.
        */
        i8253_clockevent.cpumask = cpumask_of(smp_processor_id());

        clockevents_config_and_register(&i8253_clockevent, PIT_TICK_RATE,
                                        0xF, 0x7FFF);
}
#endif
```

CPU local timer

PIT is a global timer, and interrupts raised by it that can be handled by any CPU in an SMP system. In some cases, having such a common timer is beneficial, whereas in other cases, a per-CPU timer is more desirable. In an SMP system, keeping process time and monitoring allotted time slices to a process in each CPU would be much easier and efficient with a local timer.

Local APIC in recent x86 microprocessors embeds such a CPU local timer. A CPU local timer can issue interrupts either once or periodically. It uses a 32-bit timer and can issue interrupts at a very low frequency (this wider counter allows more ticks to occur before an interrupt is raised). The APIC timer works with the bus clock signal. The APIC timer is quite similar to PIT except that it's local to the CPU, has a 32-bit counter (PIT has a 16-bit one), and works with the bus clock signal (PIT uses its own clock signal).

High-precision event timer (HPET)

The HPET works with clock signals in excess of 10 Mhz, issuing interrupts once every 100 nano seconds, hence the name high-precision. HPET implements a 64-bit main counter to count at such a high frequency. It was co-developed by Intel and Microsoft for the need of a new high-resolution timer. HPET embeds a collection of timers. Each of them is capable of issuing interrupts independently, and can be used by specific applications as assigned by the kernel. These timers are managed as groups of timers, where each group can have a maximum of 32 timers in it. An HPET can implement maximum of 8 such groups. Each timer has a set of *comparator* and *match register*. A timer issues an interrupt when the value in its match register matches the value of the main counter. Timers can be programmed to generate interrupts either once or periodically.

Registers are memory mapped and have relocatable address space. During system bootup, the BIOS sets up the registers' address space and passes it to the kernel. Once the BIOS maps the address, it's seldom remapped by the kernel.

ACPI power management timer (ACPI PMT)

The ACPI PMT is a simple counter that has a fixed frequency clock at 3.58 Mhz. It increments on each tick. The PMT is port mapped; the BIOS takes care of address mapping in the hardware initialization phase during bootup. The PMT is more reliable than the TSC, as it works with a constant clock frequency. The TSC depends on the CPU clock, which can be underclocked or overclocked as per the current load, resulting in time dilation and inaccurate measurements. Among all, the HPET is preferable since it allows very short time intervals if present in the system.

Hardware abstraction

Every system has at least one clock counter. As with any hardware device in a machine, this counter too is represented and managed by a structure. Hardware abstraction is provided by struct clocksource, defined in the include/linux/clocksource.h header file. This structure provides callbacks to access and handle power management on the counter through the read, enable, disable, suspend, and resume routines:

```
struct clocksource {
        u64 (*read)(struct clocksource *cs);
        u64 mask;
        u32 mult;
        u32 shift;
        u64 max_idle_ns;
        u32 maxadj;
#ifdef CONFIG_ARCH_CLOCKSOURCE_DATA
        struct arch_clocksource_data archdata;
#endif
        u64 max_cycles;
        const char *name;
        struct list_head list;
        int rating;
        int (*enable)(struct clocksource *cs);
        void (*disable)(struct clocksource *cs);
        unsigned long flags;
        void (*suspend)(struct clocksource *cs);
        void (*resume)(struct clocksource *cs);
        void (*mark_unstable)(struct clocksource *cs);
```

```
        void (*tick_stable)(struct clocksource *cs);

        /* private: */
#ifdef CONFIG_CLOCKSOURCE_WATCHDOG
        /* Watchdog related data, used by the framework */
        struct list_head wd_list;
        u64 cs_last;
        u64 wd_last;
#endif
        struct module *owner;
};
```

Members `mult` and `shift` are useful in obtaining elapsed time in relevant units.

Calculating elapsed time

Until this point we know that in every system there is a free-running, ever-incrementing counter, and all time is derived from it, be it wall time or any duration. The most natural idea here to calculate the time (seconds elapsed since the start of counter) would be dividing the number of cycles provided by this counter with the clock frequency, as expressed in the following formula:

Time (seconds) = (counter value)/(clock frequency)

There is a catch with this approach, however: it involves division (which works on an iterative algorithm, making it the slowest among the four basic arithmetic operations) and floating point calculations, which might be slower on certain architectures. While working with embedded platforms, floating point calculations are evidently slower than they are on PC or server platforms.

So how do we overcome this issue? Instead of division, time is calculated using multiplication and bitwise shift operations. The kernel provides a helper routine that derives the time this way. `clocksource_cyc2ns()`, defined in `include/linux/clocksource.h`, converts the clocksource cycles to nanoseconds:

```
    static inline s64 clocksource_cyc2ns(u64 cycles, u32 mult, u32 shift)
    {
            return ((u64) cycles * mult) >> shift;
    }
```

Here, the parameter cycles is the number of elapsed cycles from the clock source, `mult` is the cycle-to-nanosecond multiplier, while `shift` is the cycle-to-nanosecond divisor (power of two). Both these parameters are clock source dependent. These values are provided by the clock source kernel abstraction discussed earlier.

Clock source hardware are not accurate all the time; their frequency might vary. This clock variation causes time drift (making the clock run faster or slower). In such cases, the variable *mult* can be adjusted to make up for this time drift.

The helper routine `clocks_calc_mult_shift()`, defined in `kernel/time/clocksource.c`, helps evaluate `mult` and `shift` factors:

```
void
clocks_calc_mult_shift(u32 *mult, u32 *shift, u32 from, u32 to, u32 maxsec)
{
        u64 tmp;
        u32 sft, sftacc= 32;

        /*
         * Calculate the shift factor which is limiting the conversion
         * range:
         */
        tmp = ((u64)maxsec * from) >> 32;
        while (tmp) {
                tmp >>=1;
                sftacc--;
        }

        /*
         * Find the conversion shift/mult pair which has the best
         * accuracy and fits the maxsec conversion range:
         */
        for (sft = 32; sft > 0; sft--) {
                tmp = (u64) to << sft;
                tmp += from / 2;
                do_div(tmp, from);
                if ((tmp >> sftacc) == 0)
                        break;
        }
        *mult = tmp;
        *shift = sft;
}
```

Time duration between two events can be calculated as shown in the following code snippet:

```
struct clocksource *cs = &curr_clocksource;
cycle_t start = cs->read(cs);
/* things to do */
cycle_t end = cs->read(cs);
cycle_t diff = end - start;
duration =  clocksource_cyc2ns(diff, cs->mult, cs->shift);
```

Linux timekeeping data structures, macros, and helper routines

We will now broaden our awareness by looking at some key timekeeping structures, macros, and helper routines that can assist programmers in extracting specific time-related data.

Jiffies

The jiffies variable holds the number of ticks elapsed since system bootup. Every time a tick occurs, *jiffies* is incremented by one. It's a 32-bit variable, meaning for a tick rate of 100 Hz, overflow will occur in approximately 497 days (and in 49 days, 17 hours for a 1000 Hz tick rate).

To overcome this issue, a 64-bit variable jiffies_64 is used instead, which allows for thousands of millions of years before the overflow occurs. The jiffies variable is equated to the 32 least significant bits of jiffies_64. The reason for having both jiffies and jiffies_64 variables is that in 32-bit machines, a 64-bit variable can not be accessed atomically; some synchronization is required in order to avoid any counter update while these two 32-bit halves are processed. The function get_jiffies_64() defined in the /kernel/time/jiffies.c source file returns the current value of jiffies:

```
u64 get_jiffies_64(void)
{
        unsigned long seq;
        u64 ret;

        do {
                seq = read_seqbegin(&jiffies_lock);
                ret = jiffies_64;
        } while (read_seqretry(&jiffies_lock, seq));
        return ret;
}
```

While working with jiffies, it's crucial to take into account the possibility of wraparound, because it leads to unpredictable results while comparing two time events. There are four macros that serve this purpose, defined in include/linux/jiffies.h:

```
#define time_after(a,b)             \
        (typecheck(unsigned long, a) && \
         typecheck(unsigned long, b) && \
         ((long)((b) - (a)) < 0))
```

```
#define time_before(a,b)        time_after(b,a)

#define time_after_eq(a,b)      \
        (typecheck(unsigned long, a) && \
         typecheck(unsigned long, b) && \
         ((long)((a) - (b)) >= 0))
#define time_before_eq(a,b)     time_after_eq(b,a)
```

All these macros return Boolean values; parameters **a** and **b** are time events to be compared. If a happens to be the time after b, `time_after()` returns true, otherwise false. Conversely, if **a** happens to be before **b**, `time_before()` returns true, else false. Both `time_after_eq()` and `time_before_eq()` return true if both a and b are equal. Jiffies can be converted to other time units such as milliseconds, microseconds, and nanoseconds using routines `jiffies_to_msecs()`, `jiffies_to_usecs()`, defined in `kernel/time/time.c`, and `jiffies_to_nsecs()`, in `include/linux/jiffies.h`:

```
unsigned int jiffies_to_msecs(const unsigned long j)
{
#if HZ <= MSEC_PER_SEC && !(MSEC_PER_SEC % HZ)
        return (MSEC_PER_SEC / HZ) * j;
#elif HZ > MSEC_PER_SEC && !(HZ % MSEC_PER_SEC)
        return (j + (HZ / MSEC_PER_SEC) - 1)/(HZ / MSEC_PER_SEC);
#else
# if BITS_PER_LONG == 32
        return (HZ_TO_MSEC_MUL32 * j) >> HZ_TO_MSEC_SHR32;
# else
        return (j * HZ_TO_MSEC_NUM) / HZ_TO_MSEC_DEN;
# endif
#endif
}

unsigned int jiffies_to_usecs(const unsigned long j)
{
        /*
         * Hz doesn't go much further MSEC_PER_SEC.
         * jiffies_to_usecs() and usecs_to_jiffies() depend on that.
         */
        BUILD_BUG_ON(HZ > USEC_PER_SEC);

#if !(USEC_PER_SEC % HZ)
        return (USEC_PER_SEC / HZ) * j;
#else
# if BITS_PER_LONG == 32
        return (HZ_TO_USEC_MUL32 * j) >> HZ_TO_USEC_SHR32;
# else
        return (j * HZ_TO_USEC_NUM) / HZ_TO_USEC_DEN;
# endif
```

```
#endif
}

static inline u64 jiffies_to_nsecs(const unsigned long j)
{
        return (u64)jiffies_to_usecs(j) * NSEC_PER_USEC;
}
```

Other conversion routines can be explored in the `include/linux/jiffies.h` file.

Timeval and timespec

In Linux, the current time is maintained by keeping the number of seconds elapsed since midnight of January 01, 1970 (called epoch); the second elements in each of these represent the time elapsed since the last second in microseconds and nanoseconds, respectively:

```
struct timespec {
        __kernel_time_t  tv_sec;                        /* seconds */
        long             tv_nsec;          /* nanoseconds */
};
#endif

struct timeval {
        __kernel_time_t          tv_sec;                /* seconds */
        __kernel_suseconds_t     tv_usec;  /* microseconds */
};
```

Time (counter value) read from the clock source needs to be accumulated and tracked somewhere; the structure `struct tk_read_base,` defined in `include/linux/timekeeper_internal.h,` serves this purpose:

```
struct tk_read_base {
        struct clocksource       *clock;
        cycle_t                  (*read)(struct clocksource *cs);
        cycle_t                  mask;
        cycle_t                  cycle_last;
        u32                      mult;
        u32                      shift;
        u64                      xtime_nsec;
        ktime_t                  base_mono;
};
```

The structure `struct timekeeper,` defined in
`include/linux/timekeeper_internal.h,` keeps various timekeeping values. It's the
primary data structure to maintain and manipulate the timekeeping data for different
timelines, such as monotonic and raw:

```
struct timekeeper {
        struct tk_read_base     tkr;
        u64                     xtime_sec;
        unsigned long           ktime_sec;
        struct timespec64 wall_to_monotonic;
        ktime_t                 offs_real;
        ktime_t                 offs_boot;
        ktime_t                 offs_tai;
        s32                     tai_offset;
        ktime_t                 base_raw;
        struct timespec64 raw_time;

        /* The following members are for timekeeping internal use */
        cycle_t                 cycle_interval;
        u64                     xtime_interval;
        s64                     xtime_remainder;
        u32                     raw_interval;
        u64                     ntp_tick;
        /* Difference between accumulated time and NTP time in ntp
        * shifted nano seconds. */
        s64                     ntp_error;
        u32                     ntp_error_shift;
        u32                     ntp_err_mult;
};
```

Tracking and maintaining time

Timekeeping helper routines `timekeeping_get_ns()` and `timekeeping_get_ns()` help
get the correction factor (delta t) between universal time and terrestrial time in
nanoseconds:

```
static inline u64 timekeeping_delta_to_ns(struct tk_read_base *tkr, u64
delta)
{
        u64 nsec;

        nsec = delta * tkr->mult + tkr->xtime_nsec;
        nsec >>= tkr->shift;

        /* If arch requires, add in get_arch_timeoffset() */
```

```
            return nsec + arch_gettimeoffset();
}

static inline u64 timekeeping_get_ns(struct tk_read_base *tkr)
{
        u64 delta;

        delta = timekeeping_get_delta(tkr);
        return timekeeping_delta_to_ns(tkr, delta);
}
```

The routine `logarithmic_accumulation()` updates mono, raw, and xtime timelines; it accumulates shifted intervals of cycles into a shifted interval of nanoseconds. The routine `accumulate_nsecs_to_secs()` accumulates the nanoseconds in the `xtime_nsec` field of `struct tk_read_base` into `xtime_sec` of `struct timekeeper`. These routines help keep track of the current time in the system, and are defined in `kernel/time/timekeeping.c`:

```
static u64 logarithmic_accumulation(struct timekeeper *tk, u64 offset,
                                u32 shift, unsigned int *clock_set)
{
        u64 interval = tk->cycle_interval << shift;
        u64 snsec_per_sec;

        /* If the offset is smaller than a shifted interval, do nothing */
        if (offset < interval)
                return offset;

        /* Accumulate one shifted interval */
        offset -= interval;
        tk->tkr_mono.cycle_last += interval;
        tk->tkr_raw.cycle_last  += interval;

        tk->tkr_mono.xtime_nsec += tk->xtime_interval << shift;
        *clock_set |= accumulate_nsecs_to_secs(tk);

        /* Accumulate raw time */
        tk->tkr_raw.xtime_nsec += (u64)tk->raw_time.tv_nsec <<
tk->tkr_raw.shift;
        tk->tkr_raw.xtime_nsec += tk->raw_interval << shift;
        snsec_per_sec = (u64)NSEC_PER_SEC << tk->tkr_raw.shift;
        while (tk->tkr_raw.xtime_nsec >= snsec_per_sec) {
                tk->tkr_raw.xtime_nsec -= snsec_per_sec;
                tk->raw_time.tv_sec++;
        }
        tk->raw_time.tv_nsec = tk->tkr_raw.xtime_nsec >> tk->tkr_raw.shift;
        tk->tkr_raw.xtime_nsec -= (u64)tk->raw_time.tv_nsec <<
```

```
tk->tkr_raw.shift;

        /* Accumulate error between NTP and clock interval */
        tk->ntp_error += tk->ntp_tick << shift;
        tk->ntp_error -= (tk->xtime_interval + tk->xtime_remainder) <<
                                        (tk->ntp_error_shift +
shift);

        return offset;
}
```

Another routine `update_wall_time()`, **defined in** `kernel/time/timekeeping.c`, **is** responsible for maintaining the wall time. It increments the wall time using the current clock source as reference.

Tick and interrupt handling

To provide the programming interface, the clock device generating the ticks is abstracted through the structure `struct clock_event_device`, **defined in** `include/linux/clockchips.h`:

```
struct clock_event_device {
        void                    (*event_handler)(struct clock_event_device
*);
        int                     (*set_next_event)(unsigned long evt, struct
clock_event_device *);
        int                     (*set_next_ktime)(ktime_t expires, struct
clock_event_device *);
        ktime_t                  next_event;
        u64                      max_delta_ns;
        u64                      min_delta_ns;
        u32                      mult;
        u32                      shift;
        enum clock_event_state   state_use_accessors;
        unsigned int            features;
        unsigned long           retries;

        int                     (*set_state_periodic)(struct
clock_event_device *);
        int                     (*set_state_oneshot)(struct
clock_event_device *);
        int                     (*set_state_oneshot_stopped)(struct
clock_event_device *);
        int                     (*set_state_shutdown)(struct
clock_event_device *);
        int                     (*tick_resume)(struct clock_event_device
```

```
*);

        void                    (*broadcast)(const struct cpumask *mask);
        void                    (*suspend)(struct clock_event_device *);
        void                    (*resume)(struct clock_event_device *);
        unsigned long           min_delta_ticks;
        unsigned long           max_delta_ticks;

        const char              *name;
        int                     rating;
        int                     irq;
        int                     bound_on;
        const struct cpumask    *cpumask;
        struct list_head  list;
        struct module           *owner;
} ____cacheline_aligned;
```

Here, `event_handler` is the appropriate routine, assigned by the framework to be called by the low-level handler to run the tick. Depending on the configuration, this `clock_event_device` could be `periodic`, `one-shot`, or `ktime` based. Out of these three, the appropriate operating mode for the tick device is set through the `unsigned int features` field, using any of these macros:

```
#define CLOCK_EVT_FEAT_PERIODIC 0x000001
#define CLOCK_EVT_FEAT_ONESHOT 0x000002
#define CLOCK_EVT_FEAT_KTIME   0x000004
```

Periodic mode configures the hardware generate the tick once every *1/HZ* seconds, while one-shot mode makes the hardware generate the tick after the passage of a specific number of cycles from the current time.

Depending on the use cases and the operating mode, event_handler could be any of these three routines:

- `tick_handle_periodic()`, which is the default handler for periodic ticks and is defined in `kernel/time/tick-common.c`.
- `tick_nohz_handler()` is the low-resolution interrupt handler, used in low res mode. It's defined in `kernel/time/tick-sched.c`.
- `hrtimer_interrupt()` is used in high res mode and is defined in `kernel/time/hrtimer.c`. Interrupts are disabled when it's called.

A clock event device is configured and registered through the routine `clockevents_config_and_register()`, defined in `kernel/time/clockevents.c`.

Tick devices

The `clock_event_device` abstraction is for the core timing framework; we need a separate abstraction for tick devices per CPU; this is achieved through the structure `struct tick_device` and macro `DEFINE_PER_CPU()`, defined in `kernel/time/tick-sched.h` and `include/linux/percpu-defs.h`, respectively:

```
enum tick_device_mode {
 TICKDEV_MODE_PERIODIC,
 TICKDEV_MODE_ONESHOT,
};

struct tick_device {
        struct clock_event_device *evtdev;
        enum tick_device_mode mode;
}
```

A `tick_device` could be either periodic or one shot. It's set through the `enum tick_device_mode`.

Software timers and delay functions

A software timer allows a function to be invoked on expiry of a time duration. There are two types of timers: dynamic timers used by the kernel and interval timers used by the user-space processes. Apart from software timers, there is another type of commonly used timing function called delay functions. Delay functions implement a precise loop, which is executed as per (usually as many times as the) delay function's argument.

Dynamic timers

Dynamic timers can be created and destroyed at any time, hence the name dynamic timers. Dynamic timers are represented by the `struct timer_list` object, defined in `include/linux/timer.h`:

```
struct timer_list {
        /*
        * Every field that changes during normal runtime grouped to the
        * same cacheline
        */
        struct hlist_node entry;
        unsigned long           expires;
        void                    (*function)(unsigned long);
```

```
        unsigned long              data;
        u32                        flags;

#ifdef CONFIG_LOCKDEP
        struct lockdep_map         lockdep_map;
#endif
};
```

All timers in a system are managed by a doubly linked list, and are sorted in order of their expiry time, represented by the expires field. The expires field specifies the time duration, after which the timer expires. As soon as the current `jiffies` value matches or exceeds this field's value, the timer decays. Through the entry field, a timer is added into this timer linked list. The function field points to the routine to be invoked on expiry of the timer and the data field holds the parameter to be passed to the function, if needed. The expires field is constantly compared with `jiffies_64` values to determine whether the timer has expired or not.

A dynamic timer can be created and activated as follows:

- Create a new `timer_list` object, let's say `t_obj`.
- Initialize this timer object using macro `init_timer(&t_obj)`, defined in `include/linux/timer.h`.
- Initialize the function field with the function's address to be invoked on expiry of the timer. If the function requires a parameter, initialize the data field too.
- If the timer object is already added to a timer list, update the expires field by calling the function `mod_timer(&t_obj, <timeout-value-in-jiffies>)`, defined in `kernel/time/timer.c`.
- If not, initialize the expires field and add the timer object into the timer list using `add_timer(&t_obj)`, defined in `/kernel/time/timer.c`.

The kernel removes a decayed timer from its timer list automatically, but there are other methods too to remove a timer from its list. The `del_timer()` and `del_timer_sync()` routines and the macro `del_singleshot_timer_sync()` defined in `kernel/time/timer.c` help in doing so:

```
int del_timer(struct timer_list *timer)
{
        struct tvec_base *base;
        unsigned long flags;
        int ret = 0;

        debug_assert_init(timer);
```

```
                timer_stats_timer_clear_start_info(timer);
                if (timer_pending(timer)) {
                        base = lock_timer_base(timer, &flags);
                        if (timer_pending(timer)) {
                                detach_timer(timer, 1);
                                if (timer->expires == base->next_timer &&
                                    !tbase_get_deferrable(timer->base))
                                        base->next_timer = base->timer_jiffies;
                                ret = 1;
                        }
                        spin_unlock_irqrestore(&base->lock, flags);
                }

                return ret;
        }


        int del_timer_sync(struct timer_list *timer)
        {
        #ifdef CONFIG_LOCKDEP
                unsigned long flags;

                /*
                 * If lockdep gives a backtrace here, please reference
                 * the synchronization rules above.
                 */
                local_irq_save(flags);
                lock_map_acquire(&timer->lockdep_map);
                lock_map_release(&timer->lockdep_map);
                local_irq_restore(flags);
        #endif
                /*
                 * don't use it in hardirq context, because it
                 * could lead to deadlock.
                 */
                WARN_ON(in_irq());
                for (;;) {
                        int ret = try_to_del_timer_sync(timer);
                        if (ret >= 0)
                                return ret;
                        cpu_relax();
                }
        }

        #define del_singleshot_timer_sync(t) del_timer_sync(t)
```

`del_timer()` removes both active and inactive timers. Particularly useful in SMP systems, `del_timer_sync()` deactivates the timer and waits until the handler has finished executing on other CPUs.

Race conditions with dynamic timers

While removing a timer, special care must be taken as the timer function might be manipulating some dynamically de-allocatable resources. If the resource is released before deactivating the timer, there is a possibility of the timer function being invoked when the resources it operates on do not exist at all, causing data corruption. So to avoid such scenarios, the timer must be stopped before releasing any resources. The following code snippet replicates this situation; `RESOURCE_DEALLOCATE()` here could be any relevant resource deallocation routine:

```
...
del_timer(&t_obj);
RESOURCE_DEALLOCATE();
....
```

This approach, however, is applicable to uni-processor systems only. In an SMP system, it's quite possible that when the timer is stopped, its function might already be running on another CPU. In such a scenario, resources will be released as soon as the `del_timer()` returns, while the timer function is still manipulating them on other CPU; not a desirable situation at all. `del_timer_sync()` fixes this problem: after stopping the timer, it waits until the timer function completes its execution on the other CPU. `del_timer_sync()` is useful in cases where the timer function can reactivate itself. If the timer function doesn't reactivate the timer, a much simpler and faster macro, `del_singleshot_timer_sync()`, should be used instead.

Dynamic timer handling

Software timers are complex and time consuming, and therefore should not be handled by the timer ISR. Rather they should be performed by a deferrable bottom-half softirq routine called `TIMER_SOFTIRQ`, and its routine is defined in `kernel/time/timer.c`:

```
static __latent_entropy void run_timer_softirq(struct softirq_action *h)
{
        struct timer_base *base = this_cpu_ptr(&timer_bases[BASE_STD]);

        base->must_forward_clk = false;
```

```
        __run_timers(base);
        if (IS_ENABLED(CONFIG_NO_HZ_COMMON) && base->nohz_active)
                __run_timers(this_cpu_ptr(&timer_bases[BASE_DEF]));
}
```

Delay functions

Timers are useful when the timeout period is relatively long; in all other use cases where a shorter duration is desired, delay functions are used instead. While working with hardware such as storage devices (namely *flash memory* and *EEPROM*), it's is very crucial for the device driver to wait until the device finishes the hardware operations such as writing and erasing, which in most cases is in the range of a few microseconds to milliseconds. Going ahead and executing other instructions without waiting for the hardware to complete such operations would result in unpredictable read/write operations and data corruption. In cases such as these, delay functions come in handy. The kernel provides such short delays by means of the `ndelay()`, `udelay()`, and `mdelay()` routines and macro, which receive arguments in nanoseconds, microseconds, and milliseconds, respectively.

The following functions can be found in `include/linux/delay.h`:

```
static inline void ndelay(unsigned long x)
{
        udelay(DIV_ROUND_UP(x, 1000));
}
```

These functions can be found in `arch/ia64/kernel/time.c`:

```
static void
ia64_itc_udelay (unsigned long usecs)
{
        unsigned long start = ia64_get_itc();
        unsigned long end = start + usecs*local_cpu_data->cyc_per_usec;

        while (time_before(ia64_get_itc(), end))
                cpu_relax();
}

void (*ia64_udelay)(unsigned long usecs) = &ia64_itc_udelay;

void
udelay (unsigned long usecs)
{
        (*ia64_udelay)(usecs);
}
```

POSIX clocks

POSIX provides software timers to multithreaded and real-time user space applications, known as POSIX timers. POSIX provides the following clocks:

- CLOCK_REALTIME: This clock represents the real time in the system. Also known as the wall time, it's similar to the time from a wall clock and used for timestamping as well as providing actual time to the user. This clock is modifiable.

- CLOCK_MONOTONIC: This clock keeps the time elapsed since the system bootup. It's ever increasing and non modifiable by any process or user. Due to its monotonic nature, it's the the preferred clock to determine the time difference between two time events.

- CLOCK_BOOTTIME: This clock is identical to CLOCK_MONOTONIC; however, it includes time spent in suspend.

These clocks can be accessed and modified (if the selected clock allows it) through the following POSIX clock routines, defined in the time.h header:

- int clock_getres(clockid_t clk_id, struct timespec *res);
- int clock_gettime(clockid_t clk_id, struct timespec *tp);
- int clock_settime(clockid_t clk_id, const struct timespec *tp);

The function clock_getres() gets the resolution (precision) of the clock specified by *clk_id*. And if the resolution is non-null, it stores it in the struct timespec pointed to by the resolution. Functions clock_gettime() and clock_settime() read and set the time of the clock specified by *clk_id*. *clk_id* could be any of the POSIX clocks: CLOCK_REALTIME, CLOCK_MONOTONIC, and so on.

CLOCK_REALTIME_COARSE

CLOCK_MONOTONIC_COARSE

Each of these POSIX routines has corresponding system calls, namely `sys_clock_getres()`, `sys_ clock_gettime()`, and `sys_clock_settime`. So every time any of these routines is invoked, a context switching occurs from user mode to kernel mode. If calls to these routines are frequent, context switching can result in low system performance. To avoid context switching, two coarse variants of the POSIX clock were implemented as the vDSO (virtual Dynamic Shared Object) library:

vDSO is a small shared library with selected kernel space routines that the kernel maps into the address space of user-space applications so that these kernel-space routines can be called by them in process from user space directly. The C library calls the vDSOs, so the user space applications can be programmed in the usual way through standard functions and the C library will utilize the functionalities available through vDSO without engaging any syscall interface, thus avoiding any user mode-kernel mode context switching and syscall overhead. Being an vDSO implementation, these coarse variants are faster and have a resolution of 1 milliseconds.

Summary

In this chapter, we looked in detail at most of the routines that the kernel provides to drive time-based events, in addition to comprehending the fundamental aspects of Linux time, its infrastructure, and its measurement. We also briefly looked at POSIX clocks and some of their key time access and modification routines. Effective time-driven programs however rest on careful and calculated use of these routines.

In the next chapter, we will briefly look at the management of dynamic kernel modules.

11
Module Management

Kernel modules (also referred as LKMs) have accentuated the development of kernel services owing to their ease of use. Our focus through this chapter will be to understand how the kernel seamlessly facilitates this entire process, making loading and unloading of modules dynamic and easy, as we look through all core concepts, functions and important data structures involved in module management. We assume readers are familiar with the basic usage of modules.

In this chapter, we will cover the following topics:

- Key elements of a kernel module
- Module layout
- Module load and unload interfaces
- Key data structures

Kernel modules

Kernel module is an easy and effective mechanism to extend the functionality of a running system without the baggage of rebuilding the whole kernel, they have been vital in ushering dynamism and scalability to the Linux operating system. Kernel modules not only satiate the extendable nature of the kernel but also usher the following functionalities:

- Allowing kernel the ability to only keep features which are necessary, in-turn boosting capacity utilization
- Allowing proprietary/non-GPL compliant services to load and unload
- The bottom-line feature of extensibility of the kernel

Elements of an LKM

Each module object comprises of the *init(constructor)* and *exit(destructor)* routines. The *init* routine is invoked when a module is deployed into kernel address space, and the *exit* routine is called while the module is being removed. As the name innately suggests, the *init* routine is usually programmed to carry out operations and actions which are essential to set up the module body: such as registering with a specific kernel subsystem or allocating resources that are essential for the functionality being loaded. However, specific operations programmed within the *init* and *exit* routines depend on what the module is designed for and the functionality it brings to the kernel. The following code excerpt shows template of the *init* and *exit* routines:

```
int init_module(void)
{
  /* perform required setup and registration ops */
    ...
    ...
    return 0;
}
void cleanup_module(void)
{
    /* perform required cleanup operations */
    ...
    ...
}
```

Notice that the *init* routine returns an integer—a zero is returned if the module is committed to the kernel address space and a negative number is returned if it fails. This additionally provides flexibility for programmers to commit a module only when it succeeds in registering with the required subsystem.

The default names for the init and exit routines are `init_module()` and `cleanup_module()`, respectively. Modules can optionally change names for the *init* and *exit* routines to improve code readability. However, they will have to declare them using the `module_init` and `module_exit` macros:

```
int myinit(void)
{
        ...
        ...
        return 0;
}

void myexit(void)
{
```

```
        . . .
        . . .
    }

module_init(myinit);
module_exit(myexit);
```

Comment macros form another key element of a module code. These macros are used to provide usage, licence, and author information of the module. This is important as modules are sourced from various vendors:

- MODULE_DESCRIPTION(): This macro is used to specify the general description of the module
- MODULE_AUTHOR(): This is used to provide author information
- MODULE_LICENSE(): This is used to specify legal licence for the code in the module

All the information specified through these macros is retained into the module binary and can be accessed by users through a utility called *modinfo*. MODULE_LICENSE() is the only mandatory macro that a module must mention. This serves a very handy purpose, as it informs users about proprietary code in a module, which is susceptible to debugging and support issues (kernel community in all probability ignores issues arising out of proprietary modules).

Another useful feature available for modules is of dynamic initialization of module data variables using module parameters. This allows data variables declared in a module to be initialized either during module deployment or when module is *live* in memory (through the sysfs interface). This can be achieved by setting up selected variables as module parameters through the appropriate module_param() family of macros (found in kernel header <linux/moduleparam.h>). Values passed to module parameters during deployment of the module are initialized before the *init* function is invoked.

Code in modules can access global kernel functions and data as needed. This enables the code of the module to make use of existing kernel functionality. It is through such function calls a module can perform required operations such as printing messages into kernel log buffer, allocation and de-allocation of memory, acquiring and releasing of exclusion locks, and registering and unregistering module code with appropriate subsystem.

Similarly, a module can also export its symbols into the global symbol table of the kernel, which can then be accessed from code in other modules. This facilitates granular design and implementation of kernel services by organizing them across a set of modules, instead of having the whole service implemented as a single LKM. Such stacking up of related services leads to module dependency, for instance: if module A is using the symbols of module B, then A has dependency on B, in that case, module B must be loaded before module A and and module B cannot be unloaded until module A is unloaded.

Binary layout of a LKM

Modules are built using kbuild makefiles; once the build process completes, an ELF binary file with a *.ko* (kernel object) extension is generated. Module ELF binaries are appropriately tweaked to add new sections, to differentiate them from other ELF binaries, and to store module-related metadata. The following are the sections in a kernel module:

`.gnu.linkonce.this_module`	**Module structure**
`.modinfo`	Information about the module (Licenses and so on)
`__versions`	Expected versions of symbols that the module depends on during compile time
`__ksymtab*`	The table of symbols exported by this module
`__kcrctab*`	The table of versions of symbols exported by this module
`.init`	Sections used when initializing
`.text`, `.data` etc.	Code and data sections

Load and unload operations

Modules can be deployed through special tools that are part of an application package called *modutils*, of which *insmod* and *rmmod* are widely used. *insmod* is used to deploy the module into kernel address space and *rmmod* is used for unloading a live module. These tools initiate load/unload operations by invoking appropriate system calls:

```
int finit_module(int fd, const char *param_values, int flags);
int delete_module(const char *name, int flags);
```

Here, `finit_module()` is invoked (by `insmod`) with the file descriptor of the specified module binary file (.ko) and other relevant arguments. This function steps into kernel mode by invoking the underlying system call:

```
SYSCALL_DEFINE3(finit_module, int, fd, const char __user *, uargs, int,
flags)
{
        struct load_info info = { };
        loff_t size;
        void *hdr;
        int err;

        err = may_init_module();
        if (err)
                return err;

        pr_debug("finit_module: fd=%d, uargs=%p, flags=%i\n", fd, uargs,
flags);

        if (flags & ~(MODULE_INIT_IGNORE_MODVERSIONS
                        |MODULE_INIT_IGNORE_VERMAGIC))
                return -EINVAL;

        err = kernel_read_file_from_fd(fd, &hdr, &size, INT_MAX,
                                        READING_MODULE);
        if (err)
                return err;
        info.hdr = hdr;
        info.len = size;

        return load_module(&info, uargs, flags);
}
```

Here, `may_init_module()` is called to verify the `CAP_SYS_MODULE` privilege of the calling context; this function returns a negative number on failure and zero on success. If the caller has the required privilege, a specified module image is accessed through *fd* using the `kernel_read_file_from_fd()` routine that returns address of the module image, which is populated into an instance of `struct load_info`. Finally, the `load_module()` core kernel routine is invoked with address to instance of `load_info` and other user arguments passed down from the `finit_module()` call:

```
static int load_module(struct load_info *info, const char __user *uargs, int
flags)
{
        struct module *mod;
        long err;
        char *after_dashes;
```

```
err = module_sig_check(info, flags);
if (err)
        goto free_copy;

err = elf_header_check(info);
if (err)
        goto free_copy;

/* Figure out module layout, and allocate all the memory. */
mod = layout_and_allocate(info, flags);
if (IS_ERR(mod)) {
        err = PTR_ERR(mod);
        goto free_copy;
}

. . . .
. . . .
. . . .


}
```

Here, `load_module()` is a core kernel routine that attempts to link module image into kernel address space. This function initiates a series of sanity checks, and finally commits the module by initializing module parameters to values provided by the caller, and invokes the *init* function of the module. The following steps detail these operations with names of the relevant helper functions invoked:

- Checking for the signature (`module_sig_check()`)
- Checking for the ELF header (`elf_header_check()`)
- Checking the module layout and allocate the necessary memory (`layout_and_allocate()`)
- Appending the module to the modules list (`add_unformed_module()`)
- Allocate per-cpu areas used in the module (`percpu_modalloc()`)
- As module is in final location, finding the optional sections (`find_module_sections()`)
- Checking for module license and versions (`check_module_license_and_versions()`)
- Resolving the symbols (`simplify_symbols()`)
- Setting up the module parameters as per values passed in the args list
- Checking for duplication of symbols (`complete_formation()`)

- Setting up the sysfs (`mod_sysfs_setup()`)
- Freeing the copy in the *load_info* structure (`free_copy()`)
- Calling to the *init* function of the module (`do_init_module()`)

The unloading process is quite similar to the loading process; the only thing different is that there are certain sanity checks to ensure the safe removal of the module from kernel without affecting the system stability. A module's unloading is initialized with the call to the *rmmod* utility, which calls the `delete_module()` routine, which steps into the underlying system call:

```
SYSCALL_DEFINE2(delete_module, const char __user *, name_user,
                unsigned int, flags)
{
        struct module *mod;
        char name[MODULE_NAME_LEN];
        int ret, forced = 0;

        if (!capable(CAP_SYS_MODULE) || modules_disabled)
                return -EPERM;

        if (strncpy_from_user(name, name_user, MODULE_NAME_LEN-1) < 0)
                return -EFAULT;
        name[MODULE_NAME_LEN-1] = '\0';

        audit_log_kern_module(name);

        if (mutex_lock_interruptible(&module_mutex) != 0)
                return -EINTR;

        mod = find_module(name);
        if (!mod) {
                ret = -ENOENT;
                goto out;
        }

        if (!list_empty(&mod->source_list)) {
                /* Other modules depend on us: get rid of them first. */
                ret = -EWOULDBLOCK;
                goto out;
        }

        /* Doing init or already dying? */
        if (mod->state != MODULE_STATE_LIVE) {
                /* FIXME: if (force), slam module count damn the torpedoes
*/
                pr_debug("%s already dying\n", mod->name);
```

```
                              ret = -EBUSY;
                              goto out;
                      }

              /* If it has an init func, it must have an exit func to unload */
              if (mod->init && !mod->exit) {
                      forced = try_force_unload(flags);
                      if (!forced) {
                              /* This module can't be removed */
                              ret = -EBUSY;
                              goto out;
                      }
              }

              /* Stop the machine so refcounts can't move and disable module. */
              ret = try_stop_module(mod, flags, &forced);
              if (ret != 0)
                      goto out;

              mutex_unlock(&module_mutex);
              /* Final destruction now no one is using it. */
              if (mod->exit != NULL)
                      mod->exit();
              blocking_notifier_call_chain(&module_notify_list,
                                      MODULE_STATE_GOING, mod);
              klp_module_going(mod);
              ftrace_release_mod(mod);

              async_synchronize_full();

              /* Store the name of the last unloaded module for diagnostic
purposes */
              strlcpy(last_unloaded_module, mod->name,
sizeof(last_unloaded_module));

              free_module(mod);
              return 0;
out:
              mutex_unlock(&module_mutex);
              return ret;
      }
```

On invocation, the system call checks whether the caller has the requisite permissions, then it checks for any module dependencies. If there are none, the module is good to be removed (else, an error is returned). After this, the module state is verified (*live*). Finally, the exit routine of the module is called and at last the `free_module()` routine is called:

```
/* Free a module, remove from lists, etc. */
static void free_module(struct module *mod)
{
        trace_module_free(mod);

        mod_sysfs_teardown(mod);

        /* We leave it in list to prevent duplicate loads, but make sure
         * that no one uses it while it's being deconstructed. */
        mutex_lock(&module_mutex);
        mod->state = MODULE_STATE_UNFORMED;
        mutex_unlock(&module_mutex);

        /* Remove dynamic debug info */
        ddebug_remove_module(mod->name);

        /* Arch-specific cleanup. */
        module_arch_cleanup(mod);

        /* Module unload stuff */
        module_unload_free(mod);

        /* Free any allocated parameters. */
        destroy_params(mod->kp, mod->num_kp);

        if (is_livepatch_module(mod))
                free_module_elf(mod);

        /* Now we can delete it from the lists */
        mutex_lock(&module_mutex);
        /* Unlink carefully: kallsyms could be walking list. */
        list_del_rcu(&mod->list);
        mod_tree_remove(mod);
        /* Remove this module from bug list, this uses list_del_rcu */
        module_bug_cleanup(mod);
        /* Wait for RCU-sched synchronizing before releasing mod->list and
   buglist. */
        synchronize_sched();
        mutex_unlock(&module_mutex);

        /* This may be empty, but that's OK */
        disable_ro_nx(&mod->init_layout);
```

```
        module_arch_freeing_init(mod);
        module_memfree(mod->init_layout.base);
        kfree(mod->args);
        percpu_modfree(mod);

        /* Free lock-classes; relies on the preceding sync_rcu(). */
        lockdep_free_key_range(mod->core_layout.base,
mod->core_layout.size);

        /* Finally, free the core (containing the module structure) */
        disable_ro_nx(&mod->core_layout);
        module_memfree(mod->core_layout.base);

#ifdef CONFIG_MPU
        update_protections(current->mm);
#endif
}
```

This call removes the module from the various lists where it was placed during loading (sysfs, module list, and so on) to initiate the cleanup. An architecture-specific cleanup routine is invoked (can be found in `</linux/arch/<arch>/kernel/module.c>`). All dependent modules are iterated and the module is removed from their lists. As soon as the cleanup is over, all resources and the memory that was allocated to the module are freed.

Module data structures

Every module that is deployed in the kernel is as usual represented through a descriptor, called `struct module`. Kernel maintains a list of module instances, with each representing a specific module in memory:

```
struct module {
        enum module_state state;

        /* Member of list of modules */
        struct list_head list;

        /* Unique handle for this module */
        char name[MODULE_NAME_LEN];

        /* Sysfs stuff. */
        struct module_kobject mkobj;
        struct module_attribute *modinfo_attrs;
        const char *version;
        const char *srcversion;
        struct kobject *holders_dir;
```

```c
        /* Exported symbols */
        const struct kernel_symbol *syms;
        const s32 *crcs;
        unsigned int num_syms;

        /* Kernel parameters. */
#ifdef CONFIG_SYSFS
        struct mutex param_lock;
#endif
        struct kernel_param *kp;
        unsigned int num_kp;

        /* GPL-only exported symbols. */
        unsigned int num_gpl_syms;
        const struct kernel_symbol *gpl_syms;
        const s32 *gpl_crcs;

#ifdef CONFIG_UNUSED_SYMBOLS
        /* unused exported symbols. */
        const struct kernel_symbol *unused_syms;
        const s32 *unused_crcs;
        unsigned int num_unused_syms;

        /* GPL-only, unused exported symbols. */
        unsigned int num_unused_gpl_syms;
        const struct kernel_symbol *unused_gpl_syms;
        const s32 *unused_gpl_crcs;
#endif

#ifdef CONFIG_MODULE_SIG
        /* Signature was verified. */
        bool sig_ok;
#endif

        bool async_probe_requested;

        /* symbols that will be GPL-only in the near future. */
        const struct kernel_symbol *gpl_future_syms;
        const s32 *gpl_future_crcs;
        unsigned int num_gpl_future_syms;

        /* Exception table */
        unsigned int num_exentries;
        struct exception_table_entry *extable;

        /* Startup function. */
        int (*init)(void);
```

```
        /* Core layout: rbtree is accessed frequently, so keep together. */
        struct module_layout core_layout __module_layout_align;
        struct module_layout init_layout;

        /* Arch-specific module values */
        struct mod_arch_specific arch;

        unsigned long taints;      /* same bits as kernel:taint_flags */

#ifdef CONFIG_GENERIC_BUG
        /* Support for BUG */
        unsigned num_bugs;
        struct list_head bug_list;
        struct bug_entry *bug_table;
#endif

#ifdef CONFIG_KALLSYMS
        /* Protected by RCU and/or module_mutex: use rcu_dereference() */
        struct mod_kallsyms *kallsyms;
        struct mod_kallsyms core_kallsyms;

        /* Section attributes */
        struct module_sect_attrs *sect_attrs;

        /* Notes attributes */
        struct module_notes_attrs *notes_attrs;
#endif

        /* The command line arguments (may be mangled).  People like
          keeping pointers to this stuff */
        char *args;

#ifdef CONFIG_SMP
        /* Per-cpu data. */
        void __percpu *percpu;
        unsigned int percpu_size;
#endif

#ifdef CONFIG_TRACEPOINTS
        unsigned int num_tracepoints;
        struct tracepoint * const *tracepoints_ptrs;
#endif
#ifdef HAVE_JUMP_LABEL
        struct jump_entry *jump_entries;
        unsigned int num_jump_entries;
#endif
#ifdef CONFIG_TRACING
        unsigned int num_trace_bprintk_fmt;
```

```
            const char **trace_bprintk_fmt_start;
#endif
#ifdef CONFIG_EVENT_TRACING
        struct trace_event_call **trace_events;
        unsigned int num_trace_events;
        struct trace_enum_map **trace_enums;
        unsigned int num_trace_enums;
#endif
#ifdef CONFIG_FTRACE_MCOUNT_RECORD
        unsigned int num_ftrace_callsites;
        unsigned long *ftrace_callsites;
#endif

#ifdef CONFIG_LIVEPATCH
        bool klp; /* Is this a livepatch module? */
        bool klp_alive;

        /* Elf information */
        struct klp_modinfo *klp_info;
#endif

#ifdef CONFIG_MODULE_UNLOAD
        /* What modules depend on me? */
        struct list_head source_list;
        /* What modules do I depend on? */
        struct list_head target_list;

        /* Destruction function. */
        void (*exit)(void);

        atomic_t refcnt;
#endif

#ifdef CONFIG_CONSTRUCTORS
        /* Constructor functions. */
        ctor_fn_t *ctors;
        unsigned int num_ctors;
#endif
} ____cacheline_aligned;
```

Let's now look at some of the key fields of this structure:

- `list`: This is the double linked list that contains all the loaded modules in the kernel.
- `name`: This specifies the name of the module. This must be an unique name as the module is referenced with this name.
- `state`: This indicates the current state of the module. A module can be in either of the states specified in `enum module_state` under *<linux/module.h>*:

```
enum module_state {
        MODULE_STATE_LIVE,          /* Normal state. */
        MODULE_STATE_COMING,        /* Full formed, running module_init. */
        MODULE_STATE_GOING,         /* Going away. */
        MODULE_STATE_UNFORMED,      /* Still setting it up. */
};
```

While loading or removing a module, it's important to know its current state; for instance, we need not insert an existing module if its state specifies that it is already present.

`syms, crc and num_syms`: These are used to manage symbols that are exported by the module code.

`init`: This is the pointer to a function which is called when the module is initialized.

`arch`: This represents the architecture specific structure which shall be populated with architecture-specific data, needed for the modules to run. However, this structure mostly remains empty as most architectures do not need any additional information.

`taints`: This is used if the module is tainting the kernel. It could mean that the kernel suspects a module to do something harmful or a non-GPL complaint code.

`percpu`: This points to per-CPU data belonging to the module. It is initialized at the module load time.

`source_list and target_list`: This carries details on module dependencies.

`exit`: This simply is the opposite of init. It points to the function that is called to perform the cleanup process of the module. It releases memory held by the module and does other cleanup specific tasks.

Memory layout

A module's memory layout is shown through an object, `struct module_layout`, defined in *<linux/module.h>*:

```
struct module_layout {
        /* The actual code + data. */
        void *base;
        /* Total size. */
        unsigned int size;
        /* The size of the executable code.  */
        unsigned int text_size;
        /* Size of RO section of the module (text+rodata) */
        unsigned int ro_size;

#ifdef CONFIG_MODULES_TREE_LOOKUP
        struct mod_tree_node mtn;
#endif
};
```

Summary

In this chapter, we briefly covered all the core elements of modules, its implications, and management details. Our attempt has remained to give you a quick and comprehensive view of how kernel facilitates its extensibility through modules. You also understood the core data structures that facilitate module management. Kernel's attempt at remaining safe and steady in this dynamic environment is also a notable feature.

I really hope this book serves as a means for you to go out there and experiment more with Linux kernel!

Index

Made in the USA
Middletown, DE
27 November 2018